FOLDING
THE
UNIVERSE

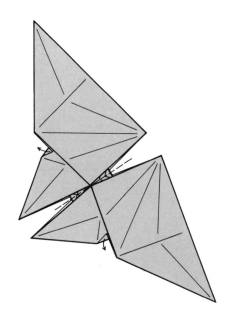

FOLDING
THE
UNIVERSE

ORIGAMI FROM
ANGELFISH TO ZEN

PETER ENGEL

VINTAGE BOOKS
A Division of Random House, Inc.   New York

Published in the United States by Random House, Inc., New York, and simultaneously in Canada by Random House of Canada Limited, Toronto.

Library of Congress Cataloging-in-Publication Data
Engel, Peter, 1959–
   Folding the universe.
   "Vintage original."
   Bibliography: p. 313
   Includes index.
   I. Origami.   I. Title.
TT870.E54   1988   736'.982   87-45940
ISBN 0-394-75751-3 (pbk.)

Portions of this text were originally published in *Discover, Nippon Origami Association Magazine,* and *TWA Ambassador.*

Grateful acknowledgment is made to the following for permission to reprint previously published material:

The Friends of The Origami Center of America: Four articles by Peter Engel: "Creativity in Origami: A Panel Discussion," "Humblest Before Nature, Proudest Among Men: An Interview with Akira Yoshizawa," "Profile: Peter Engel," and "On Discovering Origami" (including drawings and photographs which were originally published in *The Origamian*). Reprinted by permission of The Friends of The Origami Center of America.

The Sciences: "Snowflakes, Coastlines, and Clouds" and "A Paper Folder's Finding" by Peter Engel. These articles are reprinted by permission of *The Sciences* and are from the September/October 1983 and May/June 1984 issues.

Book design by Jennifer Dossin and Peter Engel

Manufactured in the United States of America

CONTENTS

ACKNOWLEDGMENTS

This book has been a labor of love for half a lifetime. For fifteen years, I have invented original origami figures, each of which can be constructed from a single, uncut piece of paper. (Paperfolders call these figures "models.") Some of my models, like the simple fish and birds included in this book, employ traditional folding techniques and are easy to recreate. Others, like the mammals and insects that appear toward the end of the book, use original techniques and are a challenge to fold. In devising the more advanced models, I have drawn upon the groundwork laid by the ancient Japanese, adding layer upon layer of complexity without sacrificing the simple rules that give origami its austere and timeless beauty.

Over the years, many people have encouraged my investigations into mathematics and art, and I would like to thank them. Martin Gardner's column in *Scientific American* was an early inspiration, and he unfailingly replied to letters written in my childish scrawl. Many years later, when my penmanship had improved, Douglas Hofstadter, his successor, responded with equal enthusiasm.

The Origami Center of America, located in New York City, provides a haven for paperfolders young and old. Three of its members, Alice Gray, Lillian Oppenheimer, and Michael Shall, watched me grow up and nurtured my development as a folder. Fellow folders Robert Lang, John Montroll, and Stephen Weiss have continued to offer constructive criticism of my designs and drawings.

During my visit to Japan, many folders opened their homes to me and talked candidly about their lives and work. I am grateful to Kunihiko Kasahara, Saburo Kase, Toyoaki Kawai, Jun Maekawa, Eiji Nakamura, Dokuotei Nakano, Toshie Takahama, and Akira Yoshizawa. Mrs. Takahama doubled as an invaluable guide and interpreter.

I owe an immeasurable debt, both intellectual and personal, to Albert Alcalay, Gunther Gerzso, Owen Gingerich, Stephen Jay Gould, Walter Gruen, Erwin Hiebert, Shinya Inoué, Stanislaw Lem, Masahiro Mori, Cyril Stanley Smith, and Peter Stevens. I am particularly indebted to Arthur Loeb and the members of the Design Science Studio at Harvard University. Over the years, these artists, architects, mathematicians, scientists, and writers have shared with me their curiosity about nature and the creative process. They are mentors all.

Amy Anderson and Ann Kalla taught me that being passionate about drawing and design is really the same thing as enjoying yourself immensely. This is perhaps the most valuable lesson I could pass along to a prospective designer.

This book benefits from the contributions of many people. Scott Kim and Xu Yunshu prepared original calligraphy. James Crutchfield, Fereydoon Family, Benoit Mandelbrot, Douglas McKenna, and Allan Wilks generated computer graphics. Wasma Chorbachi shared her original research on Islamic geometry. Carmen Quesada and Christopher Burke of Quesada/Burke, New York, brought skill and sensitivity to their photographs of the origami models. My friends Sarah Boxer, David Brittan, Ted Conover, Jeanne Heifetz, Walter Jacob, Allen Kurzweil, and Peter Stein read early drafts of the manuscript and made valuable suggestions. Margaret Lem provided an acute aesthetic sense to guide the drawings while they were in progress. Finding time between careers as an animator and landscape architect, Kathleen Bakewell carefully inked many of the final drawings. When the book went into extra innings, Suenn Ho took over and got the save.

The manuscript was still in its formative stage when it got to Random House. It took shape under the keen editorial eye of Becky Saletan and Miranda Sherwin and the fine designing hands of Cathy Aison, Jennifer Dossin, Tasha Hall, and Susan Mitchell. Victoria Mathews, Quinn O'Neill, Linda Rosenberg, and Harold Vaughn upheld exacting standards throughout the production of a complicated book, no mean feat.

Cheryl Schofner emerged from Florida to provide inspiration and humor during the home stretch. She has been a wise and humble sounding board, an affectionate and loving friend. It is no exaggeration to say that without her, this book would not have an alligator.

My parents and brother have encouraged my passion for paperfolding longer than anyone else. For their love and support, this book is dedicated to them—Marjorie, Stephen, and John.

FOREWORD

If it is true that play is the honing and rehearsing of skills and strategies that may at some time become useful for survival, then the term *recreation* should probably be replaced by *precreation*. When students come to me, unsure of finding a topic for their thesis, I tend to ask them what they enjoyed when they were small: Usually going back to these basic skills will bring to mind a suitable thesis topic.

Peter Engel never was one of those students at a loss for things to do. As this book, ostensibly on paperfolding, indicates, his tastes are broad and varied, and the connections between origami, Beethoven's Seventh Symphony, and *Alice in Wonderland* are crystal clear to him. Peter finds recreation in his work, and work in his recreation. It is hard to say whether what gives him the greatest satisfaction is the image he designs by folding paper or rather the pattern created by the folds, and displayed when the origami figure is once again unfolded into the square from whence it came.

The process of creating a complex pattern and the rich variety that may be obtained from a sequence of very simple operations are close to the spiritual and the molecular basis of life. It is therefore small wonder that the art of origami would have appealed to Leonardo da Vinci as well as to Lewis Carroll, to name but a few predecessors Peter refers to.

Peter asks whether the result of a notated linear sequence of essentially binary decisions, which is therefore entirely predictable and one of a finite, enumerable set of patterns, can be considered art. He himself partially answers this question when he tells us that the origami figure folded out of a single sheet is at once more pleasing and more challenging to the designer than a composite made from several sheets. The awareness that a sequence of events must be capable of being notated rather than being entirely improvisatory imposes a considerable constraint on artists, be (s)he paperfolder, choreographer, or composer. The nature of this notation and the subtleties of detail it permits both determine and are determined by the style of the composition. The ingenuity with which the creator responds to the stylistic constraints gives the creation its artistic value.

The reader will find enjoyment on many levels in this book. Its subject is recreational, but it may as well prove to be precreational: Skills developed through paperfolding will prove useful in computer programming and molecular biology. However, regardless of ulterior motives induced by our achievement-oriented culture, the reader will find peace and joy in Peter Engel's patterns and in the ruminations and insights that he presents alongside them.

Arthur L. Loeb
Harvard University

FOLDING
THE
UNIVERSE

M. C. Escher, *Tiles in the Alhambra*, 1936.

CROSSING THE DIVIDE

In 1936, the Dutch artist M. C. Escher visited the Alhambra, the fourteenth-century Moorish palace in southern Spain, and experienced a revelation. Until that time, Escher, who lived from 1898 to 1972, had directed his gaze toward the natural world. His work had consisted of portraits, plant and figure studies, and renderings of Italian hill towns and the Mediterranean coastline. An extraordinary craftsman who worked primarily in woodcutting and lithography, Escher had painstakingly studied natural form and explored techniques for transforming three-dimensional objects into two-dimensional graphic designs. He had not yet devised the tile patterns, geometric solids, impossible structures, and optical illusions for which he would become famous.

Escher's trip to the Alhambra gave new direction to his work. The walls and floors of the palace are decorated with colorful and intricately carved tessellations, patterns of tiles capable of covering an entire surface without leaving space between them. Escher filled sketchbook after sketchbook with pencil drawings reproducing the patterns and analyzing their geometry. Excited by his discovery, he wrote, years later:

> What a pity it was that Islam forbade the making of "images." In their tessellations they restricted themselves to figures with abstracted geometrical shapes. So far as I know, no single Moorish artist ever made so bold (or maybe the idea never dawned on him) as to use concrete recognizable figures such as birds, fish, reptiles, and human beings as elements of their tessellations. Then I find this restriction all the more unacceptable because . . . it is precisely *this crossing of the divide* between abstract and concrete representations, between "mute" and "speaking" figures, which leads to the heart of what fascinates me above all in the regular division of the plane. [My italics.]

When Escher settled in Holland in 1941, the experience of the Alhambra remained with him. After a decade of traveling in southern Europe, his return to the cold, spare landscape of his native country triggered a turn away from the natural world toward a more personal, inner world of geometric form. In 1937 Escher's art began to bridge both worlds. He wrestled with the disparity between an object and its image, creating works that reveal the illusion of representation—the

M. C. Escher, *Regular Division of the Plane II*, plate from *The Regular Division of the Plane*, 1958. Escher copied panels A and C from tessellations in the Alhambra and panel B from a Japanese woodcut. Panels 1, 2, and 3 are his own invention.

M. C. Escher, *Regular Division of the Plane I*, plate from *The Regular Division of the Plane*, 1958.

building that appears solid but is impossible to construct, the hands that seem to draw themselves, the water that flows uphill in apparent perpetual motion. The theme to which he returned most often—the one he called "the richest source of inspiration I have ever struck"— was the depiction of three-dimensional objects emerging by a process of metamorphosis from two-dimensional tessellations. Dissatisfied with the Moors' refusal to render the natural world, he devoted the remainder of his life to crossing the divide.

Escher's epiphany at the Alhambra has helped me to understand my own fascination with origami. The joy of "crossing the divide" is so simple and childlike that it must be an important component of human experience. We delight in endowing patterns with meaning, finding faces in the clouds and figures in the trees. When we glance up at the night sky, we cannot help but give significance to constellations that are no more than chance configurations of stars in space.

To fold a piece of paper into an object is to transform a mute, geometric shape into a recognizable figure. From the blank square emerges a chaotic pattern of angles and edges, a pattern we imbue with order and meaning—this flap resembles the head, that flap the body—until eventually, by slow, awkward steps, the living creature emerges. It is impossible to identify the moment of metamorphosis, for the transformation takes place within our own minds.

Crossing the divide is a spiritual act. At its most abstract, folding an origami animal replicates both the growth of the animal from fertilized egg to adult (the early, symmetrical folds paralleling the highly mechanical process of mitosis) and the origin of life itself. In the paper, as in the primordial cosmic soup, chaos yields to order, formlessness to form, darkness to light. When Escher reflected on the origin of his tessellations, the neutral gray background from which the black-and-white figures emerge, he felt transcendent:

> I consider the indeterminate, misty grey plane as a means of expressing static peace, of rendering the absence of time and the absence of dimension that preceded life and that will follow it; as a formless element into which all contrasts will dissolve again, "after death."

Let us begin, then, like Escher, with the formless element into which all contrasts dissolve—the empty square.

GETTING TO KNOW THE SQUARE

In the beginning was the square.

To the paperfolder, the square is the origin of all form. Geometric shapes, animals, objects, and human beings arise from the square and then, unfolded, dissolve back into it. The empty square is the alpha, the genesis, and the prime mover of origami. In Taoist philosophy, the square is the First Form, the undifferentiated void from which the opposing Yin and Yang forces arise. Where others see only the void—dull, blank, meaningless—the folder sees a world already overflowing with possibilities. His mission is to discover those possibilities and bring the square to life.

Because paper is the folder's only medium—his canvas, paint, and brush—he must get to know it intimately. What is its color? Its texture? If you fold it in half and press it flat, will it hold the crease or spring open? How far will it stretch before it rips? Rub it back and forth between your fingers. How does it *feel*?

There are many things you can do with an ordinary sheet of paper. You can crumple it and throw it away. You can roll it against the edge of a ruler and make it curl. You can write on it, and it becomes a letter. Then, if you put it in another piece of paper (an envelope) and fasten a smaller piece of paper onto that one (a stamp), it can be delivered to a friend. "Dear fellow folder..."

But there are some things you can do only with a *square* sheet of paper. The square has geometric properties that can be exploited for folding. To begin, it is regular. It has four corners, all of them measuring the same angle, 90 degrees. It has four sides, all of them the same length. And it has a vast, undifferentiated middle —as yet, unpromising. The corner of the square takes up 90 degrees of paper, the edge 180 degrees, and the middle 360 degrees.

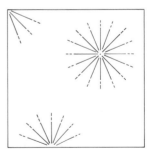

The three portions of the square: corner, edge, middle.

Our tool is geometry; our purpose, to create a representation of an animal, an object, or a human being. To do so, we must transform the square into a new shape and manufacture a separate flap from the corners, edges, and middle for each feature of the figure we're trying to create: head, neck, arms, legs, wings, horns, antennae, tail. As these appendages become long and

Family portrait: The class of all rectangles. The square is third from left.

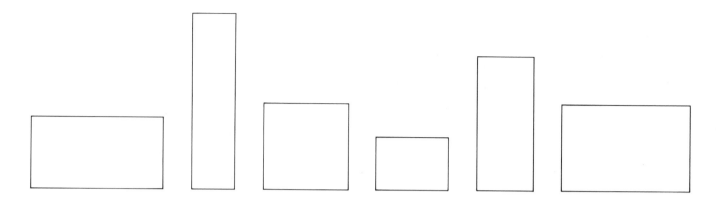

Family portrait: The class of all rhombuses. The square is fourth from left.

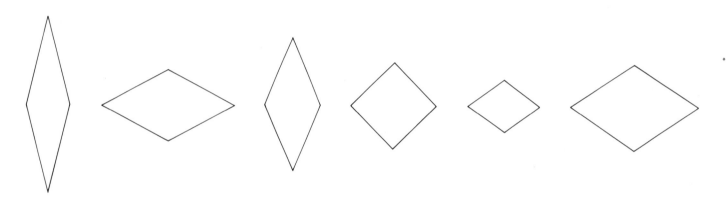

Symmetry of a square.

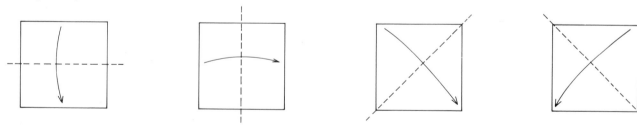

Symmetry of a rectangle.   **Symmetry of a rhombus.**

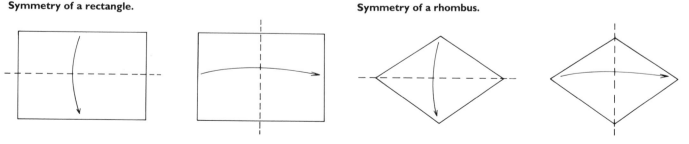

thin, the body of the animal becomes concentrated and thick, and paper that serves no function must be tucked out of sight.

For this reason, the finished model must be efficient and compact. When angles and edges line up, there is little excess paper to hide from view. The regularity and symmetry of the square mean that when you fold it, the angles and edges often align. The square is the only shape that is both a rectangle (a form with four identical angles) and a rhombus (a form with four identical sides).

Both rectangles and rhombuses exhibit a kind of symmetry called left-right symmetry or mirror-symmetry. Rectangles have mirror-symmetry along their orthogonals: If you fold the *adjacent* corners together, the sides will meet. Rhombuses have mirror-symmetry along their diagonals: If you fold the *opposite* corners together, the sides will meet. A square has both properties, which means that there are many ways of folding it so that both the angles and the edges line up.

Now that we've covered the geometry of the square, we're ready to start folding. But first, we have to review the materials, tools, and language of origami.

MATERIALS AND TOOLS

To begin, we need paper. The best paper is thin and crisp and absolutely square. For the simpler models, try Japanese origami paper, available at most art supply stores. When attempting complex models for the first time, use a sheet measuring as least 18 inches to a side. Foil-backed wrapping paper comes in rolls up to 30 inches wide and is a good kind to start with.

It is also possible to make your own paper. A method passed on to me by the folder Robert Lang requires making a sandwich of aluminum foil and two pieces of tissue paper. (For the models in this book, I used hand-made Japanese rice paper instead of tissue paper.) Tear off a piece of aluminum foil (heavy-duty Reynolds Wrap comes in a width of 18 inches), and spray one side with an aerosol adhesive (such as Scotch Spray Mount). Place the foil atop a large piece of tissue paper and smooth out the creases with a roller or the edge of a ruler. Repeat on the other side. When the sandwich is complete, mark out a square lightly with a pencil and trim with an X-acto knife. The composite sheet combines the ductility of foil (which holds its shape better than paper) and the durability of paper (foil by itself rips too easily). Experiment and invent your own techniques.

Useful tools to have on hand include a letter opener or burnisher to stiffen creases and a pair of tweezers to negotiate minute folds. It will help to have a smooth, horizontal surface to lean on, though many Japanese fold in the air.

SYMBOLS AND PROCEDURES

Origami diagrams are like a composer's score or an architect's plans: They are the key to interpreting the design, the means by which the performer or builder realizes the creator's intentions. Learning to read folding instructions takes practice, just like learning to follow a musical score. Paying attention to a few folding tips will improve your results:

- Study each diagram carefully and read the accompanying text before commencing a fold. Look ahead to the next diagram to examine the result.
- Make creases crisp. A sloppy fold made early on will grow even sloppier over the course of folding.
- Remember that paper has a thickness. Layers of paper accumulate and in the more complicated models may reach a quarter to half an inch. It is often best to leave space between two adjacent edges so that in subsequent folds they will not overlap and bunch.
- Be patient. A careless maneuver in the late stage of a model can rip the paper and mar the result. If a model proves too complicated, try another, and then return to the first. The initial attempt at folding a model rarely yields a masterpiece, but repeated tries will almost certainly improve the finished product.

The symbols and terms used in this book derive from a notational system popularized by Akira Yoshizawa in the East and by Samuel Randlett and Robert Harbin in the West. It is now the internationally accepted set of symbols, so when you have mastered the ones here, you should be able to follow the instructions in virtually any origami book. Nevertheless, books differ slightly depending upon the whim of their authors (everyone is always trying to perfect the system), and in some instances I have added my own variants and eliminated symbols or terms I have felt unnecessary. Many folding procedures have colloquial names, and I have retained them.

Symbols consist of two types: arrows and lines. There are many types of arrows, whose expressive shapes suggest the motion of the paper.

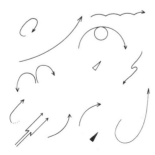

Arrows.

This arrow means "turn the paper over":

There are five types of lines.

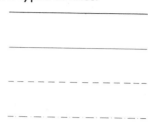

A *thick* line represents an edge of the paper, either the original edge or one produced by folding.

A *thin* line represents a crease in the paper that was formed in an earlier step.

A *dashed* line represents a valley fold.

A *dotted and dashed* line represents a mountain fold.

A *dotted* line represents a fold hidden from view, or occasionally a fold about to be formed.

A piece of paper has two sides. Thus, it can be folded in either of two directions. Each of these folds has a name. This is a *valley fold*:

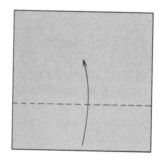

Swing the lower edge upward.

The completed valley fold.

This is a *mountain fold*:

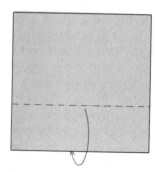

Swing the lower edge underneath.

The completed mountain fold.

Every folding procedure is a valley fold, a mountain fold, or a combination of valley and mountain folds.

In a *reverse fold*, two layers of paper are folded together symmetrically along a single crease. The reverse fold comes in two types. This is an *inside reverse fold*:

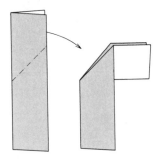

Crease firmly to form the line of the reverse fold. Spread the open edges of the paper, and turn the top portion inside out. Flatten.

The completed inside reverse fold.

This is an *outside reverse fold*:

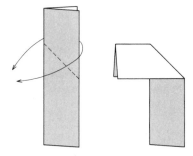

Crease firmly to form the line of the reverse fold. Spread the open edges of the paper, and turn the top portion outside in. Flatten.

The completed outside reverse fold.

All told, there are only about two dozen folding procedures, and the valley fold, mountain fold, inside reverse fold, and outside reverse fold are by far the most common. They are also the only ones you need to know for now. The remainder of the procedures will be introduced throughout the book as they become necessary. The first time a term appears, it is printed in italics and receives a full explanation. In subsequent appearances, the same name is used but an explanation may not be given. To locate the explanation of each folding procedure, consult the INDEX TO TERMS.

FOUR EASY PIECES

We're now ready to make a simple animal. Remembering that our goal is to make a compact body with long, slender appendages, let's take the logical first step. We'll begin by narrowing the portion of the square that is already the narrowest, the corner.

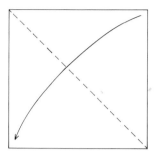

Valley-fold along the diagonal and unfold.

The completed valley fold.

We've divided the opposing corners into angles of 45 degrees. Narrow, but not narrow enough. Let's divide the corner again.

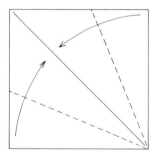

Valley-fold two edges to the centerline.

We'll also make a crease to show where the flaps fall.

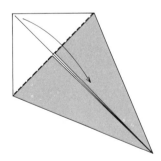

Valley-fold the corner triangle and unfold.

The completed kite base.

This shape is more promising. Because it looks like a kite, it is often called the *kite base*. *Base* is a term loosely used for a shape made from the original square that gives rise to a variety of models. The kite base is the simplest of the origami bases and was discovered hundreds of years ago by the Japanese. One of the many traditional designs that have been made from the kite base is this duck.

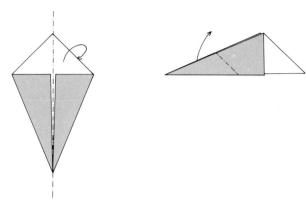

Mountain-fold the kite base in half.

Inside reverse–fold the left half upward to make the neck.

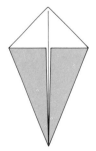

Inside reverse–fold the neck to make the head. Inside reverse–fold the right side to make the tail.

The completed duck.

We've made our first origami model, and it was pretty simple. But if we analyze it, we find that despite its simplicity, the duck possesses interesting properties.

The best way to understand an origami model is to unfold it, lay the paper flat, and draw a picture showing its important creases—not the details but the folds that constitute its essential geometry. I call this kind of drawing a *folding pattern*. Each origami model has its characteristic folding pattern; there is one reproduced for each model in this book.

The folding pattern is, by necessity, an abstraction, a reduction of a complicated form to its underlying structure. To understand that people and cows are both mammals, you have to look beyond their surface differences to their common form. The same is true of two origami models. The folding pattern is a tool enabling the folder to understand and to group models according to their fundamental similarities and differences. That knowledge, in turn, allows him to create new models.

Latent in every pristine piece of paper are undisclosed geometric patterns, combinations of angles and ratios that permit the paper to assume interesting and

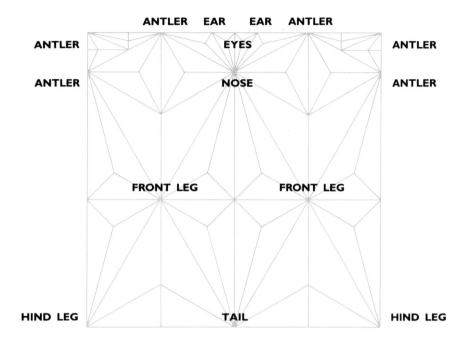

ANTLER EAR EAR ANTLER

ANTLER

EYES

ANTLER

ANTLER

NOSE

ANTLER

FRONT LEG

FRONT LEG

HIND LEG

TAIL

HIND LEG

Folding pattern to the butterfly.

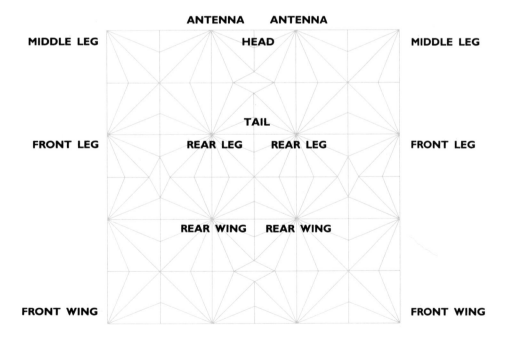

ANTENNA ANTENNA

MIDDLE LEG

HEAD

MIDDLE LEG

FRONT LEG

TAIL

REAR LEG REAR LEG

FRONT LEG

REAR WING REAR WING

FRONT WING

FRONT WING

symmetrical shapes: isosceles right triangles, twisting configurations of equilateral triangles, perfect hexagons and octagons, grids of squares within squares, rectangles with the satisfying proportions of $1 \times \sqrt{2}$ and $1 \times \sqrt{3}$. Unusual figures that at first appear to have no mathematical foundation prove on inspection to be aggregates of simpler forms. There is enough geometry in a single origami model to have kept Pythagoras busy for weeks.

In the case of the duck, the folding pattern is given by the kite base. Unfold the duck and you see this configuration of creases:

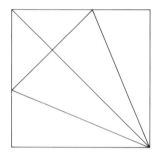

Folding pattern to the duck.

Even a form this simple has repetition. The pattern comprises two different elements, two triangles of one type and four of another. One small triangle and two large triangles make up a repeating *module:*

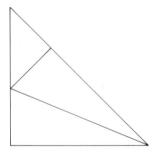

The module.

Assemble two modules, and you have the kite base. Strange as it seems, nearly every model in this book is made from multiples of this simple module!

Now suppose we want to make a slightly more complicated animal. The duck has a head, a body, and a tail. How would we make an animal with a head, a body, a tail, and two fins? One way would be to narrow not one but two corners of our square. It would be like making two kite bases on opposite corners of the square.

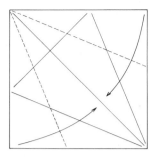

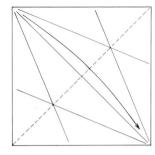

Begin with the kite base. Valley-fold two edges to the centerline and unfold.

Valley-fold the diagonal and unfold.

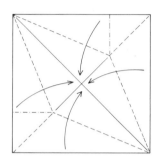

Fold all four edges to the centerline.

The completed fish base.

This shape is called the *fish base*. It is the source of another traditional Japanese model, the whale.

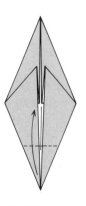

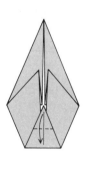

Begin with the fish base. Valley-fold the bottom tip to the center of the square.

Valley-fold the tip in half the other way.

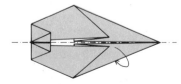

Mountain-fold the model in half.

Swing the triangular flap to the other side. Repeat on the identical flap behind.

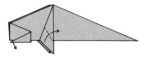

Narrow the triangular flap with a valley fold. Repeat behind.

Valley-fold the triangular flap to the right to make a fin. Repeat behind. Pull down the mouth.

Valley-fold the fin to the right. Valley-fold the tip of the mouth to form an eye. Repeat both steps behind. Inside reverse–fold the tail.

The completed whale.

Now let's open up the whale and examine its folding pattern:

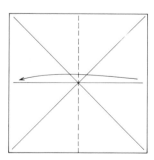

Folding pattern to the whale.

The pattern reveals a total of four small triangles and eight large ones, all of the type we encountered before. All told, it comprises four modules.

Now to the next level of complexity. What happens if we try to narrow all the corners into fourths? It would be like making four kite bases, one on each corner. Somehow we will have to resolve the configuration of the paper in the middle, where they all meet. The easiest way to do this is first to fold a figure known as the *preliminary fold*.

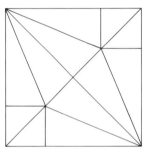

Begin with a square folded along the diagonals. Valley-fold the top half to the bottom. Unfold.

Valley-fold the right half to the left. Unfold.

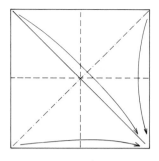

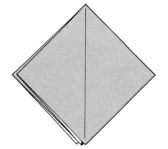

Collapse all four sides at once.

The completed preliminary fold.

We're ready to narrow the four sides. To do this, we will use a procedure called a *petal fold*. In a petal fold, a flap is lifted out of the plane of the paper and stretched. The stretching causes the flap's two sides to come together. When the flap has stretched as far as it will go, the sides touch and the flap lies flat. The petal fold can take many forms. The most common is the following:

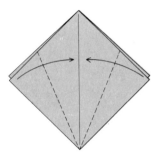

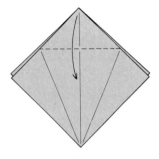

Begin with the preliminary fold. Valley-fold the edges to the centerline. Unfold.

Valley-fold the top triangle down and press firmly. Unfold.

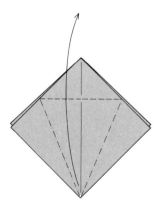

Lift the bottom corner.

Stretch the corner upward as far as it will go.

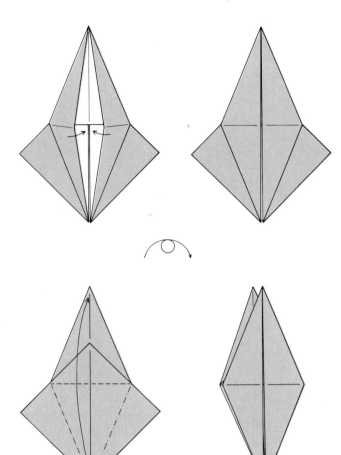

Flatten.

The completed petal fold. Turn the paper over.

Repeat the previous steps.

The completed bird base.

This is the *bird base,* the source of the famous Japanese flapping bird. The flapping bird is easy to make:

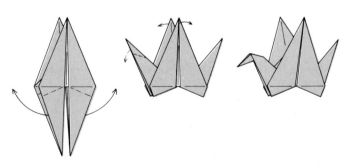

Begin with the bird base. Inside reverse–fold two flaps upward to make the neck and tail.

Inside reverse–fold the neck to make the head. Spread the wings.

Grasp the tail with one hand and the bottom of the neck with the other. Pull apart to make the wings flap.

Unfolding the flapping bird reveals a more intricate folding pattern than the ones we have seen before:

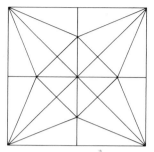

Folding pattern to the flapping bird.

Nevertheless, we recognize a familiar form—the module, now repeated eight times. Could this be a coincidence?

Nothing in mathematics is a coincidence! If a pattern or form or formula recurs, you can bet that there is an underlying reason for it. (We'll find out later why we keep running into these shapes.)

Now that we have narrowed first one corner, then two corners, and finally four corners, we have run out of corners. The next step is less obvious. In order to get a base offering more than four flaps, we have to turn to the center of the paper, to a point that is as far away from the four corners as the square permits. To narrow the center of the paper, along with the four corners, we go back to the preliminary fold. Along the way we will encounter a new procedure, the *squash fold*, and a different version of the petal fold.

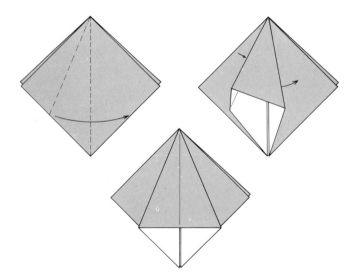

Begin with the preliminary fold. Lift the left-hand flap and swing it to the right.

Squash the flap so that it lands symmetrically. Flatten.

The completed squash fold.

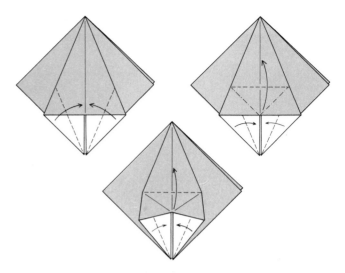

This is a preliminary fold with one flap squashed. Valley-fold the edges of the flap to the centerline and unfold.

Lift the center of the horizontal edge, and stretch it upward.

Continue stretching until the sides meet and the flap has stretched as far as it can. Flatten.

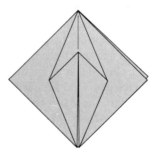

The completed petal fold. Repeat this procedure on the remaining three sides.

The completed frog base.

This configuration is called the *frog base* because it is the source of the traditional Japanese jumping frog:

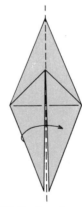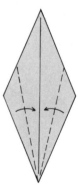

Begin with the frog base. Swing the left-hand flap over to the right.

Valley-fold the two sides to the centerline.

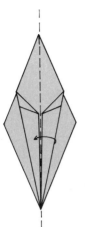

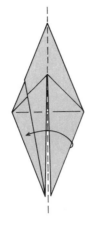

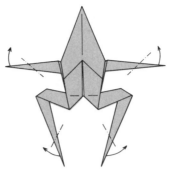

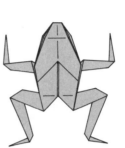

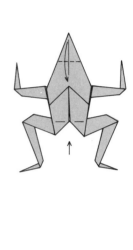

Swing the right-hand flap over to the left.

Repeat the previous steps on the three remaining pairs of flaps.

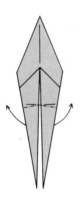

Inside reverse–fold both pairs of legs again.

Valley-fold the tip of the head to the tip of the loose triangle. Press firmly and unfold. Inflate the frog by blowing gently through the hole.

The completed jumping frog. Tap on its back to make the frog jump.

Unfolding the frog yields the next step in the evolution of the bases, the folding pattern to the frog base:

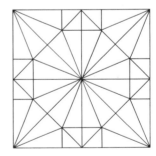

Folding pattern to the jumping frog.

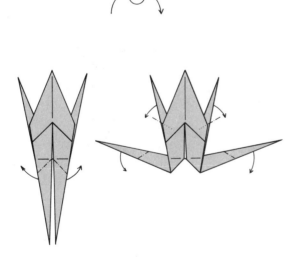

Inside reverse–fold the two top flaps upward.

These are the front legs. Turn the model over.

Inside reverse–fold the two top flaps out to the sides. These are the back legs.

Inside reverse–fold both pairs of legs.

Scrutinizing this pattern reveals even more complexity than before. Counting the number of modules in the frog base yields sixteen.

BASE	NUMBER OF MODULES
Kite	2
Fish	4
Bird	8
Frog	16

THE FOUR FUNDAMENTAL BASES AND THEIR FOLDING PATTERNS

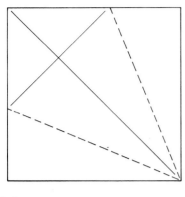 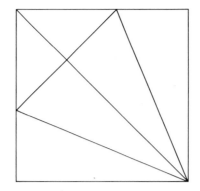 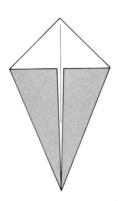

Kite base.

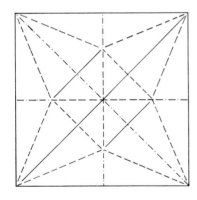 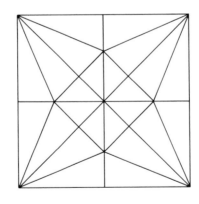 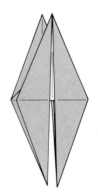

Fish base.

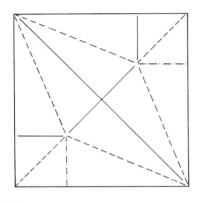 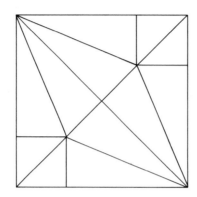 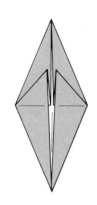

Bird base.

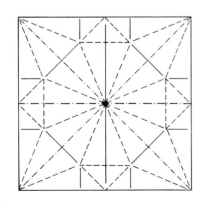 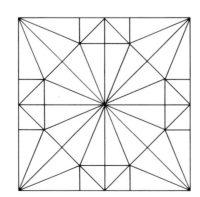 

Frog base.

Two, four, eight, sixteen... Something's going on here! We have glimpsed a rare order, the repetition of simple elements to create complex patterns in the paper. The key is a module, a form so simple, yet so essential, that we have only begun to grasp its importance.

The frog base completes the set of simple bases that I call the *four fundamental bases*. The bases share both geometry and history: They were discovered by the ancient Japanese and for over a thousand years served as the source of many origami models made in Japan. Yet, strangely enough, the Japanese stumbled on them by accident. They paid little attention to the geometry of the square, and there is no indication that they recognized patterns in the paper. To my knowledge, this is the first time that the geometric relationship among the four bases has appeared in print.

FOLDING: A COMPACT HISTORY

Paperfolding originated in China around the first or second century A.D. and reached Japan by the sixth century. The Japanese called this new art form *origami* (the name coined from *ori*, "to fold," and *gami*, "paper") and cultivated it as an art of understatement. Origami suggests; it implies without announcing outright, intimates without brashness. It exists best in a kind of light the Japanese call *ke*, a soft, gentle light for intimate occasions. Why use a bright light when you can see in a dim one? Why shout when you can whisper? For that matter, why draw the entire bamboo tree when a few brushstrokes suffice? Just as a three-line haiku evokes a setting or a season, the placement of a rock and a pond in a Japanese garden recalls the universe. It is a short imaginative leap from the rock to a mountain, from the pond to the sea.

Origami is an art of economy. A few simple creases evoke an animal; modify the sequence slightly, and an entirely new beast appears. To the Japanese sensibility, the success of a completed origami figure depends on the creator's eye for form, structure, and proportion. Does it capture the creature's true form, the placement of its head and limbs, the shape of its shoulders and hips? Does it suggest the animal's motion, its stride, glide, or gallop? And finally, is the paper figure a mere likeness of the original, or does it delve deeper, into its essential character?

Over many generations, the Japanese developed and refined a small repertoire of models that are stylized and abstract, often involving cuts and painted or printed details. (For a while, the Chinese produced their own individualized models, including the famous Chinese

A Japanese word is a complex pattern composed of simple elements. This word consists of two characters which derive, like much of Japanese writing, from Chinese characters. The left-hand element of a character is a radical, or root, which suggests the character's etymological origin. The radical at the top left derives from a picture of a hand; the character means "to fold." The radical at the bottom left derives from a picture of silk; the character means "paper." Together, the two characters form the word "to fold paper"—origami.

junk, but their work was soon subsumed into the Japanese tradition.) By the Heian period, from 794 to 1185, origami had become a significant part of the ceremonial life of the Japanese nobility. Since paper was still a rare and precious commodity, paperfolding was a diversion only the rich could afford. Samurai warriors exchanged gifts adorned with *noshi,* good-luck tokens of folded paper and strips of abalone or dried meat. Shinto noblemen celebrated weddings with glasses of *sake,* rice wine, wrapped in male and female paper butterflies representing the bride and groom. Tea ceremony masters received their diplomas specially folded to prevent misuse in case the documents should fall into the wrong hands. (Once the paper was opened, it could not be resealed without allowing extra creases to show.) Even today, the expression *origami tsuki* means "certified" or "guaranteed."

When paper became inexpensive enough to be used by everyone, origami assumed a new ceremonial role, as a means of social stratification. During the Muromachi period, a time of military rule from 1338 to 1573, origami styles served to distinguish the aristocratic samurai —who folded in the so-called Ise manner—from farmers and peasants, followers of the school of Ogasawara. People knew their place, and they folded accordingly.

The democratization of origami came only in the Tokugawa period, from 1603 to 1867, the great efflorescence of Japanese art and culture often likened to the Elizabethan Age in England. The Tokugawa period saw the emergence of the bird base, documented in the oldest surviving publication on origami, the *Senbazuru Orikata* ("How to Fold One Thousand Cranes") of 1797. The Tokugawa period also witnessed the publication in 1845 of the *Kan no mado* ("Window on Midwinter"), the first comprehensive collection of origami figures, which includes the first appearance of the frog base.

With the development of the frog base, origami acquired still another ceremonial usage. In Japanese the word for "frog" and the verb for "to return" are pronounced the same way, and it became customary for a geisha to pin a paper frog to a pillar after entertaining a favorite patron, in the hope that he would return. With the union of these two universal pastimes, origami had become the consummately democratic art form. But there were few other developments, and until the resurgence of origami in this century, only about 150 simple models, handed down from generation to generation, remained to attest to a millennium of Japanese folding.

The Japanese were not, however, the only ones to cultivate paperfolding. It developed simultaneously under the Moors, Muslims who flourished in North Africa and brought paperfolding to Spain when they invaded in the eighth century. The Moors were expert

Traditional Japanese models are the legacy of a thousand years of folding. The butterflies *ocho* and *mecho*, from the Heian period, are reprinted from the *Kan no mado*.

Early models from the Heian period include three good-luck tokens called *noshi*. They are reprinted from the book *Hanatsu tsumi* ("Flower Wrappings") by K. Ashida, published in 1900.

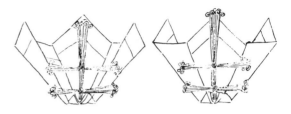

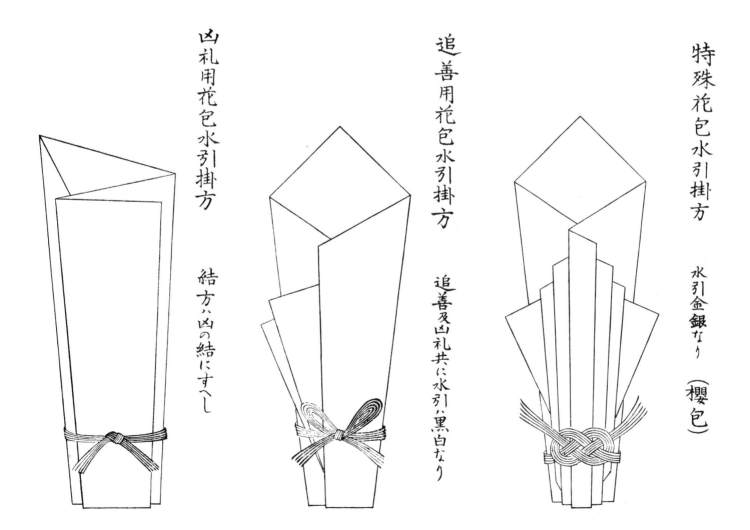

凶礼用花包水引掛方　　結方ハ凶の結にすへし

追善用花包水引掛方　　追善及凶礼共に水引ハ黒白なり

特殊花包水引掛方　　水引金銀なり（櫻包）

The *Senbazuru Orikata* dates from the Tokugawa period and contains instructions for folding forty-nine different families of cranes from sheets of cut paper. The woman standing at the right of the woodcut holds a family of eight cranes; a family of eighteen cranes and a family of ninety-seven cranes are also shown, along with their respective cutting patterns. The crane is a Japanese symbol of longevity; folding 1,000 cranes is said to assure a long and peaceful life.

The crane is similar to the flapping bird, and it is possible to construct a family of flapping birds from the same cutting pattern. To construct the family at left, cut the paper as shown. Match the lower-left-hand square with the upper-right-hand square and fold them together to make a single crane or flapping bird. (Study the drawing of the finished model to locate the position of the head, tail, and wings.) Moving counterclockwise from the corners, repeat with the six loose squares at top and bottom. Fold the remaining squares into individual birds.

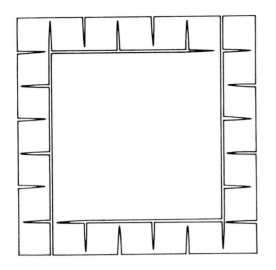

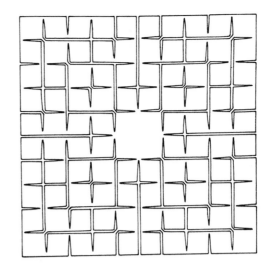

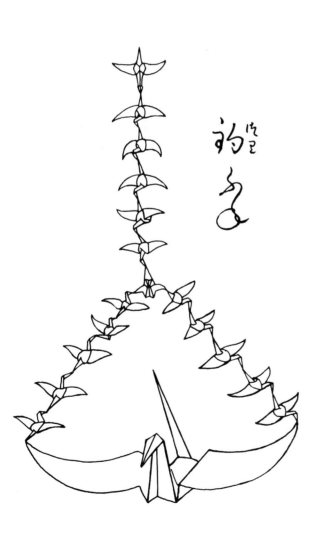

The *Kan no mado* also dates from the Tokugawa period and contains instructions for folding forty-eight popular models, including both animals and human figures. The left-hand panel, clockwise from top left, shows Ariwara no Narihira (one of the six poets), a prawn, a snail, a wrestler, and a spider. The right-hand panel, clockwise from top left, shows Ono no Komachi (a woman poet), a crab, a lobster, a comic dancer, an octopus, and a dragonfly. Of the models shown, only the snail does not require cutting.

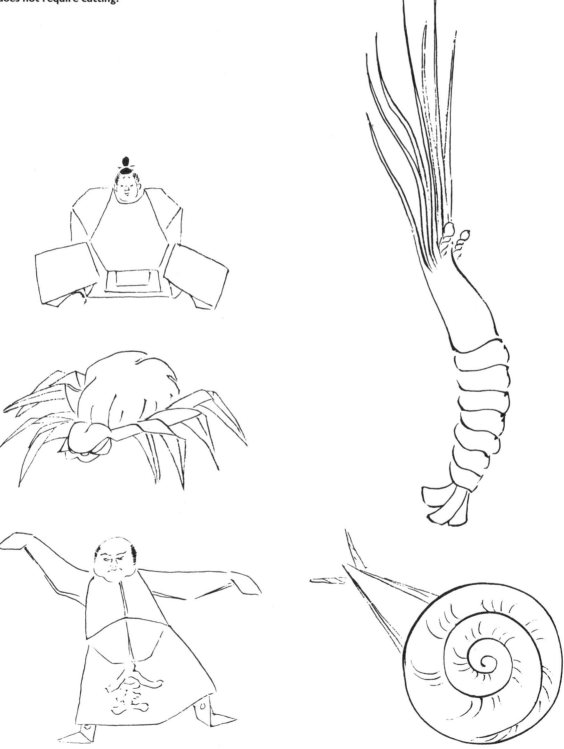

A helmet with tortoise and crane is a recent Japanese creation, dating from the Meiji Restoration (1868–1912).

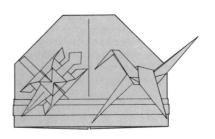

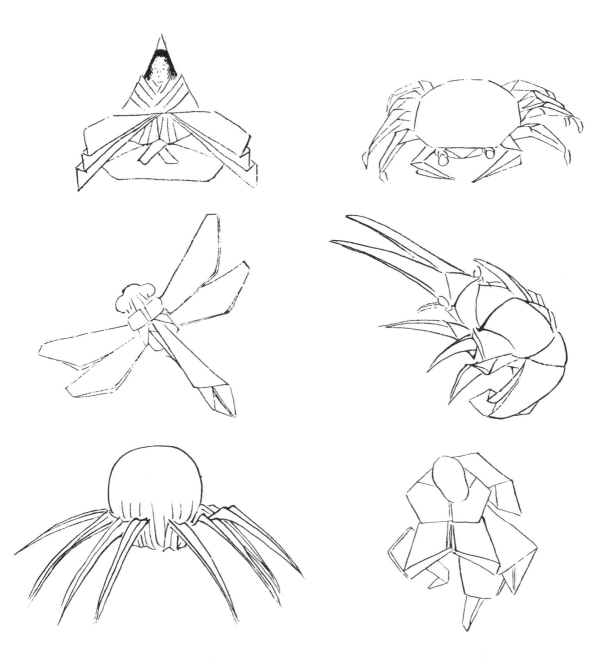

The Moors' paperfolding studies probably resembled Islamic tessellations of the square, shown here in a seventeenth-century Persian manuscript that is a copy of an earlier text in Arabic. The square tile at the lower-right-hand corner of the page is generated by a series of six geometric operations related to folding. In the fourth step, the angle formed by the two dashed lines is sixty degrees; if it is reduced to forty-five degrees, the proportions are those of the folding pattern to the alligator. Nine tiles produce the tessellation at right.

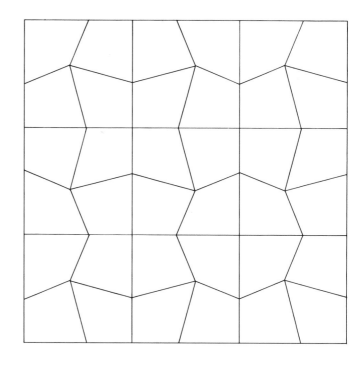

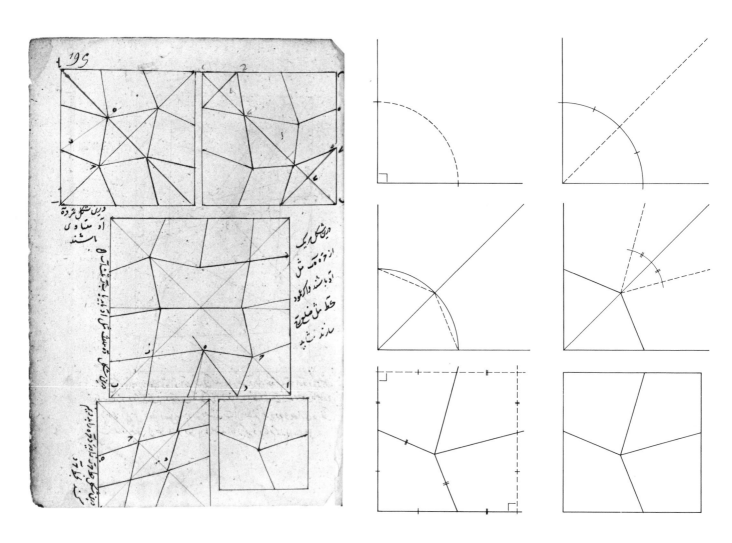

mathematicians and astronomers (they gave us Arabic numerals and the term *algebra*), and they instilled paperfolding with the principles of geometry. What a pity it is that they did not allow themselves to make representational figures! This practice (to echo Escher) would have contradicted Islam. Instead, they investigated the many folding properties of the square, much as they explored ways of covering the walls of the Alhambra with tessellations and applied their advanced knowledge of trigonometry to mapping the stars.

The Moors' activity flourished throughout the High Middle Ages, and if they had not been expelled during the Spanish Inquisition, folding might today be considered a predominantly Spanish pastime. Nevertheless, an indigenous tradition of folding survived in Spain to the early twentieth century, when it came under the tutelage of philosopher and poet Miguel de Unamuno (1864–1936). Unamuno wrote two treatises on paperfolding and was a popular figure in Salamanca, where he could often be seen folding animals while sipping his midday coffee at a café. (By then, the restriction on representational origami had lapsed.) Many of Unamuno's creations and those of his followers are still in the repertoire, and an Unamuno "school" exists in Spain and South America even today.

It remained for twentieth-century folders to tie the two strands together. The inheritors of the Japanese and Moorish traditions now communicate freely through books, magazines, and conferences, the result of movements that have sprung up throughout the world. The dissemination of Japanese aesthetics throughout Europe and America and of Western science in Japan has produced a new generation of paperfolders equally at home in both traditions. And a remarkable cross-fertilization has taken place.

In the West, where origami is most widely practiced by children, it has never achieved the status of an art. For generations, European and American schoolchildren have made water bombs and fortune-tellers, flapping birds and jumping frogs. The highly ordered process of folding is their means of apprehending nature in a systematic way: It imposes a rigid order on the flux of the external world and gives them mastery over their environment. I believe that in this child's impulse lies a key to creativity. The fundamental urge to discover order in a nebulous world—or to impose it on the world— remains with us as we grow older, and it is one of the underpinnings of both art and science. It is hardly surprising that educators from Friedrich Froebel, the nineteenth-century inventor of Froebel blocks, to Laszlo Moholy-Nagy, a leader of the Bauhaus, incorporated paperfolding exercises into their lessons.

But a child's activity—especially one in a perishable medium, like paper—is a suspect art, with little cachet and even less commercial value. Here, in America, paper

Traditional Spanish models are the legacy of the Moors' experiments with the geometry of folding. Shown are the traditional praying Moor and six models by Miguel de Unamuno. Clockwise from the top left, they are an eagle, a teapot, a gorilla, a table, a bear, and a vulture.

Western paperfolders have included Leonardo da Vinci, Lewis Carroll, Miguel de Unamuno, and Harry Houdini.

Leonardo da Vinci entered into his *Codex Atlanticus* a number of geometric exercises in paperfolding along with a study of the velocity and motion of paper airplanes. Shown at right are some of his paperfolding studies.

The Reverend Charles Lutwidge Dodgson taught mathematics at Oxford and published puzzles, humorous verse, and two children's fantasies written under the pen name Lewis Carroll. He also entertained the children of royalty at his country home with toys folded from paper and recorded the events with delight in his diary. Shown at far right are two scenes from John Tenniel's illustrations for Carroll's *Through the Looking-Glass* (1871). In the railway car scene, Alice's fellow passenger is dressed entirely in white paper. In the walrus and carpenter scene, the carpenter wears an origami hat. The hat was later appropriated by printing press operators to keep the ink out of their hair.

Miguel de Unamuno wrote two treatises on paperfolding and invented dozens of models that are still in the origami repertoire. Shown at lower right is a portrait of Unamuno by Ignacio Zuloaga y Zamora from 1925. On the table to Unamuno's right are two origami birds.

Harry Houdini, better known as an escape artist and the author of *Handcuff Secrets*, also published in 1922 one of the first books on origami in English, *Houdini's Paper Magic*, shown below.

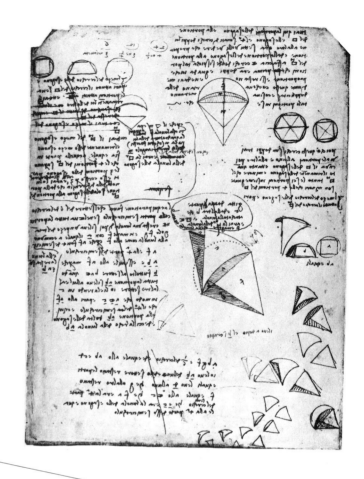

is made to be discarded: There are always more trees. Not so in Japan, where the wrapping is often more valuable than the gift.

In this country, origami was taken up not by artists but by mathematicians. Its practitioners are scientists, engineers, and architects, heirs to the Moorish tradition of paperfolding. Enter a new set of aesthetic standards, the values of the geometer. The mathematician's idea of beauty draws its inspiration from an ideal world, a world of regularity, pattern, and order. Beauty is identified by simplicity and economy: the brevity of a proof, the compactness of a crystal, the symmetry of the Moorish mosaics at the Alhambra. Euclid's axioms, the Pythagorean theorem, harmonic motion, and the four-color-map theorem achieve maximal ends through minimal means. Why use more colors if four suffice?

To the mathematician, the beauty of origami is its simple geometry. The mathematician asks: Does the finished design make the greatest use of the existing geometry? Is the folding procedure elegant and pristine, with crisp lines, compact folds, simple and regular proportions? Is there no wasted paper, awkward thickness, or arbitrary fold? Is utility served in each step?

Today, a work of origami must exemplify both the artist's and the mathematician's standards of beauty. It must be anatomically accurate—an American demand, not a Japanese one—yet suggest more than it shows. It may employ folding techniques that are unexpected, but never arbitrary, and whose logic may become clear only when the entire figure has been completed. To the folder who meets these demands head-on, the constraints of the medium are not a limitation but a stimulus to greater imagination.

I MEET THE MASTER

If one man can be said to have brought about origami's present renaissance, it is Akira Yoshizawa of Japan. Yoshizawa, called *sensei*, master, may be the most prolific folder in the history of origami. In his younger days (he was born in 1911), he created new origami models with abandon, working twenty hours at a stretch and churning out extraordinarily lifelike, sculpted representations of mammals, plants, birds, fish, reptiles, masks, gliders, tops, and geometric solids that expand or collapse with a flick of the wrist. Yoshizawa, the Linnaeus of paperfolding, turned out six, eight, ten versions of each model, refining and streamlining them, categorizing and classifying everything that swims, runs, or flies.

While other paperfolders busied themselves with hats and cups, water bombs and fortune-tellers, Yoshizawa produced butterflies, moths, ladybugs, bees, dragonflies, and the ubiquitous Japanese beetle. Another

A GALLERY OF OLD (AND YOUNG) MASTERS

Dukuotei Nakano has had a lifetime fascination with the crane. Among his hundreds of variations on this two-century-old model are standing cranes, swimming cranes, seated cranes, pleated cranes, stooping, swooping, and whooping cranes. His origami correspondence course on the crane is known worldwide, and he has completed a television videotape to expand his audience still further. Nakano now divides his time between origami and cat's cradle. He has invented some thirty original string patterns, including a giraffe that wiggles as it walks from hand to hand. Shown is one of his variations on the crane.

folder might have been satisfied to invent a deer, but for Yoshizawa that was not specific enough—would it be an antelope, springbok, dik-dik, or wapiti? His models were designed with proportion, crafted with sensitivity, and charged with life; anything that moves he captured in midmotion, leaping, charging, hovering, diving, gliding. And in time the models accumulated, filling up boxes and drawers, closets and shelves, basements and attics at a rate of three new models a day, twenty a week, a thousand a year: 50,000 over a lifetime of folding.

As Yoshizawa approaches the apogee of his career, a new sense of urgency has overtaken him. Although he is still creating models at a prodigious rate, he has begun preparing for posterity. An origami model is a delicate thing: Fire, rain, wind, human carelessness spell its doom. Using a special long-lasting paper that is manufactured by only one company in Japan, Yoshizawa is folding one copy of each of his most important models to last for hundreds of years. When each is finished, it is wrapped in gauze and placed in a succession of wooden boxes on a shelf in a humidity-controlled room in Yoshizawa's house.

But even under perfect conditions, no origami model lives forever. Paper crumbles, colors fade, creases broaden. So Yoshizawa is establishing his legacy in another way, one that will withstand all time. In recent years he has begun drawing diagrams that show, step by step, how to fold each of his models. Yet so far Yoshizawa has illustrated only a dozen books, a mere 300 models, little more than half a percent of his total output. And still he continues to invent new models faster than he can illustrate them. Only a madman would continue alone in the face of such a Sisyphean task, but Yoshizawa refuses to entrust such important work to his pupils. His strenuous regimen of creating, teaching, and illustrating allows for only three or four hours' sleep a night. If Yoshizawa were to stop creating today and turn all his effort to producing a book a year, it would still take him two thousand years to complete the task. The world waits for Akira Yoshizawa.

Only in Japan would such single-minded devotion to a hopeless cause be taken as a matter of course. As an origami *sensei,* Yoshizawa is treated with the same respect accorded any great craftsman, whether calligrapher, cook, poet, painter, or Buddhist priest. Now, as in centuries past, the pupil of a master craftsman must undergo an extended apprenticeship before he is permitted to produce original work. If he is apprenticed to a painter, he will wash brushes, look after the studio, cook meals, and entertain guests; and slowly, by observation, acquire the skills and style of his master. One sushi cook informed me that as the apprentice to a master chef, he had spent fifteen years washing dishes and sweeping floors before he was even allowed to make the sushi rice ball. Now, after fifteen years of

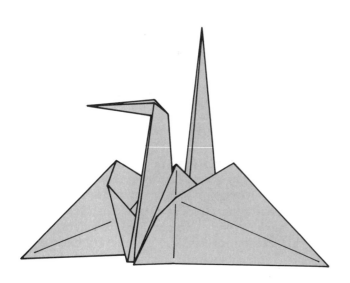

preparing rice balls, he considers himself barely proficient. "I think in maybe ten more years I will be good," he said.

It is less true now, but in the past this posture of servility continued even after the master's death. When a master printmaker died, his favorite pupil would continue to make prints in the master's style, and even, on occasion, assume the master's name—hence the proliferation in art books of Toyokunis, Hiroshiges, Kunisadas. A pupil of the printmaker Harunobu, who took the master's name after his death, finally had to change his name back: The public had begun to believe that he was Harunobu.

Yoshizawa's role as origami master would be straightforward if he were the only one, but in fact Japan has many of them. Their divisiveness runs deep. Some refuse to recognize any model that involves cutting or glue. Others allow cutting or glue, but reject metallic foil. Another group actually prefers foil, but refuses to fold from more than one piece of paper. Still another insists that some models must be folded from more than one piece of paper, but they must all be square. One defiant individual refuses to fold from a square; he folds only from the "true" rectangle, measuring $1 \times \sqrt{2}$, a shape that evolved, he explained to me, sometime in the early days of Creation, a little after the circle but (significantly) before the square. Seen individually, each of these master folders is a model of Japanese politeness and grace. Put them in a room together and it would be an ugly scene indeed.

To protect his work from plagiarism, Yoshizawa has devised a system of rules and regulations of Byzantine complexity. With the exception of close friends and select pupils, Japanese folders cannot enter his home. Although, like other masters, he exhibits his work in museums and department stores, he displays only those models he has already published and stands guard at the door to screen visitors. Yoshizawa has made himself a political entity. As the president of the International Origami Centre, he is venerated throughout Japan. In addition to his intensive, four-day mountain retreat each summer, he teaches group classes twice a week and grants private lessons to a select few.

Attempts by other masters to enter Yoshizawa's circle have been rudely rebuffed. Some years ago, Saburo Kase, a master folder who has been blind since childhood, showed up at Yoshizawa's door and petitioned to be his pupil. By Kase's account, Yoshizawa rejected the request and forbade him to enter the house, proclaiming, "Origami is not for the blind." Such tales, apocryphal or true, are hardly the harbinger of good relations. If Yoshizawa stands alone among paperfolders, the reason is simple: No one else will approach him.

I had always dreamed of meeting Yoshizawa, and a few years ago I summoned the courage to request an

Saburo Kase, blind since childhood, began folding at the age of thirty and has since become one of Japan's best-loved origami masters. Folding entirely by feel, he invents simple, charming, and often whimsical figures, such as a scuttling crab, a crouching frog, a mountain goat, a butterfly ring, a stand-up valentine, and a "double penguin," two linked penguins formed from a single sheet. Kase is a world traveler who lectures and teaches origami to organizations for the blind. One of his most prized possessions is a string tie, a souvenir from a visit to Texas. Shown is his model of a swordfish.

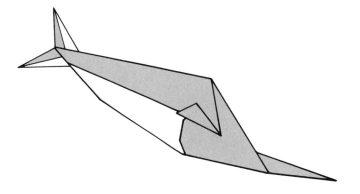

Toyoaki Kawai is a maker of masks. His tastes range from the sacred to the profane; among his thousands of creations are Buddha masks, priest masks, human masks, animal masks, Chinese opera masks, two-faced masks, many-colored masks, and ghost, goblin, and devil masks. Kawai favors the esoteric and the bizarre. In addition to masks, his models include a panoply of beetles (scarab, ground, long-horned, rhinoceros, hercules, Japanese, stag), a giant panda (life-size), an electric snake (it coils and strikes with the aid of a motor), and a series of models on erotic themes, best left undescribed. Shown is his model of a Daruma priest mask.

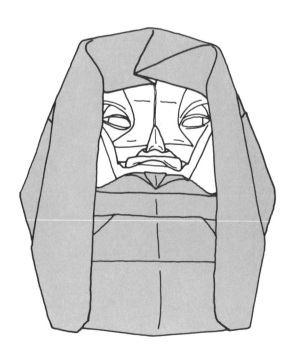

audience. Along with my humble letter I enclosed a reindeer, a modest sample of my work. Six weeks later I received a reply. "I believe your deep understanding of origami," Yoshizawa wrote, in gracious but not quite grammatical English. "Let's talk about my thoughts of origami and your work when we see each other." He had agreed to see me! I felt like a peasant summoned to meet the shogun.

It was my first meeting with a Japanese master, and I wanted to make a good impression. On a July afternoon in the middle of Japan's rainy season (paperfolders are particularly sensitive to humidity), I rode the Japan National Railroad from Tokyo to Ogikubo, the affluent suburb where Yoshizawa lives. The trip afforded me an hour and a half to rehearse the few Japanese phrases I had thought necessary to learn for the occasion: "Good afternoon," "Good evening," "Where is the rest room?" and "Master, I throw myself at your feet." I struggled to recall the appropriate rules of etiquette. Is it an insult to bow lower than your host, or not low enough? Do I dip the sushi in the mustard and then the soy sauce—or is it the other way around? I was sure to commit a disastrous faux pas. If I spilled tea on Yoshizawa's favorite model, I would never be asked back.

At the station in Ogikubo I was greeted by Hiromi Nakamura, a paperfolding friend of Yoshizawa's who had agreed to interpret. She led the way to Yoshizawa's home, and we soon stood at the doorstep of a modern two-story house, the portal so few had crossed. The door swung inward, and there stood Yoshizawa: small, wiry, unassuming. With a grin and an outstretched hand, he beckoned us in.

Following custom, we removed our shoes at the door and exchanged them for cloth slippers. We shuffled over straw tatami mats to a room like a den, a spacious study equipped with a long wooden table and chairs, diverse lighting apparatuses, and a special humidity control. Lining the four walls were shelves supporting large cardboard boxes. It was not hard to guess what they contained.

Yoshizawa hopped up on the table and retrieved one of the boxes from a shelf. He undid the top and removed a large wooden box, then undid the top of the wooden box and removed a smaller wooden box, each one planed, stained, and polished. Box within box within box, when suddenly, from inside the smallest, shrouded in protective rice-paper gauze, nearly lost among the packaging, emerged a tiny, exquisitely crafted woolly mammoth. Yoshizawa lovingly removed it and placed it on the table, turning it this way and that. I had hardly had a chance to see it when he snatched it away and returned it to the box, consigning it to another long, lonely period of hibernation. The unwrapping repeated itself in reverse: rice paper, small box, large box, cardboard box, Yoshizawa up on the table to fetch a new model.

This procedure went on for hour after hour, as the most extraordinary origami figures I have ever seen paraded before me for tantalizing glimpses of only a few seconds apiece. Yoshizawa's hands darted among the models like a pair of tiny sparrows, flickering, deft. As I watched, entranced, Yoshizawa related to me the story of a life spent folding.

"I never learned from a teacher," he began. "My teacher is nature, the animals and the birds and the flowers. When I do origami, I listen to nature, not with these ears but with the ears of my heart. I look at the actual creatures, and I also study on my own. I read constantly—in physiology, zoology, anatomy, neurobiology, embryology. It's important to know the structure of each object. Whenever I fold from nature, I think about the structural lines, how the object grows and develops, starting from the womb.

"When I fold an octopus, for instance, I don't fold it the way you do, based on an eight-pointed star. A real octopus never passes through a star shape. It starts from the egg and develops gradually, in the simplest and shortest way, into an octopus. I try to follow that process. It's also important to understand the evolution of whole species. That's why I study the different classifications of bone structure in the dinosaurs, the bird hip and the lizard hip. If you learn the basic form, it's easy to go on to other species."

I asked if he had folded many dinosaurs.

"All of them! Tyrannosaurus rex. Iguanodon. Triceratops. Brontosaurus. Stegosaurus. I'd show them to you, but they're in the attic."

Yoshizawa's claim that in his models folding recapitulates ontogeny was extraordinary, and, somewhat skeptically, I asked whether it extended to insects. Butterflies, I reminded him, spend their larva stage as caterpillars, occupying a form that is completely different.

Without answering, Yoshizawa reached into the box and removed a small insect, placing it in the palm of his hand: a life-sized cicada. Six legs, wings, head, thorax, abdomen, antennae—it was impeccably crafted, a masterpiece.

"It took me thirty years to invent," he said, breaking the silence. "I began with the earliest stage, developed it, and gradually it improved. You seem astonished that it took so long to invent, but for one insect to become that insect in nature, for its entire species to evolve, takes thousands and thousands of years. Of course, it's easier to imitate the things that nature has already made, so it doesn't take as long. But even to imitate it took thirty years!

"I have lots of fish, too, beginning with the coelacanth. Also mammals. Here are some dogs. Saint Bernard. Alaskan husky. Greyhound. Borzoi. Great Dane.

Eiji Nakamura was a professional cameraman and amateur aviator before he turned to origami. A photojournalist and documentary filmmaker (he supervised the filming of the 1964 Olympic games in Tokyo), he gave up photography in 1967 to fulfill his dream of inventing a fully human-powered aircraft. Buoyed by the success of his hot-air dirigible, Nakamura began work on a hand-built, bicycle-powered plane but was sidetracked when his car crashed on the way to the test site. "Although this seemed a serious misfortune at the time," one of his book jackets reads, "it had a brighter side because it gave him an opportunity to begin research on origami aircraft." While still in traction, folding exclusively from a rectangle, Nakamura began producing the flying storks, cranes, gliders, fighters, bombers, cruisers, and biplanes that have made him the preeminent creator of flying origami. His bicycle-powered plane never got off the ground. Shown is his model of a jet fighter plane.

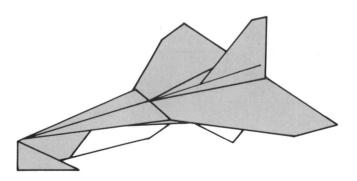

These leaves, grass, and buds you won't find in a book —they're too hard to write down. Those shelves over there are just for masks. These two boxes contain tops. I don't include any that stop spinning in less than five seconds. The center of the paper is not necessarily in the center of the top. To understand that, you'd have to study with me for more than three months, because I studied that long before I developed my own theory of tops. I had to learn gyroscopics, the study of stability. And for the gliders I learned aerodynamics. They're closely related to the tops. I have more than a hundred kinds, and I'm quite strict with them. Take a piece of paper fifty centimeters [about 20 inches] square. Wet it, make it into a ball, tie it with thread, squeeze it tight. When it dries it becomes hard, like a ball made of wood. Now, if you throw it, it will go quite far. But my gliders must go farther than that or they might as well not be gliders."

A ZEN PHILOSOPHY

Yoshizawa continued: "Because I was originally an iron-smith, I know a lot about materials. But mostly I learned from nature. Nature is cleverer than we are. The ground seems flat to our eyes, but if you make an indentation and put in a little bit of water, the water always flows from the highest point to the lowest. No matter how clever the human being is, he won't know which way the ground tilts. But the water knows where to go. Like the water, the glider finds which way to go through the air. It knows how to glide most naturally, how to adjust its wings for uplift, how long to fly before falling to the ground. It's not something you can see, but the structure's there. I'm working on a new way of studying origami with shadows. I use this spotlight to make shadows so I can study aspects of models, like gliders, that cannot otherwise be seen.

"I think no one in origami has gone as far as I have, so that must mean I'm the smartest person in origami. But in other words that means I'm also the stupidest person, the biggest maniac. Look, here is the crane, folded from a three-millimeter [about 0.12-inch] square."

He held out a plastic box that appeared empty but on second glance revealed the smallest models I have ever seen: a miniature crab, with all eight legs and claws, a tiny jumping frog, and an almost microscopic crane.

"I made the crane without using a magnifying glass," he explained. "It's folded from paper of the lotus flower. And the frog is made from the inside of a bamboo shoot. To make them I used very dim light. I covered a light bulb with a black lampshade and made a hole four millimeters [about 0.16 inch] in diameter. It's much

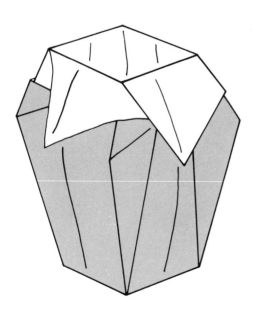

more accurate that way. The reason has to do with the structure of the eye. There are hundreds of thousands of nerve cells, in the shape of rods and cones, behind each eye. You could fit as many on a postage stamp as there are people in the United States. So even if there's only a little stimulation, the eye adjusts to it.

"Japanese are accustomed to using dim light. For a long period we used paper-shade lanterns, which don't tire out the eyes. Once you get used to dim light, you see quite easily. Nowadays, of course, we use fluorescent bulbs, but there are still some places, like the Imperial Hotel in Tokyo, where they imitate the lighting of the old Katsura Palace. So when you walk in you feel comfortable, not excited or uneasy.

"In Japan we have two ways of seeing. One is called *hare*, and the other is *ke*. *Hare* means shiny and outward. It's the way you enjoy things in the sunshine, in very bright places, and on formal and fancy occasions. *Ke* is the way you appreciate things in ordinary light, in a quiet and comfortable atmosphere, like at home. To see art exhibits or hold lectures, we always use dim light, and for religious ceremonies we turn the lights off. On the other hand, when you make a monument for a big hall, soft-textured materials won't match the size of the hall. So you use marble or metal or a hard piece of wood. In my origami exhibitions I use a spotlight for some models and a dim light for others. It depends on the theme of the model and where it will be seen.

"That's one reason I don't use metallic foil. Foil shines like metal and reflects like a mirror. When people see an animal made of foil, they feel metal and not the animal's natural structure. They see *hare* when they should be seeing *ke*. But if you use fine paper, old Japanese paper, you have to struggle to make it into a beautiful shape that won't fall apart. In the course of the struggle, you reach a level where you are learning from your fingers. And sometimes the paper won't go the way you expect it to. So you have to be humble before the paper, you have to have a conversation with it. That's why everyone feels my models are different from other people's, because of the warmth in my paper. With foil you will never start to feel that *sense*.

"Origami, if you compare it to a painting, is the canvas, the brush, and the paint, all in one. So you have to be careful to choose the right sheet of paper for each model. If you're going to make a horse, you have to use paper which fits the horse. If I feel the paper is too thin, I put two pieces of paper together with paste and brush it into the thickness I want. All of the tools you see here —the brushes, the pincers, the paste—are specially ordered for that purpose."

Yoshizawa told me that forty years ago he had dyed his own paper, and he produced a sheet colored with persimmon to prove it. "You can see it's still in perfect condition," he said. "Because of its high acid content,

Kunihiko Kasahara is Japan's most prolific origami author. He has written and illustrated more than 100 books of original folds, the most recent on the creation of geometric solids composed of interlocking pieces of paper. His polyhedra display startling color combinations and often become different solids when turned inside out. One seemingly innocuous cube opens up to reveal an entire Japanese village. Shown is his model of a panda.

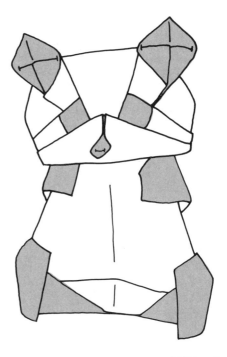

Jun Maekawa is a likely bet to become Japan's youngest origami master. A recent graduate in physics from Tokyo Metropolitan University, Maekawa works out the geometry of a model in his head and sketches it on paper before he begins to fold it. His original figures, among the most complicated in the repertoire, include a tyrannosaurus, a stag with antlers, a frog with webbed feet, and such Western personalities as Santa Claus, Frankenstein's monster, and E.T. His best-known creation is a horned, winged Japanese devil, shown here.

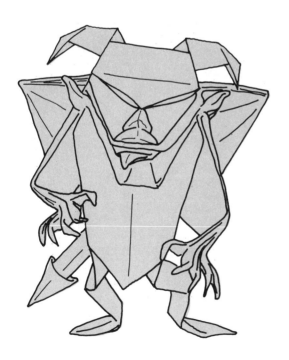

paper made today doesn't last very long, and in libraries all over the world books are falling to pieces. One of my dreams is to go up into the mountains and learn to make paper from trees the way people did in the old days. I want to go with the young people and start my own origami village, and there we will make and dye paper so it will last a long, long time. But this is not only a problem of Japan. I want to have these origami villages all over the world, and each one will make the kind of paper which suits its own country."

I asked Yoshizawa why he allowed himself to fold with pieces of paper that are not square, since some of the models in his books use equilateral triangles, right triangles, pentagons, and hexagons.

"It doesn't have to be square," he explained, "so long as the corners point out, not in, as in a star shape. A star is unacceptable because to make it from a square sheet of paper you have to cut it and fold in the edges. If I started to use that shape, there would be no borderline between folding paper and cutting it, and I could use endless shapes. But I will use an unusual shape, like a triangle, only if I can make a good structure from it. I see that your knight on horseback is made from one piece of paper, but in this case I feel that two pieces would be better. God made the human being and the horse as separate creatures, not connected, as in your model. The same applies to your model of a kangaroo with a baby in the pouch—the baby should be a separate piece. It's different when you're carving stone or wood or casting metal. Then it's possible to start from one piece."

We were interrupted by a knock at the door, a signal by Yoshizawa's wife that it was time for dinner. Throughout the afternoon, she had puttered silently about the room, dusting off boxes, picking up models when they fell, serving green tea. She now brought in a five-course meal. When we finished, she returned to clear the dishes. We settled down to a potent cup of sake and resumed our talk.

It had struck me earlier that unlike most Japanese, Yoshizawa seemed to value innovation over imitation, and I asked him about that.

"I know what you mean. In calligraphy and opera, for instance, people imitate whatever is beautiful. They listen to the great singers and imitate their style and don't develop one of their own. In the early days, origami was just the same. Everyone matched up corner to corner and edge to edge, and they all ended up with the same shape. Learning those traditional models is just like playing music written by other composers, and origami books are still like that. But it's very hard to go from that style into free and creative origami. It's not a matter of time. People who can't create won't create, even if they spend the whole of their lives.

"Of course it helps to start young. To be a composer,

for example, the child needs exposure to music, though it doesn't mean he himself has to be a good piano player. I saw my first origami model when I was four. A young lady in the neighborhood made me a ship out of newspaper, and that impressed me quite a lot. Because my family was poor, I had to work and didn't have time for origami. But I was always thinking about origami, and that's what was important. I started folding while I was working as an engineer at an ironworks. Many of the workers couldn't read blueprints because they hadn't had much education, so I began using origami to teach them. The owner was impressed, and he allowed me to spend all my time studying origami. That's how I got started."

I told Yoshizawa I was amazed that he had found the time to create 50,000 models, since in my own experience the process of invention can be extremely laborious. Yet sometimes models develop instantaneously, as if they had folded themselves. I asked if his experience was the same.

"Yes, some fold quickly, while others, like the cicada, take a long time," he replied. "When they fold easily, it's not by accident or coincidence. I'm always thinking of how to create, how to solve the particular problem I'm facing, even when I'm asleep. When I start to create and run into trouble, I won't sleep in my bed. I will just rest at my desk and doze for a while, and when I'm dreaming I try to set aside my personal feelings and desires. I will pray to God in order to concentrate on just one thing. As a Buddhist, I believe that when I'm struggling and cannot fold, God will always help me. So I sleep, and dream, and pray to God—and when I wake up, I can solve the problem."

"I've always thought that scientists and artists invent in more similar ways than people suspect," I said. "And the way you talk about structure, about gyroscopics, about how the eye works, you sound as much like a scientist as an artist. Do you consider yourself a little of both?"

"I want to have two sides to my life. One, of course, is the scientific side, a precise way of thinking and of acquiring knowledge. But I also feel strongly about the wisdom that comes from old Japanese myths and legends, and I want that in my life to help me create origami. Knowledge is like something you keep in a barrel —you save it, and if you use all of it up, you won't have any more. But wisdom comes like a spring, and it will never dry up. People today think about how to gather knowledge, but they don't bother about wisdom.

"Japanese legends often have a lot of nonsense, like the saying that babies come from the top of the head of the god or goddess, or the story about the mountain that marries the lake. Of course, we don't believe that the mountain actually marries the lake, but these legends are a tradition and we accept them anyway. In a

THE MASTER IN THE CLASSROOM

In addition to meeting me privately at his home, Yoshizawa allowed me to sit in on one of his weekly classes. By the time I entered the classroom, most of the twenty or so students had taken their designated places behind rows of long, narrow tables and were awaiting the arrival of the teacher. I sat in the back and tried to look inconspicuous, a difficult feat for a twenty-four-year-old American man in a roomful of elderly Japanese women. A hush fell over the room. The master entered and took attendance. The class began.

Yoshizawa started by demonstrating the different structural properties of a piece of paper. He was businesslike but playful as he systematically crumpled it, crimped it, curled it along the edge of a ruler with his palm. Next he reviewed the bird base, showing how the traditional shape formed from a square is but a special case of the generalized, asymmetrical bird base that can be folded from any four-sided form.

The bird base quickly became a flapping bird, a standing crane, and an ostrich, pausing in each incarnation only long enough for the teacher to point out the structural similarities among the different species. Now came time for show-and-tell. Yoshizawa pulled from a cardboard box a menagerie of models that included a spirited kangaroo, a one-hump camel, and a sinuous octopus. The octopus, he announced, would be the model taught this class.

The students set to work, and I watched with hypnotic fascination as they pulled from their identical paper kits identical pieces of 10-inch red paper and proceeded to fold them in perfect synchronism, step by meticulous step. I leaned over the table and had begun to make the first folds in my piece when a student tapped me on the arm and pointed to the front of the classroom. I noticed that I was the only one using the desk for support. The rest, including the teacher, were folding in the air. To my further chagrin, I saw that everyone else had turned the paper inside out. Nonplussed, but eager to conform, I followed suit.

Under Yoshizawa's direction we had soon folded a charming red octopus, and I now understood why we had reversed the color of the paper: the mottled red skin of the octopus was captured perfectly by the splotches of dye that had seeped through to the back of the paper. I made a clandestine attempt to adjust the legs of my octopus to a more realistic pose, but Yoshizawa caught me. Even without an interpreter, the message was clear. Seizing my model, he returned the legs to the *correct* position, his own.

By now, time was running out, so Yoshizawa launched into a short lesson on octopus anatomy, using illustrations from a zoology textbook to show how the model he had just taught aspired, however crudely, to capture the beauty and elegance of the octopus's own natural structure. The lesson ended with a hilarious pantomime of an octopus squeezing through the top of a bottle, the act performed by none other than the master himself. It was a strange but somehow fitting conclusion to a class in which Akira Yoshizawa had proved himself to be in teaching, as I already knew him to be in creating, passionate, inspired, dogmatic, and slightly crazy, the humblest of men before God and nature, the proudest of men among men.

symbolic way, the mountain is man, and the lake is woman. The symbolism has to do with the shapes—I think you can see the connection. So the story really does have a meaning, one that we hold deep in our feelings.

"The way the ancient people lived, the way of the legends, was to accept everything as it is—to accept the sun and the rain and the wind and the ideas of others and put them all into your life. That's what the old books say. There are two ways to the Zen style of living. One is to know the space around you, to know the world, and accept it. We all inhale the same air, for one thing, so we share nature with one another. The other way is to know yourself, your feelings and what's inside you. Imagine that you have a map of the entire world and also a vehicle that can go anywhere—in the air, on land, in the water. If you don't have a destination in mind, they won't help. That's why I need to know my purpose and also the world around me. If you know yourself and at the same time love nature and the people around you, the two ways of Zen will be united."

It was dusk. The last remaining rays of light filtered through the paper window shades and cast kaleidoscopic patterns on the floor. A gentle rain had begun to patter on the roof. Through the rhythmic pattering, the plucking of a koto beckoned from a house down the street. The fading of the light, the beating of the rain, the calling of the koto produced an atmosphere of timeless calm. (I think the sake had also begun to take effect.) I could have listened forever, but I knew it was time to go. As Yoshizawa and I prepared to say farewell, I could not resist asking a final question. After 50,000 models and fifty years of folding, was there anything he had never been able to fold?

"A lot! A Zen priest meditating, for instance. Of course, it's easy to make the shape of a priest meditating, but that's only the surface. I want to make a model where everybody will not only see the priest meditating, but also feel him meditating, feel his inner feelings along with him. Those abstract feelings—that's what I've been waiting to make. Like the feeling before you die. Everyone has to die, even healthy people, wealthy people, successful people. And everyone must have that feeling. I also want to make in origami the joy of living. In Buddhism we call it 'throwing your body to the ground to thank God.' It might be a little hard to understand, but that's the feeling I've been searching for and trying to put into origami my whole life."

THE FLOATING SQUARE: SIX STAGES IN THE EVOLUTION OF THE RATTLESNAKE

Zero seconds

Most origami snakes look like this.

0.5 seconds

My first mental image: a free-floating square ruled with horizontal lines.

1.0 seconds

My second mental image: the square rolled into a tube, forming a series of parallel rings.

1.5 seconds

My third mental image: with one line shifted, the tube forms a spiral.

2.5 seconds. Stop the clock!

My fourth mental image: the spiral becomes a coiled snake, sprouting a head and tail.

—Two months later—

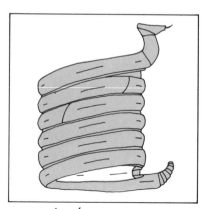

The rattlesnake, finished at last.

THE FLOATING SQUARE

I saw a square of paper floating through space.

One day, I decided to invent an origami snake. I knew of dozens of snakes in the origami repertoire—pythons and sidewinders, diamondbacks and boas—but they were all pretty much the same. To make the longest possible snake from a square, the folders had lined up the body with the diagonal and collapsed the two other corners accordion-style to narrow the body. That was it. Subtle variations in the position of the head and tail were the only clues to distinguish one model from another. The exercise seemed trivial.

When I had seen one too many pythonsidewinderdiamondbackboas, I knew it was time to invent a snake of my own. I couldn't get the idea out of my head: *My* snake would be different. But I had no idea how to start. I conjured up images of snakes that I had seen in photographs or in zoos and sought the traits that most stood out. What do snakes do that no other animal does? What aspects of their anatomy, their evolution, their movement define "snakeness"? In short, what makes a snake a snake? Snakes slither, I thought, they undulate, they hang from trees, they strike—and they coil. I couldn't think of any other animal that coils. I made up my mind to invent a coiled snake.

At that moment, images flashed before me as my mind raced to find a solution. I saw a square of paper floating through space. On the square was a pattern of horizontal lines. I pictured the square rolled into a tube. The horizontal lines turned into parallel rings running up and down the tube. I pictured the square rolled into a tube, but now the edges of the square were shifted by one line. Instead of rings, there was a spiral—one long coil running all the way around the tube, like the stripe on a barber pole. The pattern changed again; the edges sealed, and a head and a tail sprouted from each end of the spiral. I had my snake. The conceptual part of the process was over and done. Two, maybe three seconds had elapsed.

The rest of the task, the execution, took two months.

Like many American folders, I came to origami through mathematics. Before I began folding paper, I was a devoted reader of Martin Gardner's popular "Mathematical Games" column in *Scientific American*. I initiated a correspondence with Gardner and plied him with such inventions of mine as a tetrahedron puzzle, a four-sided geometric solid that was fiendishly difficult to assemble;

an approximate trisection of the angle, my own solution to an age-old mathematical challenge; and puzzle pieces made from hexagonal tiles, capable of being rearranged into different shapes.

Gardner's replies were warm and polite, but there was no disguising the content of his message. The tetrahedron I sent had been independently invented and discussed in his column five years earlier; my mathematical derivation had been well known for three centuries; a team of engineers had already worked out all the possible configurations of my puzzle pieces on a high-speed computer in about seven minutes. Gardner always concluded by noting that he appreciated my writing and was happy to have my contributions "on file."

I despaired. No matter how much time and effort I gave to creating and solving a puzzle or problem, some mathematician or computer scientist or amateur puzzler had already created and solved it in a fraction of the time. Would I never invent anything entirely of my own?

My plea was answered when I discovered origami. In little time I had read all the origami books I could find. (There aren't very many.) I learned how to fold traditional models like the duck, the whale, the flapping bird, and the jumping frog, and also the water bomb, the fortune-teller, the Chinese junk, and the printer's hat. The second time around, I improvised and improved them. I mastered the kite base, the fish base, the bird base, and the frog base, though I had not yet discovered that they were geometrically related. (None of the books had pointed this out, either.) When I had perfected the traditional models, I began to devise figures I had seen nowhere else.

My first attempts were crude and unoriginal. Like the traditional models, mine derived from the four fundamental bases. As time went on, my efforts improved, and I began turning out dozens of variations, some of which appear in this book: the three tropical fish, the hummingbird, the penguin, the giraffe, the dollar-bill folds. (Most of the others I have since destroyed.) I had bags and bags of models that *almost* made it (an elephant with three legs, a rhinoceros without a horn) and a pile of discarded paper equal to several trees. I was making things that were unique, my own! I felt joy—the joy of crossing the divide.

But creativity is a fickle muse. Just when we get it, we don't know how to keep it. It maddens us with its quirky rhythms. It comes in fits and starts, bursts and flashes: First you had it then you lost it *now* what do you do? Or it can be slow, methodical, tedious: the working out of possibilities, the ruling out of options.

And so it was that in the midst of my creative plenitude, my imagination dried up. Variations on familiar folds no longer interested me. The legacy of a thousand years of Japanese folding became bland and uninspiring. Constrained to the four fundamental bases, my creativity suffocated. The kite base offered one flap, the fish base two, the bird base four, and the frog base five. More complicated animals that required six, eight, twelve flaps seemed unattainable. Was it possible that four simple bases exhausted the potential of the square? Was this all that origami could offer? Incapable of creating new forms, I became bored and listless. (I stopped making lists of animals to invent.) At the age of fifteen, imagination betrayed, I was finished.

Or so I thought. I now realize that this early loss of creativity was not an ending but a beginning. It marked the first time I had asked myself, How do you create? because, for the first time, I could not create. The question initiated a long investigation into the creative process, one that continued as I went on to study the history of science and become an architect and designer. I now know that the creative lapses never cease; they are merely overcome, one by one. The origami impasse was merely my first, and the resulting breakthrough enabled me to invent my finest and most complicated models.

LEARNING FROM NATURE

With the question "How do you create?" my search for new forms had begun. All artists, I knew, go through periods of malaise and stagnation. The greatest ones survive to make breakthroughs in their fields. Was I, like them, an artist in search of inspiration? Was I an artist at all? Was origami an art? The books had invariably called paperfolding "the ancient Japanese *art* of origami," but I felt like a mathematician or a scientist: a discoverer, not a creator. The models never felt as if they came from deep inside, the way I thought an artist's inspiration springs from within. I had not set out to invent new artistic forms. I had merely lined up corners with corners and edges with edges to try to capture the shape of a particular animal. Then, when I had labored with the paper a long time and a fish or a bird or a giraffe appeared, I felt as if I had come across forms that had lain dormant for years. I was just the lucky investigator who had unearthed them.

This feeling matched an important observation I had made earlier, during my prolific days. I had noticed patterns in the paper. When I compared my handful of finished models with the voluminous contents of my discard pile, I saw that the successful models inevitably contained regular angles and simple proportions. The patterns they formed were crisper, cleaner, and more beautiful than the lines of the discards. The paper had yielded to the pressure of my fingers and had either collapsed into a more compact configuration of folds or else become a crumpled wad offering no promise of long appendages or a compact body. Despite my best attempts to produce models based on arbitrary folds, geometry had fought back and put me in my place. Clearly the patterns were "out there," somehow contained within the potential of the piece of paper rather than in my own head. I felt like the filter for some indomitable natural law.

Gradually, on reflection, the reason for that feeling became clear. Like Molière's *bourgeois gentilhomme,* a man who spoke prose all his life without realizing it, I had been speaking mathematics, the language of form. The world about us is geometric. The cracks in porcelain almost always cross at 90-degree angles. Soap bubbles invariably meet three to a junction, forming angles of 120 degrees. The petals of the sunflower, the horns of the mountain goat, and the shell of the chambered nautilus grow in logarithmic spirals. The same principle holds for more complicated processes. Mathematics determines the formation of clouds (variations in atmospheric pressure), the branching of rivers (the momentum of the stream, the resistance of the terrain), the pattern of fractures in a struck block of ice (the crystalline structure of frozen water, the force of the blow). Whatever the object or process, geometric laws govern its birth, growth, movement, shape, size, death, and decay.

Why should this be? "Space is not a passive vacuum, but has properties which impose powerful constraints on any structure that inhabits it," writes the crystallographer Arthur Loeb in his afterword to R. Buckminster Fuller's *Synergetics.* Buffeted by the powerful forces of nature, trapped in a battle between energy and entropy, phenomena take the shapes and sizes that enable them to hold those forces in check. Simple mathematical laws dictate each of these configurations. Geometry is a clever negotiator, working out compromises to keep energy and entropy on good terms.

Discovering geometry in nature renewed my confidence. What if I looked for inspiration not within, but without, in the world around me? As I examined nature, I saw patterns, complex patterns, road maps to forces in conflict. Even without a conscious mind to guide it, nature was a prodigious inventor, devising patterns to suit every need. And the patterns were beautiful! Often, at first glance, they seemed to lack sense and harmony, but a closer look revealed their disarming simplicity. Each configuration was composed of just a few simple elements. The elements would appear at different or-

Nature generates complex patterns by repeating simple processes at varying scales. Patterns can be produced by different mechanisms, including the following.

Cracking:

Cracks in a glazed ceramic surface.

Dividing:

Soap film pressed between two parallel glass plates.

Stretching and shrinking:

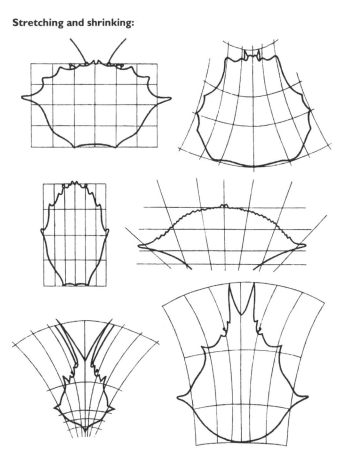

Comparative study of the carapaces of six crabs by the biologist D'Arcy Thompson.

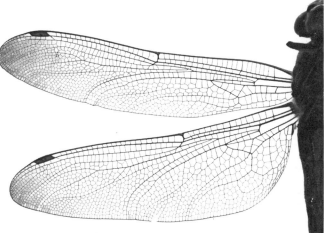

Wings of a dragonfly.

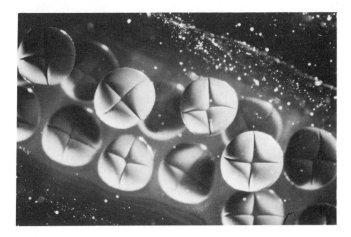

Division of fertilized eggs during mitosis.

Aggregating:

Chambered nautilus shell.

Branching:

The ridges on the fractured surface of a brittle compound of magnesium and copper.

Aluminum crystals.

Leaves in a fern.

The delta of the Colorado River on the Gulf of California.

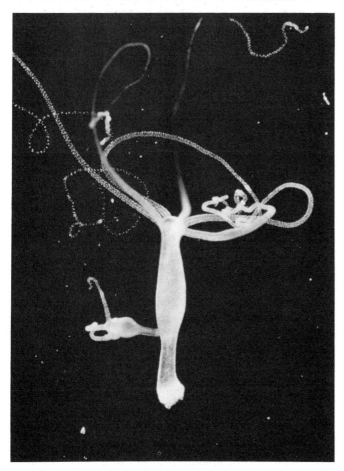

Budding of a *Hydra oligactis.*

The surface of an ingot of antimony, showing dendritic crystals that have grown to interference with each other.

The undersurface of a *Victoria amazonica* leaf.

ders of magnitude, recombined, shuffled—but always identical. They would appear at full size, half size, quarter size, eighth size, and also doubled, quadrupled, octupled. Because the appearance is independent of scale, this property of patterns has come to be known as *self-similarity* or *scaling*. The beauty of those patterns derives from nature's efficiency and economy, not its occasional profligacy and waste.

The curious thing is that so many objects and processes are self-similar. Galaxies form clusters, superclusters, and perhaps even "cluster complexes"—superduperclusters. Rivers branch into brooks, brooks into creeks, and creeks into ever and ever smaller tributaries. Along a mountain ridge, distances are notoriously difficult to estimate because the terrain looks everywhere the same; it, too, is self-similar. Meteors strike the moon at random, but their size and distribution are self-similar; photographs of the moon, whether taken from the height of 1 mile or 100, invariably give no clue as to the craters' true size. In the lungs, blood vessels go through about fifteen self-similar bifurcations before they reach the size of capillaries and the self-similarity ends. Turbulence is self-similar: In the ocean, bigger whorls beget lesser whorls, while in the atmosphere, gusts of wind create lesser gusts. The complex appearance of these shapes merely masks their innate simplicity.

Years ago, grappling with my youthful creative impasse, I understood little about the process behind these shapes. But I could appreciate this fundamental lesson of invention in nature: Simple elements make complex patterns. While no single definition encompasses every act of invention, the essential similarity in the process, no matter what the field of endeavor, hints at something profound about nature. Reflecting on all that I had learned from my investigation, I came to the conclusion that nature invents new forms by

unconsciously playing with simple elements,
rearranging them to form patterns, and
choosing the patterns that are most *efficient*.

Simple elements make complex patterns. Could nature's way of inventing new forms be applied to origami?

X AND X'

To manufacture new forms, nature uses a process called *iteration*. An iterative process (it can also be called a recursive process or a feedback loop) is an efficient mechanism for generating form, creating elaborate structures with a minimum expenditure of energy and information. The results, not surprisingly, are structures that appear self-similar.

In a typical iterative process, an operation is performed and produces a result, x. That result is then fed back into the process to produce another result, x'. x' is fed back into the process to produce x'', and so on. (An alternative notation uses the terms x_n, x_{n+1}, x_{n+2}, etc.) Each stage is called an iteration. In the last forty years, iterative processes and their patterns have come under scrutiny by information theorists, crystallographers, developmental cell biologists, geneticists, and artificial intelligence researchers. New examples of iteration have come to light that could scarcely have been imagined without the aid of technological advances in observational devices and computers. Cloud chamber patterns of subatomic particles undergoing fission, scanning electron micrographs of the cell, aerial photographs of the earth, and satellite images of the surfaces of other planets have transformed the way we see the world. The phenomena they reveal existed long before humanity, but it has taken us this long to catch on. It has become clear that iterative processes lie at the origin of life itself.

Some of the most beautiful forms I have ever seen are the product of mathematical discoveries less than twenty years old. They are strange and enigmatic shapes known as *fractals*: Koch snowflakes, Mandelbrot sets, bifurcation diagrams, Hénon attractors. Until recently, even the most complex mathematical descriptions of nature still fell short of capturing the subtlety of a mountain range or a waterfall. But using the principles of fractal geometry, a branch of the discipline known as chaos theory, human beings can finally capture the forms of nature.

One of the easiest forms to represent is a snowflake. Like other natural shapes, a snowflake is more or less self-similar, so we can use an iterative process to generate it. Of course, no two snowflakes are exactly the same, and our artificial snowflake is but a rough approximation of the real thing. Whereas a real snowflake is a three-dimensional structure made of ice crystals, the shape that we will construct is flat and made of equilateral triangles. It was discovered by Helge von Koch, a Swedish mathematician, in 1904, and would today be called a fractal.

Generally speaking, a fractal is any shape that reveals more and more detail the more finely you examine it. Most natural phenomena, it turns out, are fractals: The more closely you look at a self-similar form like a mountain ridge or a coastline, the more crenellations you find. A fractal also has a technical definition: It is an object that occupies a fractional number of dimensions, like 1.26 (somewhat more than a line and less than a plane) or 2.67 (somewhat more than a plane and less than a solid). Fractal dimension is a strange and fascinating concept, explained more fully on pages 50 and 51.

To construct the Koch snowflake, we will avail our-

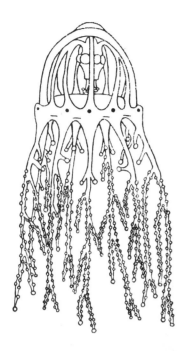
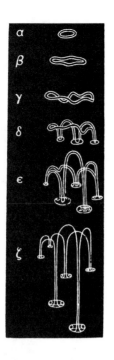

THE GROWTH OF AN ANIMAL COLONY COMPARED WITH A DROP OF INK

Left, the medusa *Cordylophora*, a colonial organism (an animal that is both a single large organism and a colony of smaller organisms). Right, a falling drop of ink in water. The resemblance was noted by D'Arcy Thompson.

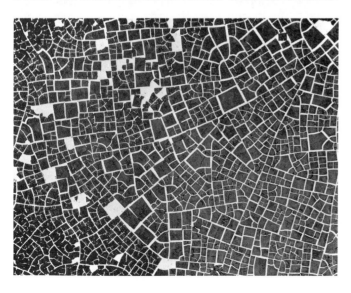

THE GROWTH OF A HUMAN COLONY COMPARED WITH A DROP OF OIL

Top, an aerial photograph of an Islamic settlement, the town of Hamadan, Iran. Bottom, the fissures in a gelatinous preparation of tin oil.

selves of one of fractal geometry's principal tools: the computer. Iteration is idiot's work. Repeating the same operation over and over requires an unthinking, untiring performer, a slave to iteration. What better worker than a computing machine? The starting point of the Koch snowflake (also called its initial condition) is a simple equilateral triangle.

Using the computer, we add to the middle of each side another simple element, a smaller equilateral triangle whose edge length is one-third that of the larger triangle. The result is a six-pointed star.

So far, the snowflake is nothing special. But now we enter the iterative part of the process. (The six-pointed star is regarded as iteration 0.) Add to the middle of each new edge a still smaller triangle, again with edge length one-third that of the existing edge. To make the second iteration, repeat the process.

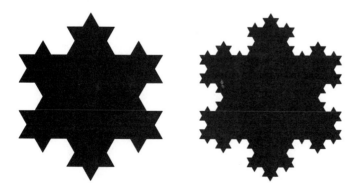

Each stage from here to eternity is exactly the same. The generating procedure is simple, even mundane—

but the result is an object of great beauty. The ultimate figure cannot, of course, be depicted, but by the fifth iteration it approximates a real snowflake:

Comparing our method of making an artificial snowflake with the real thing, we find a keen similarity:

	NATURE	MATHEMATICS
ELEMENT	Ice crystal	Equilateral triangle
PATTERN	Hexagonal packing	Insertion of new element at midsegment
CREATION	Snowflake	Koch snowflake

It's one thing to use a system to invent mathematical forms and quite another to claim that a mere mechanical process can produce an origami model or any other work of art. Why go through so much effort to capture the forms of nature using mathematics, when artists have been doing it for centuries? Because, I believe, the systematic manufacturing of new shapes is a lot closer to human creativity than most people think. Beneath the shimmering surface of a Monet landscape and the hard molecular structure of a real haystack reside similar forces of design.

I believe that people in any creative field, whether they are painters, poets, composers, mathematicians, or scientists, face the same dilemma as nature does every time they sit down to work: How do you make something out of nothing? Making something from nothing— the process I call "inventing"—is epitomized in origami as well. The folder's mandate is to make an animal or an object or a human figure from a blank square—from

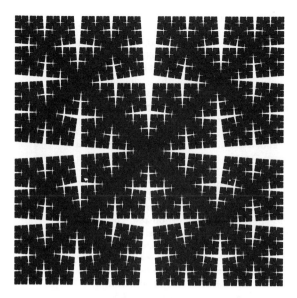

Square fractal pattern.

Arrowhead-shaped fractal pattern.

Tree-shaped fractal pattern.

SIMPLE ELEMENTS MAKE COMPLEX PATTERNS

The computer generates complex patterns by repeating simple rules in a feedback loop. The resulting fractal patterns can be used to model natural phenomena or to produce music. Compare with patterns in nature.

More sophisticated snowflakes than the Koch snowflake are based on the thermodynamics of crystal formation and on variations in atmospheric temperature, pressure, and humidity encountered as each snowflake descends.

FRACTAL DIMENSION

Determining the dimension of a fractal, like the Koch snowflake, requires a new concept of dimension. Fractal dimension cannot be described by calculus, the field of mathematics that deals with continuous change. The smooth flow of a river and the constant acceleration of a falling object are simple phenomena that can be modeled by calculus. But other phenomena are less ruly. Some are discontinuous: the velocity of a particle suspended in fluid, the distribution of galaxies in the universe. Others, like the Koch snowflake, are continuous but move in many directions at once: the erratic shape of a coastline, the branching of rivers or of blood vessels in the body. Until fractal geometry discovered their underlying order, such curves were written off as "pathological" or "monster" curves, for good reason. They have fractal dimension.

The fractal definition of dimension, devised by Benoit B. Mandelbrot, the founder of fractal geometry, is more general and abstract than the definition used in calculus. It includes the standard definition as a special case, much as the laws of special relativity reduce to those of Newtonian mechanics for subrelativistic speeds. To derive Mandelbrot's formula for dimension, consider a straight line of unit length. Divide the line into smaller copies of itself, calling the linear dimension of the copy r and the number of pieces N. By definition, then, $(N)(r) = 1$ and so $r = \dfrac{1}{N}$. This can also be written as

$$r = N^{-1}.$$

Now take a solid unit square whose edge is also divided into segments of length r. There are $(N)(N)$, or N^2, smaller squares in an area of 1. Hence $(\sqrt{N})(r) = 1$, and so

$$r = N^{-1/2}.$$

Analogously, a unit cube contains N^3 smaller cubes of length r in a volume of 1. Hence $(\sqrt[3]{N})(r) = 1$, and

$$r = N^{-1/3}.$$

A pattern emerges. For each figure, the denominator of the exponent contains its dimension: A line has one dimension, a square two dimensions, a cube three dimensions, and so on. Denoting dimension by D, Mandelbrot generalizes the relationship to

$$r = N^{-1/D}.$$

It is now easy to solve for D. Take the logarithm of each side: $\log r = \dfrac{-1}{D} \log N$, so $\dfrac{\log N}{D} = \log \dfrac{1}{r}$. Finally we get the finished equation for fractal dimension:

$$D = \frac{\log N}{\log(1/r)}.$$

Whenever this formula yields a fraction for D, the curve in question is a fractal.

Fractal dimension cannot tell us everything about the shape of an object (neither can the standard dimension), but it can say a great deal. To derive the dimension of the edge of the Koch snowflake, consider just the upper third of the flake.

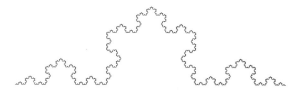

Each step divides it into four sections, each of which is one-third the size of the original.

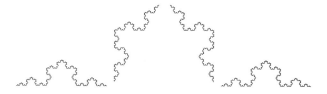

Therefore N, the number of copies, is 4, while r, the size of each copy, is ⅓. Applying Mandelbrot's formula gives

$$D = \frac{\log 4}{\log 3}.$$

The dimension of the snowflake is thus equal to 1.2618 . . . , a little more than length, a little less than area—just about right for a monster curve.

SIZING UP THE KOCH SNOWFLAKE

Calculating the area and length of the Koch snowflake takes hard work, but it is worth the effort to understand how the fractal is generated. To begin, set the area of the original triangle equal to 1, and call the area of the snowflake after each stage x. The area of the simplest Koch snowflake, the initial triangle, is thus

$$x = 1.$$

The first step is to add three new triangles. Each of those triangles turns out to be one-ninth the area of the previous triangle. (You can see this easily by dividing the original triangle up into nine little triangles.) The area of the resulting figure, a six-pointed star, is thus

$$x = 1 + 3(\tfrac{1}{9}).$$

Now the iterative process gets going. The first iteration adds 3(4) new triangles, each of which is one-ninth the size of the triangles in the six-pointed star, iteration zero. The second iteration adds 3(4)(4) new triangles, each of which is one-ninth the size of the triangles in the *first* iteration. The third iteration adds 3(4)(4)(4) new triangles, each of which is one-ninth the size of the triangles in the *second* iteration. And so on.

In general, each stage adds four times as many triangles as the previous stage added, each of them one-ninth the size of its predecessors. The net area added in each stage is thus $4\tfrac{1}{9} = \tfrac{4}{9}$ the area added in the previous stage. To determine the total area at the nth iteration, we sum an infinite series of terms, the area of the initial triangle plus the area of the three triangles that make it a six-pointed star plus the area of all the triangles added after that:

$$x = 1 + 3(\tfrac{1}{9}) + \sum_{n=1}^{\infty} 3(\tfrac{1}{9})(\tfrac{4}{9})^n.$$

The symbol Σ tells us to sum the infinite series of terms that follow it from $n = 1$, the first iteration, to $n = \infty$, the last. A convenient formula tells us the result:

$$\sum_{n=1}^{\infty} ar^n = \frac{ar}{1-r}.$$

In our equation, a is $3(\tfrac{1}{9})$ and r is $\tfrac{4}{9}$. Hence

$$x = 1 + 3(\tfrac{1}{9}) + \frac{3(\tfrac{1}{9})(\tfrac{4}{9})}{1 - (\tfrac{4}{9})}.$$

Solving for x with simple algebra yields the answer, $x = \tfrac{8}{5}$.

To determine the snowflake's perimeter is even easier. Set the perimeter of the original triangle equal to 1 and call the length of the perimeter after each stage y. The perimeter of the simplest snowflake, the initial triangle, is thus

$$y = 1.$$

Each stage in the construction of the curve replaces the previous edge with four new edges, each one-third the length of the original. The perimeter of the six-pointed star is thus

$$y = 1(4)(\tfrac{1}{3}) = (\tfrac{4}{3})^1$$

The succeeding iteration has perimeter

$$y = (\tfrac{4}{3})(\tfrac{4}{3})^1 = (\tfrac{4}{3})^2,$$

and the one after that

$$y = (\tfrac{4}{3})(\tfrac{4}{3})^2 = (\tfrac{4}{3})^3.$$

Thus the total edge length at the nth iteration (again counting the six-pointed star as step zero) is

$$y = (\tfrac{4}{3})^{n+1}.$$

Each term is larger than the previous one, which means . . . the perimeter is infinite! The sequence grows slowly, and after eight steps the total is still less than 10. By the 500th step, though, it is a robust figure of sixty-three digits, and on precisely the 801st iteration it breaks a number called a googol—a 1 followed by a hundred zeros.

nothing. Just as nature uses ice crystals to make a snow-flake, and the mathematician assembles equilateral triangles to make a fractal, the origami artist manipulates folds of paper to manufacture a work of art.

Unfortunately, the people who use creativity the most sometimes understand it the least. Artists and scientists are notorious for obscuring the creative process. Affectation and posturing protect artists from scrutiny; the more eccentric ones (though not necessarily the better ones) are lauded and left alone. Scientific papers explain only the product of discovery, never the process; to describe the path to success would expose the detours and the dead ends. A complacent public, satisfied to be astonished but not to understand, bestows the title "genius" and stands in awe.

When people encounter my paperfolding work for the first time, they, too, are astonished. Expecting to find a simple boat or hat, they see instead an origami model so elaborate that it appears impossible to construct. A butterfly with four wings, six legs, two antennae, a head, and a tail—without cutting or pasting? Doubtful. A white knight on a black horse from a single sheet of paper? Unlikely. A 3-foot-long rattlesnake from a 10-inch square of paper? Impossible!

Yet I know that such formidable creations did not spring from my head fully formed. Instead, they were the product of weeks, months, or years of dedicated work, spurred along by timely strokes of inspiration. To generate a model as complex as the butterfly, the knight on horseback, or the rattlesnake, I had to carry out a large number of routine operations at high speed. I used a set of shortcuts developed over the years to winnow through options that inexperienced folders would have had to examine one by one. But is that "genius?" Doubtful, unlikely—impossible!

Experience has taught me a different story: that creativity, far from being a gift granted to a few, is rather a learned process, a way of cultivating a good idea and bringing it to fruition. To reach the sophistication of my recent models, I worked methodically up the ladder of complexity, adding layer upon layer of simple elements to attain a rich and varied product. Like the patterns of nature, the origami model is a skillful accumulation of simple elements. The same is true of any artwork or scientific theorem. To someone who has never composed music, Brahms's Fourth Symphony seems impossibly complex. Yet its beauty is its simplicity: A single motif, transformed and elaborated, constitutes the material of practically the entire first movement. It begins quietly, gathers strength, unfolds inexorably, and comes crashing down in an awesome, tragic conclusion. I believe this is true of every creative act: Powerful ideas, simply expressed, are beautiful.

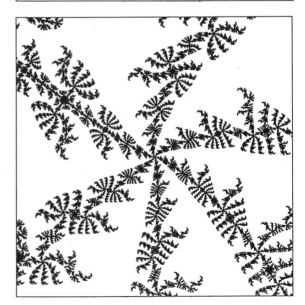

Fractal structure is apparent in computer-generated patterns relating to chaos theory. Magnified, they reveal similar structure at every scale.

Below, the Mandelbrot set, and left, three successive enlargements. Its equation is $x_{n+1} = x_n^2 + c$, where x is a complex variable and c is a complex constant. (A complex number has both a real component, like 4, and an imaginary component, like $3i$. i is the square root of -1.) The set is named for Benoit B. Mandelbrot.

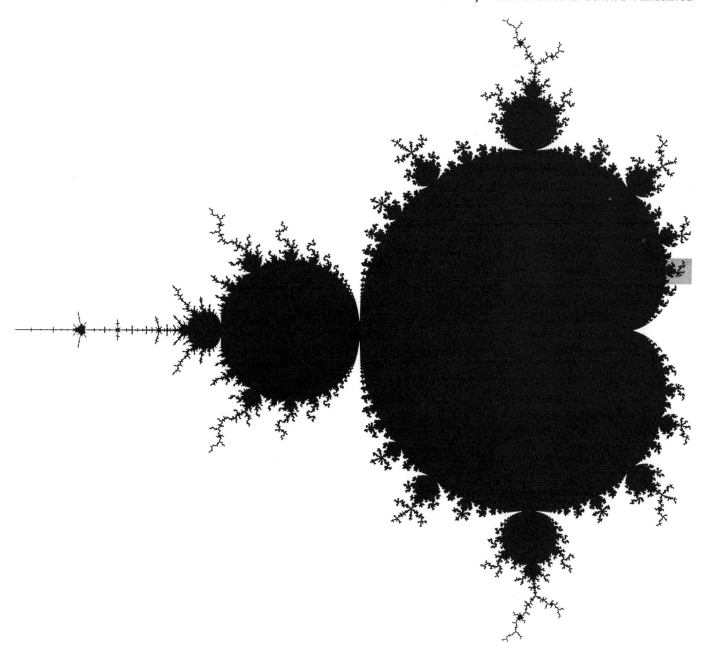

Below, the Hénon attractor, and clockwise, three successive enlargements. Its equations are $x_{n+1} = y_{n+1} - ax_n^2$ and $y_{n+1} = bx_n$, where x and y are real variables, $a = 1.4$ and $b = .3$. The attractor is named for Michel Hénon.

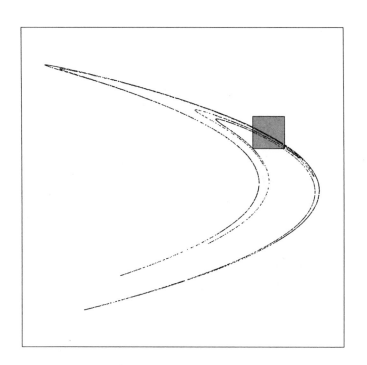

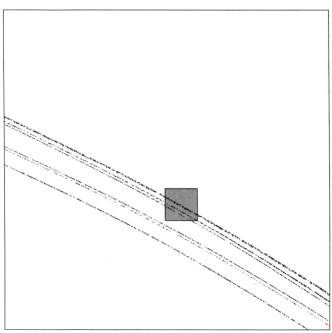

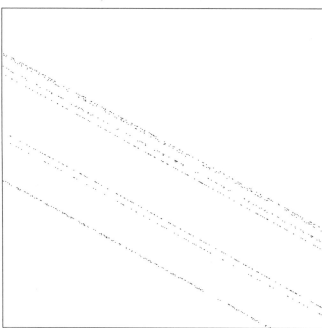

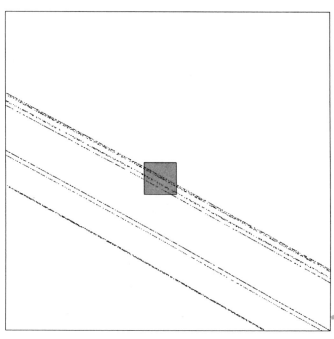

A MUSIC LESSON

If the creator's task is to weave discrete components into a meaningful and coherent whole, then the fabric of his creation, the hierarchy and interrelationship of its parts, is his personal expression. It is not just the finished origami model that is the artwork, but also how the inventor gets there—his unique process of folding. Put another way, the creator's signature lies in how he crosses the divide from reductionism to holism.

Seeing origami from the mathematical end of the telescope corresponds to a point of view called *reductionism*. The reductionist approach zooms in on the details, on the highly ordered sequence of folds in a composition. The opposite of zooming in corresponds to a point of view called *holism*. Holism means stepping back to take in the big picture, and it implies that for a time we ignore the details and concentrate on the whole: the forest, not the trees. From the point of view of holism, an origami model is irreducible, a gestalt, a completed work of art.

We often take one or the other point of view implicitly when we criticize a work of art. Advocates of the reductionist approach would, for example, be inclined to examine the minute physical components of a piece of music. The *Harvard Concise Dictionary of Music* defines rhythm as "That aspect of music concerned with the organization of time . . . by means of regularly recurring pulses or beats." At the holistic extreme is Fats Waller's famous response to a woman who asked him for an explanation of rhythm: "Lady, if you got to ask, you ain't got it!"

Once, leafing through my collection of classical records, I encountered among the liner notes this reductionist description of the second movement of Beethoven's Seventh Symphony:

> Through the subtle, simple and unheard-of device of placing the 5th of an opening chord (here, E natural) in the bass, Beethoven achieves an effect which is unique. . . . For 90 measures the tension mounts, then abates to permit the entrance of a lovely triplet section in A major. But even during this breathing spell, 'cellos and basses, pizzicato, harp insistently on the original duplet rhythmic figure.

Apart from occasional lapses into subjectivity (such as speaking of a "lovely" triplet section), the critic confines himself entirely to the quantifiable physical properties of pitch (wave frequency), intensity (wave amplitude), timbre (overtones, also known as tone color), and duration. But this explanation is somehow incomplete. Despite such observations as the "uniqueness" of Beethoven's opening chord, the description cannot communicate why this piece of music is so compelling.

Fortunately, my music collection contains *two* record-

ings of Beethoven's Seventh. The author of the second set of liner notes depicts the same movement in holistic terms. He cites critics in whom the music evokes such impressions as "a torchlight procession in the Catacombs," "a priests' march to a temple amid sacred dancing," and "innocence weep[ing] . . . sympathetic voices of widows and orphans mingl[ing] in laments and denunciations." And the composer Richard Wagner, he adds, considered the symphony as a whole an "Apotheosis of the Dance in its highest aspect, as it were the loftiest deed of bodily motion incorporated in an ideal mould of tone."

I could adduce a similar pair of criticisms about my origami rattlesnake. While the first fictitious reviewer captures it in meticulous and passionless detail,

> Engel's reptile is a helical or solenoid-shaped progression of parallel pleats . . . culminating in an elongated proboscis.
>
> —*The Reductionist Review*

the second emotes,

> This sinuous, sensuous serpent is nature incarnate, the tempter of mankind as first beheld by Adam and Eve . . . a masterpiece!
>
> —*The Histrionic Holist*

The holistic descriptions of Beethoven's symphony convey in recognizable images the emotions it expresses, but they fail to explain how the composer elicits them. Try as I might, I will never learn to write music by reading holistic liner notes. In just the same way, reciting the aesthetic rewards of my snake will not enable a reader of this book to invent a comparable origami model. Holism, too, is only half the story.

Now let's apply the principles of invention to origami. Just as we did with the Koch snowflake, we will use a computer to speed up the process. Returning to the definition we saw earlier, remember that nature invents new forms by unconsciously playing with simple elements, rearranging them to form patterns, and choosing the patterns that are most efficient. The first step is to identify the simple elements.

The discrete, reductionist components of an origami model are creases: individual mountain and valley folds. In folding the four traditional Japanese models—the duck, whale, flapping bird, and jumping frog—we saw how combinations of mountain and valley folds produced more complicated folds, such as reverse, squash, and petal folds. Assembling reverse, squash, and petal folds produced still more complicated configurations, such as the bird base and the frog base. Our second step will be to reassemble the same simple components into brand-new configurations with brand-new folding pat-

Below, the bifurcation diagram, and right, two successive enlargements. Its equation is $x_{n+1} = rx_n(1-x_n)$, where x ranges from 0 to 1 and r from 0 to 4. To my eye, this is one of the most beautiful of all fractal forms.

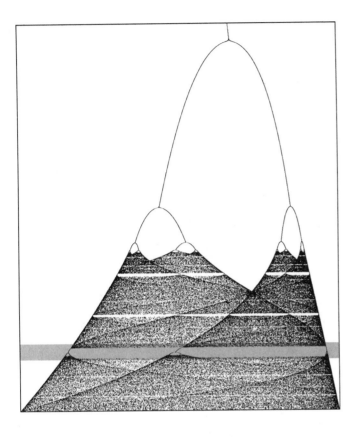

terns. Some of those patterns will prove fruitful, others not. Yet somehow, as our third step, we must find a way of selecting just the right patterns, the ones that will prove to be the bases of new and beautiful origami models. Just how to select those patterns, and cross the divide from reductionism to holism, we have yet to see.

To complete the first step of invention, we must devise a system of notation. Just as mathematicians do when they invent fractal forms like the Koch snowflake, we want to be able to translate origami's simple elements into terms a computer can understand. That means we must assign a rigorous definition to each crease in order to translate it from geometric (spatial) to arithmetic (numerical) terms. The geometric definitions are the step-by-step diagrams in this book. Put into words, a geometric definition would be something like "Fold the four corners of the paper to the center." (This is a procedure known as the blintz fold, which I will discuss in more detail later.) Once translated into numerical code, each crease could be reduced to a string of ones and zeros capable of being stored in a computer's memory bank. The strings could then be lined up end to end to produce a single binary number describing the entire sequence of folds in a model.

It happens that a system has already been devised for converting folding diagrams to a numerical notational system, John Smith's Origami Instruction Language (OIL). Smith, a British statistician and computer programmer, uses a Cartesian coordinate system to locate points on the square and identifies a crease by the two end points it connects. The success of Smith's system ensures that establishing a purely numerical representation for each model is possible. So far, so good.

The second step is to assemble the simple elements into patterns. An algorithm for devising patterns would allow the computer to call up from memory the code numbers for various types of folds and assemble them in different sequences to see what they would produce. Some combinations would work well together, while others would force the paper into impossible spatial configurations. If a model needed only four or five flaps, the potential combinations would be simple and few, and it would be easy to devise a formula for the optimal configuration of folds as a function of flaps. (Most likely, the results would be the kite base, fish base, bird base, and frog base.) With each added flap, the geometry would grow increasingly complex, but given enough time and an occasional injection of randomness to stimulate new sequences of folds, the computer would produce a continuing series of combinations. Only those combinations that allow the paper to fold itself up economically, thus ensuring long flaps for the appendages and a compact core for the body, would pass this stage. They would look something like the folding patterns in this book.

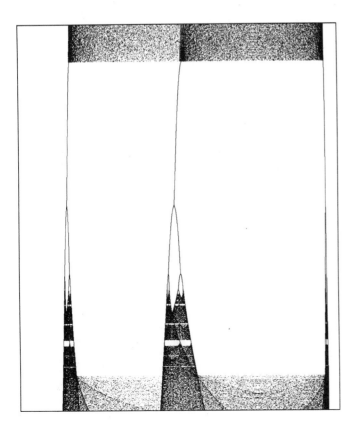

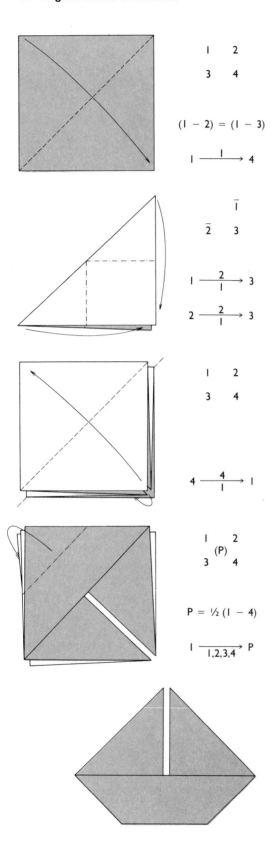

John Smith's Origami Instruction Language (OIL) converts origami diagrams into numbers. This sequence shows how to fold a sailboat, the symbol of the Origami Center of America.

The third step is by far the most difficult. It requires an algorithm for distinguishing a successful pattern of folds from an unsuccessful one. The algorithm would work like a sieve, holding back sequences that fail any of the following tests: Does the model have the same number of appendages as the animal? Is the arrangement of those appendages anatomically accurate? Do the proportions of the model correspond to those of the animal? Is the model folded efficiently, without awkward thicknesses or wasted paper? Finally, does the model possess the character and quality of the living creature? Given enough sequences of folds, a certain percentage would inevitably resemble natural forms, and of this subgroup a handful might possess the verisimilitude and charm of models devised by human folders.

Alas, I am no computer programmer. Our three-step course in origami invention remains, for now, nothing more than a thought experiment. But I do know of one attempt to program a computer to produce an origami model. In 1971, Arthur Appel directed the IBM System 360 Model 91 to print out geometric patterns at the rate of more than one hundred a minute. As our thought experiment predicted, a small portion of the patterns—about 10 percent—proved successful, and they were folded and displayed at IBM headquarters in New York.

While Appel's program produced hundreds of tantalizing patterns, it stopped short of producing an origami model. To find a computer program that has generated a *completed* work of art, we have to look to a parallel discipline with a long history of mechanized invention: music.

The comparison proves most interesting. As in our thought experiment, the programmers' first task was to reduce the artwork to its fundamental units and devise a system of notation. Just as an origami model can be reduced to an explicitly defined sequence of geometric folds, a musical composition can be broken down into notes. Using a mathematical technique called Fourier analysis, an entire composition could be represented as a single curve on an enormous oscilloscope. "This curve *is* the symphony," the physicist James Jean writes in *Science and Music,* "neither more nor less, and the symphony will sound noble or tawdry, musical or harsh, refined or vulgar, according to the quality of this curve." Today, with the advent of digital recording, we can transform that curve into a string of ones and zeros that can then be electronically decoded and heard again as music.

The programmers also handled the second step, assembling patterns, with ease. Melody, harmony, and rhythm, the building blocks of musical composition, can be manipulated merely by arranging notes in different successions, simultaneous combinations, and durations.

These permutations of notes correspond to the permutations of folds in my own second stage.

When they reached the third step, selecting patterns, however, the programmers ran into trouble. Instead of the broad consensus that had greeted the first two steps, the third step has met a cacophony of opinions. As far back as the Renaissance, people have sought to mechanize composition by tossing dice or flipping cards and looking up the results in complex musical charts. An able performer could produce hundreds of popular dances upon request, many of them with the distinct flavor of certain composers.

More recent attempts have improved in sophistication. An early approach using computers was the musicologist Wilhelm Fucks's study of musical intervals in the 1960s. Using a graphic device he called a *correlogram*, Fucks counted the number of times a certain interval occurred in a composition and discovered characteristic patterns for each composer. A few years later, in the mid-1970s, a competing musicologist named Denys Parsons compiled one of the most comprehensive studies of the patterns of composition, the *Directory of Tunes and Musical Themes*. Parsons listed some 7,000 melodies by thirty composers from Bach to Stravinsky, classifying them according to whether each note was higher than, lower than, or the same as the preceding one. He found that the underlying pattern of a melody, though not often obvious to the listener, was essential to its overall effect. For example, three pieces as diverse as the finale to Stravinsky's ballet *The Firebird,* the opening theme to Mendelssohn's overture "The Hebrides," and the second theme in the first movement of Beethoven's *Eroica* Symphony begin as follows (Parsons used the symbols D, U, and R for down, up, and repeated, with an asterisk representing the first note of the theme):

The Firebird	*DDUDD UDDUD DURDR
"The Hebrides"	*DDUDD UDDUD DUDDU
Eroica	*DDUDD UDDUD DUDDU

Parsons reasoned that composers unconsciously make up melodies on the basis of their underlying patterns, an insight that programmers have taken further to incorporate the idea of structure into computer-generated scores. At the Thomas J. Watson Research Center, in Yorktown Heights, New York, Benoit B. Mandelbrot and Richard F. Voss have used the principles of fractal geometry to specify both the deep and the surface structures of computer-generated compositions. Mandelbrot had noticed that many large-scale pieces of music are statistically self-similar: The shape of melodies has much in common with that of longer passages and with that of entire movements. In looking at individual melodies, Mandelbrot and Voss have found

through trial and error that if the statistical relationship between successive notes is too chaotic (resembling random white noise) or too ordered (resembling the motion of particles in a fluid, called Brownian motion), the melodies are unpleasant. If, however, the relationship lies somewhere in between, the resulting melodies, though mediocre, compare with tunes composed by human beings.

What have 500 years of trying to mechanize composition produced? With the aid of computers, we have combined individual notes to make patterns, much as paperfolders combine folds to make models and mathematicians assemble geometric shapes to make fractal curves that mimic the forms of nature. The products of their creation vary, but the method is universal:

	NATURE	MATHEMATICS
ELEMENT	Ice crystal	Equilateral triangle
PATTERN	Hexagonal packing	Insertion of new element at midsegment
CREATION	Snowflake	Koch snowflake

	MUSIC	ORIGAMI
ELEMENT	Note	Crease
PATTERN	Melody, harmony, rhythm, etc.	Reverse fold, petal fold, bird base, etc.
CREATION	Composition	Model

Yet 500 years of investigation have also failed to demystify the composition process. While it is possible to produce music by mechanical means, the melodies are stale and cold, and not one is as sublime as a melody by Mozart, or even as catchy as the theme to a popular song. A computer cannot distinguish between an unsuccessful melody and a successful one. That choice must be left to human beings, who will apply the same standard of beauty they would in the concert hall. The computer lays out the raw material of the composition, but the human being must refine it and declare it a work of art. The same would be true of a computerized origami model. It might resemble a reindeer or a snake in its mathematical detail, but the essential quality that breathes life into a human composition would be lost. The gap from reductionism to holism would remain unspanned, the divide uncrossed.

No less a thinker than Hermann von Helmholtz, the founder of modern acoustics, tackled this very question and threw up his hands in defeat. Remembered chiefly as a physicist, Helmholtz lectured in physiology, performed medical dissections, dabbled in optics, and made important contributions to thermodynamics. He brought all his experience to bear on the question of

Music composed by computers uses fractal geometry to produce melodies that resemble human compositions.

Typical patterns of white, Brownian, and 1/f noise.

White music is too random.

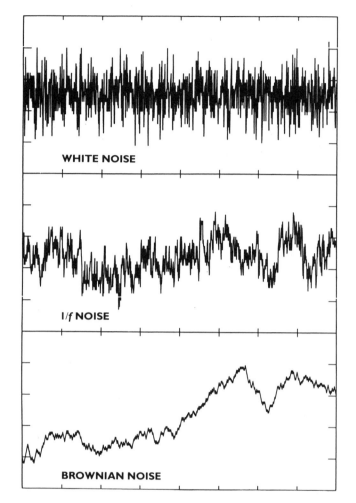

WHITE NOISE

1/f NOISE

BROWNIAN NOISE

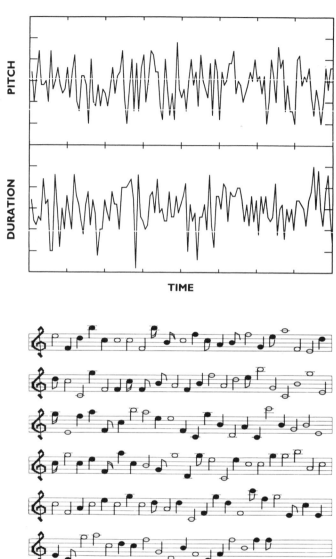

PITCH

DURATION

TIME

musical aesthetics in his treatise *On the Sensations of Tone* (1862). Helmholtz divided musical invention into three components: the physical, the physiological, and the psychological. The first component consists of the transmission and reception of pure sound waves; the second of the excitation of neurons, giving rise to sensations; and the last of the mental images or associations provoked by the sensations.

Acoustical physics can sufficiently explain the emanation of waves from a bowed string, he maintained, anat-

omy and neurobiology their reception by the eardrum and their transformation into electrochemical impulses. But when it comes to psychology, Helmholtz conceded defeat: Invention remains beyond scientific analysis. "We require every work of art to be reasonable," he wrote,

> and we show this by subjecting it to a critical examination, and by seeking to enhance our enjoyment and our interest in it by tracing out the suitability, connection, and equilibrium of all its separate parts. . . .

Brown music is too ordered.

1/f music is neither too random nor too ordered—but it is still bland.

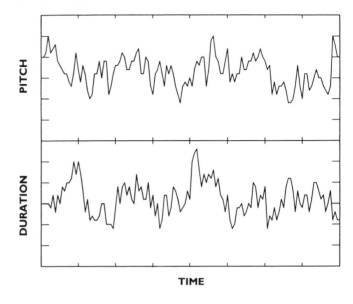

But for all this it is an essential condition that *the whole extent of the regularity and design of a work of art should not be apprehended consciously.* It is precisely from that part of its regular subjection to reason, which escapes our conscious apprehension, that a work of art exalts and delights us, and that the chief effects of the artistically beautiful proceed, not from the part which we are able fully to analyze. [My italics.]

In programming a computer to generate an origami model or a musical composition, we have seen that the first step is to gather and notate the raw material, the second step to form combinations of the constituent parts. The crucial third step consists of selecting one or several patterns from among the myriad of options. Only this step lies beyond the computer's grasp. The true source of invention—the aesthetic faculty that grasps and molds patterns into theorems or melodies or models—remains impervious to scientific investigation. It is not enough to select the patterns that are most *efficient.* What is invention's missing component?

THE PSYCHOLOGY OF INVENTION

A half century ago, the French mathematician Jacques Hadamard surveyed the working methods of his colleagues and posed a formidable question: How do you create? Hadamard was a creative thinker in his own right and knew many of the mathematicians, scientists, painters, and poets of his day. (It was a long day; Hadamard lived from 1865 to 1963.) He sent out a detailed questionnaire and in 1937 revealed the results to a symposium at the appropriately named Centre de Synthèse in Paris. His published summary—a little volume called *The Psychology of Invention in the Mathematical Field*—is one of the most exciting books I have ever read.

As Hadamard expected, no two inventors work quite the same way. Some mathematicians, like some composers, writers, and architects, are prolific, while others, equally skilled, labor intensively and produce little. Some work by day, others by night; a regular regimen aids some and distracts others. But when he had swept surface differences aside, Hadamard found that the act of invention was identical from field to field. From his findings and my own research, I have drawn some broad claims about creativity.

Hadamard began by dividing the creative process into stages: preparation, incubation, illumination, and verification. During the preparatory stage, the inventor attacks the problem with deliberation. If the problem is easy, the solution comes without effort. More often, the inventor surveys a range of possible solutions and sets the problem aside. The following period is one of incubation. While the inventor's attention is focused on other things, his mind turns the problem over and over, continuing the line of attack begun during the preparation stage. The submerged solution struggles to the surface, gasping for air. Eureka! The inventor experiences illumination. The solution appears, complete and incontrovertible. Although it must be verified, scrutinized in the light of day with patience and rigor, the hard work is done; the rest is "mopping up."

The first and last stages are easily understood, but Hadamard's respondents struggled when they tried to describe the part of thinking that produces incubation and illumination. Some called it the "unconscious," others the "subconscious"; William James, one of Hadamard's many mentors, had called it "fringe-consciousness"; the population biologist Francis Galton referred to it as the "ante-chamber" of consciousness. Whatever its name, they shared the belief that an important part of the creative process occurs in a place *beyond conscious thought*. (Helmholtz would have agreed.) After they had immersed themselves in a problem for days or weeks, the solution would come to them suddenly and without prompting. A chemist named John Edgar Teeple wrote that he had once worked on a problem for half

an hour without knowing it. He realized it only as he was about to step out of the bathtub—having just taken two baths in a row. Another of Hadamard's mentors, the mathematician Henri Poincaré, made his important discovery of Fuchsian functions while vacationing on a geological field trip. Poincaré had worked on the problem for weeks but had abandoned it before the solution struck. "Most striking at first is the appearance of sudden illumination, a manifest sign of long, unconscious prior work," Poincaré wrote. "The role of this unconscious work in mathematical invention appears to me incontestable." Upon returning home, he verified the solution through more rigorous means.

One composer had a useful metaphor for these last two stages, illumination and verification. Invention, he said, is like looking out a window into the black night of a thunderstorm. Suddenly, a flash of lightning ignites the entire landscape. Illumination! In that split second, one has seen everything—and nothing. The act of verification is the patient re-creation of that landscape, stone by stone, tree by tree.

Hadamard found that unconscious work often occurs while people dream. Many respondents wrote that they had woken from sleep to find a solution, some more than once. (Hadamard himself had done this.) An American mathematician, Leonard Eugene Dickson, told a story about his mother and her sister, rivals in geometry class at school. One night, after the two had spent the evening struggling over a problem, Dickson's mother dreamed the solution and began reciting it in a loud voice. Her sister woke up and took notes. The following morning, in class, the sister reported the right solution, which Dickson's mother didn't know.

I have no doubt that dreaming solutions is common. A friend of mine reports a similar story about his roommate at Yale. "He was a chemical engineering major and used to work on problems in his sleep," my friend told me. "Marco was quite a character. He would go on sleep binges of thirty-six hours or more and would talk in his sleep. A lot of what he said was about chemistry, but not always. We posted the best quotes on the door.

"One evening, after Marco had been asleep all day, we tried to wake him to go to dinner. We did the usual thing—shook him, beat him with pillows—but nothing worked. Suddenly, he sat straight up in bed and started shouting, 'How did we get to the zero point? How did we get to the zero point?' His eyes were wide open, and he was waving his arms about. I tried to get hold of him, but he pushed me away. Then he turned and stared directly at me and said, 'You're not in the system!' and fell back on his pillow, fast asleep. By that time we were pretty hungry, so we gave up and went to dinner."

When I was in architecture school and working twenty-hour days, I often dreamed the solutions to design problems. One time the assignment was to make a

SIMPLE ELEMENTS MAKE COMPLEX PATTERNS

Artists generate complex patterns by repeating pencil and brush strokes at varying scales. Shown are works by Western and Japanese artists that capture the iterative form of turbulence in nature.

A drawing by Leonardo da Vinci, *The Deluge*.

A wave design painted on a paper screen by Ogata Korin, c. 1704–1710.

A wood-block print by Katsushika Hokusai, *View of Mount Fuji Through High Waves off Kanagawa*, from the series *Thirty-Six Views of Mount Fuji*, 1823-1829.

A computer-generated artwork by Douglas McKenna, *Hepdragon*, 1985.

footbridge that would span 60 feet between two river-banks, one of them 10 feet higher than the other. It so happens that the origami rattlesnake was also on my mind at the time, and, in the dream, the bridge became an enormous snake that undulated across the stream. Even more remarkably, the rattles on the tail, which from above resembled a set of parallel lines, became, in three dimensions, a staircase descending the 10 feet to the lower bank. All this made plenty of sense to my feverish brain, and I recall the sadness I felt when, upon waking, I realized that the solution still eluded me.

Solutions may seem to come spontaneously, as in my rattlesnake dream, but usually they are the product of a mind working overtime, night and day, sleeping and waking. Invention does not arise from thin air. Rather, it is the transformation of the known into the unknown, the playful recombining of familiar elements in new ways. Of the hundreds or thousands of patterns that can be formed from those simple elements, only a few are fruitful, and it is the task of the unconscious to find them. "To create," wrote Poincaré, "consists precisely in avoiding useless combinations and in making those which are useful and which constitute only a small minority. Invention is discernment, selection." The Symbolist poet Paul Valéry, a speaker at the Centre de Synthèse symposium, agreed. "It takes two to invent anything," Valéry asserted.

> The one makes up combinations; the other one chooses, recognizes what he wishes and what is important to him in the mass of the things which the former has imparted to him.
> What we call genius is much less the work of the first one than the readiness of the second one to grasp the value of what has been laid before him and to choose it.

The idea that invention is a disciplined search for patterns helps explain the working method of artists whose ability is otherwise just attributed to genius. Studies of Beethoven's sketchbooks reveal, for example, that over a period of eight years he tried out no fewer than fourteen different melodies before he settled on the utterly simple first theme of the slow movement of his Fifth Symphony. Even spontaneous acts of invention, such as Johann Sebastian Bach's improvised six-part fugues, fit the pattern. It may be that what we label spontaneous invention occurs when the creation and selection of combinations follow so rapidly upon each other as to appear instantaneous.

What are the components of those combinations? The likely guess is that they belong to the inventor's field: notes for the composer, words for the poet, algebraic symbols for the mathematician. Yet this is not always the case. The components may be surrogates for the finished product, abstract quantities such as form or rhythm. A scientist might work with pictures, a painter

with sounds, a mathematician with pulsating flashes of light. Claude Lévi-Strauss, the ethnographer, invented by turning over three-dimensional images in his mind. Francis Galton, the biologist, thought in terms of nonsense words, syllables and sounds that accompanied his ideas like the notes of a song. A psychologist, Theodule Armand Ribot, refused to commit his ideas to paper until he was required to publish; he considered words about as useless and dangerous as counterfeit money. Hadamard concurred; he called words a nuisance and thought only in visual images, collections of points in space. In his now-famous letter to Hadamard, Albert Einstein wrote of using "signs" and "images" in his work:

> Words or language, as they are written or spoken, do not seem to play any role in my mechanism of thought. The psychical entities which seem to serve as elements in thought are certain signs and more or less clear images which can be "voluntarily" reproduced and combined.
> There is, of course, a certain connection between those elements and relevant logical concepts. It is also clear that the desire to arrive finally at logically connected concepts is the emotional basis of this rather vague play with the above mentioned elements. But taken from a psychological viewpoint, *this combinatory play seems to be the essential feature in productive thought*—before there is any connection with logical construction in words or other kinds of signs which can be communicated to others [My italics.]

Another example comes from chess. World-class chess players are renowned for making lightning-fast decisions. Their ability to play and defeat forty or more opponents at once appears nothing short of miraculous. Recent advances in the technology of chess-playing computers suggest a reason for their success. It appears that human chess players, like artists or scientists, rely on patterns. When they glance at the board, they overlook individual moves and instead see combinations of moves, using what one author on computer chess calls a "vocabulary of patterns" to screen out useless combinations. The best computer programs, in contrast, lack a reservoir of successful patterns and an aptitude for spotting new combinations. However, what they want in imagination they make up for in speed, exhaustively enumerating the marginal benefit of moving any piece to any possible square on the board at a rate of over 175,000 positions a second. They prey on human fallibility; eventually their opponent slips up, and then they steamroll to victory.

Once the inventor has played with the components of a problem, how does he know when he has reached the solution? Hadamard found that whatever the field, the governing factor is aesthetic. The verse or melody or equation chosen as the best is invariably the most *pleasing*. Beauty above all! "My work has always tried to unite the true with the beautiful," wrote the physicist

In the woodcuts of M. C. Escher, the extent of iteration is constrained only by the grain of the wood and the sureness of his hand.

Regular Division of the Plane VI, plate from *The Regular Division of the Plane*, 1958, and diagrammatic explanation. Compare with the folding pattern to the elephant, page 263.

Square Limit, 1964, and preliminary study showing one quadrant. Compare with the folding pattern to the butterfly, page 293.

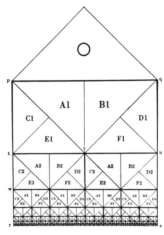

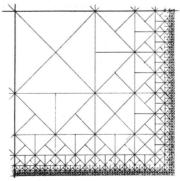

Architects generate complex patterns by repeating simple structures at varying scales. Shown are examples of ceiling vaults. The structure of a vault distributes its weight (downward force) and thrust (outward force) among its supports.

Right, Gothic ceiling vaults: axonometrics and plans of ribbed vault and fan vault. Compare with folding patterns to the flapping bird, page 15, and one-dollar bow tie, page 129.

Below, Windsor Castle, Berkshire: ceiling vaults in St. George's Chapel, 1473–1516. Compare with folding pattern to the one-dollar crab, page 133.

Opposite page, top: Westminster Abbey, ground plan, c. 1245. Dotted lines show reflections of ceiling vaults. Folding patterns everywhere!

Opposite page, bottom: Islamic ceiling vaults, Lantern of Hakim II, Great Mosque of Córdoba, 962–966 (left); central vault, Mosque of Bib Mardun, Toledo, c. 999 (right). Compare with folding patterns to the crab, page 151, and scorpion, page 195.

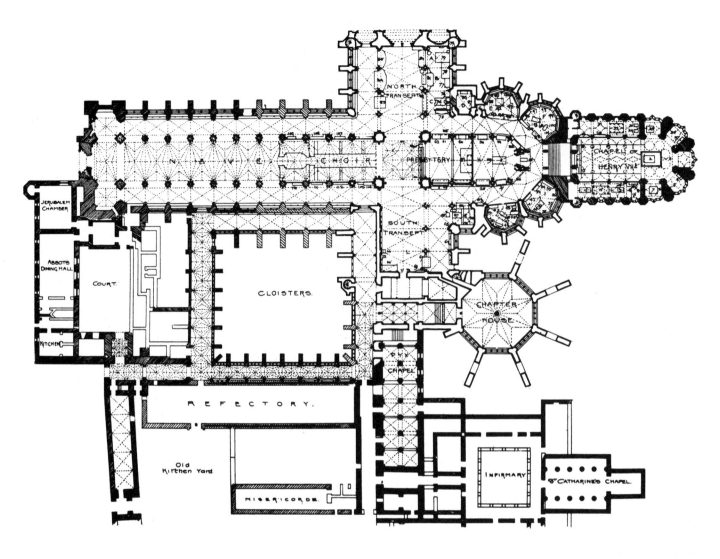

Hermann Weyl, "and when I had to choose one or the other I usually chose the beautiful." "A mathematician, like a painter or a poet, is a maker of patterns," the British mathematician G. H. Hardy recounted in his memoir, *A Mathematician's Apology*. "If his patterns are more permanent than theirs, it is because they are made with *ideas*.... The mathematician's patterns, like the painter's or the poet's, must be *beautiful*.... Beauty is the first test: there is no permanent place in the world for ugly mathematics."

Invention is universal. Scientists do it, mathematicians do it, painters, poets, and composers do it, paperfolders do it. They manipulate simple elements to form patterns. The patterns may be composed of physical forces or geometric abstractions, colors or words, notes or folds, but the act of making patterns is the same. While no single definition could encompass every act of invention, the essential similarity in the process, no matter what the field of endeavor, hints at something profound about humankind. Reflecting on all that I have learned from my investigation, I have come to the conclusion that we invent new forms by

unconsciously playing with simple elements,
rearranging them to form patterns, and
choosing the patterns that are most *beautiful*.

If that sounds like the way nature invents . . . it's no coincidence!

Encouraged by the success of Hadamard's survey, I decided to conduct one of my own. I wanted to learn whether the working habits of paperfolders parallel those of inventors in other fields. I began by compiling a list of questions. Do you set out to create one particular model, I asked, or is your method trial and error? Do you consciously use geometry in your models? How long do your models take to invent? Have you ever invented one instantaneously? Do you create in your head, or do you always begin with the paper? When you get stuck on a problem, what do you do? Finally, are there any models you have never been able to make?

I invited ten preeminent American paperfolders to a symposium at the American Museum of Natural History in New York City and sent them the questions. Much of the discussion was technical and pertained only to origami ("To create the locking mechanism for the links, I pleated the double thickness in full . . ."), but some of the comments went deeper. These, especially, pleased me, for they were uncannily like the responses Hadamard had received. "If I can't find a solution," said one folder, Stephen Weiss, "I will let the model go and come back to it in a day or a week. Often my subconscious mind has been working all along, and when I come back, I can find the solution." He continued:

The composer Richard Strauss once said that he always looked for poems that expressed a certain feeling before he began composing a song. When he found the right poem, composing the music was relatively easy and didn't take long. But if he couldn't find a suitable poem, composing took a long time and required all his technical skill, and he had to resort to artifice in order to create something that satisfied his standards.

I have the same experience in making a model. Sometimes a combination of folds will seem to lend itself to a subject almost automatically, requiring only the finishing touches. But if the pattern isn't right, I won't be able to find a solution, and I'll just forget about the problem. And maybe a year or so later, I'll rediscover it and complete the model using new techniques and fresh insight.

His comment was typical. Here are some of the others:

Sometimes, while I am asleep, I will get the solution to a problem in a dream or in a half-waking state, and if I don't get up to record it right away, I'm certain to lose it. This is not uncommon. Patricia Crawford [another folder] told me she also got her ideas in dreams, but she didn't worry about writing them down. She was sure they would surface consciously at a later date if the solution was correct.

She told me she never worked on anything for more than three days. If she couldn't get it by then, she put it aside. She said, "It's there. It'll cooperate when it's ready." Very often, after a period of subconscious investigation, she would make a model perfectly the very first time. [Alice Gray]

I never worked on a fold continuously until I arrived at a solution. Sometimes I would get lucky and the result would be spontaneous. But if, after a certain period of time, I had had no success, I'd set it aside. And maybe days, maybe weeks, maybe months later I would get back to it and work it to a conclusion. [Neal Elias]

A good deal of my process of invention consists of directed effort toward a set goal, but an awfully big part is luck and hunch. I try to be alert for accidental resemblances to things other than the subject I am working on. [Robert Lang]

The notion that the inventor should actively seek accidental resemblances was part of Escher's working method as well. He was fond of quoting the following advice, offered by Leonardo da Vinci:

If you have to depict a scene, look at some walls daubed with marks or built from stones of different kinds. In them you will see a resemblance to a diversity of mountainous landscapes, rivers, rocks, trees, sweeping plains and hills. You can also see battles and human figures, strange facial expressions, garments and countless other things, whose shapes you could straighten and improve. These crumbling walls are like the peals of church bells in which you can hear any name or word you choose.

While searching for patterns in the paper or the natural world, the painter or the folder allows his subconscious to fix upon the cracks, crevices, fissures, creases, edges, and angles that are the raw material for his construction. The inventor's experience alerts him to the appealing pattern and the fortuitous resemblance. When the opportunity comes, he is ready to seize it. "I believe in the idea of discovery," David Shall, another folder, revealed:

> I think that origami models are in the paper, just waiting to be brought out, and they can be brought out by people anywhere, anytime.
>
> Sometimes I think about a particular problem when I'm trying to go to sleep, and I fall asleep trying to work it out. I can't say that I've ever dreamt any models, but I have had the experience a couple of times of designing models when I was ill. I don't know whether this came from just lying at home—from having nothing to do but concentrate on origami for several days—or whether it had to do with being slightly delirious with fever.

The folders echoed words uttered half a century ago. Like Hadamard's respondents, they did much of their work unconsciously, often while dreaming, and looked for fortuitous resemblances to natural objects. They recognized the importance of incubation: If a solution didn't come right away, if the pattern wasn't right, they would set the problem aside and turn to another one. They experienced illumination: sudden victory. And they reinforced my own sense of being a discoverer, the feeling of calling forth forms inherent in the paper.

I had often speculated that the paperfolder is both a discoverer and a creator, that the two roles are not, as is often believed, mutually exclusive. In the early stages of inventing, when I am manipulating geometric elements to capture the structure of an animal, I feel like a scientist *discovering* patterns in the paper. As the model develops, and I turn to aesthetic decisions governing the detailed shape of the animal, I feel like an artist *creating* patterns in the paper. Clearly, I am not alone in these intuitions, since both Akira Yoshizawa and the speakers at the origami symposium reported a similar feeling. A paradox lurks here. Art is said to explore the inner world of the mind, while mathematics and science explore the outer world of experience. How could origami do both?

An act of creation is unique, the subjective vision of one person. Whether it is a spare white canvas, a blank notebook, or an empty music ledger, the artist's medium is a blank slate that must be filled with inspiration from within. A particular product of creation, it follows, could not have come into existence without the imaginative gifts of some specific creator. Could there have been a *Moby-Dick* without Melville? A Beethoven's Fifth without Beethoven? It seems inconceivable that another author or composer could have produced quite the same work. According to this argument, an origami model is a stylized work of art that bears the unmistakable stamp of its creator. This much is true: An experienced folder can recognize an original model by Fred Rohm or Patricia Crawford or John Montroll as easily as any museumgoer can distinguish a Rembrandt from a Renoir from a Rothko.

An act of discovery, by contrast, exposes an object or an idea that exists apart from its discoverer. While the scientist or mathematician may go about his work in an imaginative manner, he imparts nothing of his personality to the product of his discovery. Columbus discovered America, but it would still have been there for someone else to find had he reached Asia, his original destination, instead. Had Einstein confined his interests to his job as a patent clerk, the discovery of relativity would eventually have been made by someone else. An act of discovery is not necessarily a singular event: An object or idea may be rediscovered by different people.

Indeed, the history of science and of mathematics has recorded many instances of independent discovery. The most famous may be the separate discovery of natural selection by Charles Darwin and Alfred Russel Wallace, but there are instances in nearly every field. Both Isaac Newton and Gottfried Wilhelm Leibniz founded calculus in the 1680s. John Couch Adams and Urbain Jean Joseph Leverrier independently predicted the existence of the planet Neptune in the mid-1800s. The effectiveness of a vaccination against smallpox was proved by Edward Jenner and George Pearson in the late 1700s. Henry Cavendish, James Watt, and Antoine Lavoisier independently demonstrated the compound nature of water in the late eighteenth century. These are hardly isolated examples. The sociologist Robert K. Merton has identified 264 multiple scientific discoveries, of which 179 were made independently by pairs of scientists, 51 by three persons, 17 by four, 6 by five, 8 by six, 1 by seven, and 2 by nine. And that, Merton says, is by no means the final tally.

If an origami model is discovered—even in part—there ought to be instances of models that were devised independently by different folders. Although I cannot match Merton's exhaustive research, I know of several instances of simultaneous invention by folders located thousands of miles apart. Some of these were cited by speakers at the symposium on creativity in origami. "If you ask for my opinion on independent creation," Fred Rohm said,

> I can say from personal experience that two people can fold something simultaneously in different parts of the

country and come up with the same thing. Both Neal Elias and I were working on a seal balancing a ball on his nose. When I completed my fold, I put it in an envelope and sent it to him in the mail. In the same mail I found one from Neal that was identical in appearance. The folding techniques were absolutely different, but when you looked at the result, nobody could tell the difference. I'm just as certain as I can be that they were independent things.

It is definitely possible for two or more folders to create the same model independently. My frog shares the exact same box-pleated base as a frog by Kosho Uchiyama, although they are finished differently. Only after my model was published in the British Origami Society magazine did I obtain a copy of Uchiyama's latest book and see the same base. [Stephen Weiss]

Of the models I have invented, my favorite is a Christmas ornament that I call a lemon. The technique consists of fitting together two similar pieces to make a solid. The greatest thrill of my life was finding one folded and lying on a shelf in Philip Shen's house in Hong Kong. [Alice Gray]

I have an eight-point star that looks almost exactly like the star invented by Peter Engel. If you turn them over, you can see a slight difference, but they are nearly identical. About a few months after I made my own star, I was looking for some models for a workshop. I happened to pick out Vicente Palacios's book *Papirogami,* and there was something that looked like my star right on the front cover! [David Shall]

My own experience corroborates these claims. A few years ago, I stepped through the looking glass and met my Eastern counterpart, the Japanese folder Jun Maekawa. Maekawa was exactly my age. His interests and academic background paralleled mine. (He had studied physics at Tokyo Metropolitan University.) He had reexamined traditional Japanese folding techniques and invented something he called "folding patterns." Sound familiar? And he had produced models so similar to mine in their method of construction that they could have been my own. (We had chosen different subject matter, so his finished models do not resemble mine. But the techniques were the same.) Because Maekawa had never seen my work, nor I his, we ruled out plagiarism and unconscious influence. There was no way around it. Working independently, half the globe apart, we had followed identical paths of invention.

THE CASE OF THE PURLOINED PIG

Maekawa and I were lucky: We welcomed each other's work. But in cases of independent invention, such hospitality is rare. The most infamous controversy in ori-

gami history is a case in point. The antagonists were none other than Akira Yoshizawa and Ismael Adolfo Cerceda, the preeminent folders of the Eastern and Western hemispheres. Yoshizawa, the veteran of five decades of folding, was the standard-bearer of the Japanese origami tradition. Cerceda, an Argentine lauded for his collection of models on nationalistic and folk-art themes, was heir to the Moorish tradition. One would have hoped the transition from two dissimilar disciplines into a single field would be smooth and painless. It wasn't.

In the late 1960s, charges that Cerceda had stolen some of his finest models from Yoshizawa began to surface in origami circles. It was hard to trace the source of these claims. Allegations flew without authorship from continent to continent, and soon Cerceda's reputation was at stake. When Cerceda finally replied, he did more than parry. He had uncovered the source of the accusations: It was Yoshizawa himself! What Yoshizawa didn't know was that the shy, nationalistic Cerceda also doubled as the ferocious Carlos Corda, the Knife Thrower Extraordinaire who toured three continents performing improbable feats with knives and an Argentine bullwhip. The stage was set for a confrontation.

Cerceda sent his findings to the American origami newsletter, *The Origamian.* "I know that I invented the models ascribed to me," he wrote,

though I do not deny that Mr. Yoshizawa did too. Mr. Y published his pig in 1945, but I did not steal it from him, if that is what he means; and if I had, I would not have sent it to everybody, claiming ownership. I am not insane, yet. Neither do I agree with Yoshizawa that there is no possibility that two persons might independently invent the same model. It happens, much more often than he thinks.

He concluded, bitterly, "Because of incidents like this, many of my later models have never reached the hands of anyone else, and unless I publish them, they never will."

I cannot confirm or deny Cerceda's claim to originality. I was too young at the time; Cerceda has since died; the truth lies buried with him. (So does the Argentine bullwhip.) When I probed Yoshizawa about the incident, he changed the subject; when I inquired which Western folders he admired, he replied only, "They all copy me."

At first, naturally, I took Cerceda's side. I knew that origami is a process of discovery. Just as the mathematician or the scientist uncovers the laws of nature—laws fully independent of the discoverer—the paperfolder reveals the intrinsic patterns of the square. And so duplication occurs. But I could see Yoshizawa's side, too. The uniqueness of the folder's work resides not only in the paper but also in the folder. His signature lies in the patterns he imposes on the paper, the distinctively personal impulse he brings to the medium. Like creative artists of any epoch, the paperfolder seizes upon simple, timeless forms and manipulates them so that they emerge as never before. Do such patterns exist before we discern them? If so, we have discovered them. If not, the patterns are the constructs of our imagination, and we have created them.

The distinction between discovery and creation is subtle and illusory. Patterns formed of notes, folds, clouds, or stars are not solely the product of a single mind (as in the notion of the created object), nor do they exist exclusive of all minds (as in the notion of the discovered object). Rather, they are invented, summoned into existence by the human mind acting upon the world around it.

Invention is a search for meaning. The discoverer and the creator seek meaning in connectedness: the scientist in the hierarchies of nature, the artist in the concatenation of notes, melodies, and movements or words, sentences, and paragraphs that constitute a composition. Just as a world devoid of patterns is unintelligible, an artwork without form communicates nothing. The interconnectedness of the parts, the subtle interplay of order and disorder, gives meaning and purpose to the whole.

Today we may be closer than ever to bridging the gap between science and art. Gert Eilenberger, a German physicist specializing in dynamic systems and chaos theory, reviewed an exhibition of computer-generated fractal patterns with these words:

> The pictures in this exhibition have another, completely different aspect—they simply are beautiful. The chaotic component shown in the very fine structures does not overpower the whole work; there are large areas of order, sustained by regularity, and chaos and order appear to be joined in harmonious balance.
>
> Precisely this *mixture* of order and disorder is fascinating, and, what is crucial to these new insights, *typical* for natural processes. Here, the science of dynamic systems provides an answer to a second, emotional question: why is it that the products of our technology, the entire technical world, seem to be *un*natural when they are products of *natural* science?
>
> Why is it that the silhouette of a storm-bent, leafless tree against an evening sky in winter is perceived as beautiful, but the corresponding silhouette of any multi-purpose university building is not, in spite of all efforts of the architect?
>
> The answer seems to me, even if somewhat speculative, to follow from the new insights into dynamic systems. Our feeling for beauty is inspired by the harmonious arrangement of order and disorder as it occurs in natural objects —in clouds, trees, mountain ranges or snow crystals. The shapes of all these are dynamic processes jelled into physical forms, and particular combinations of order and disorder are typical for them.

SIMPLE ELEMENTS MAKE COMPLEX PATTERNS

The paperfolder generates complex patterns by repeating simple creases at varying scales. The first four stages in the iteration of the module produce the four fundamental bases: the kite base, fish base, bird base, and frog base. Beyond lie new and unexplored forms.

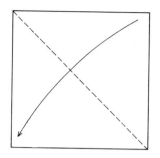

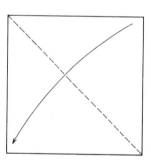
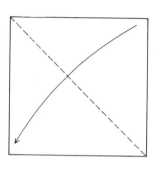
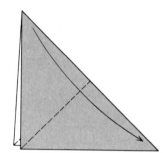

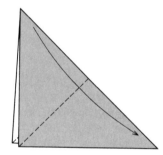
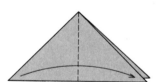

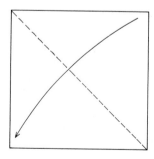
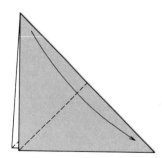
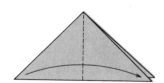

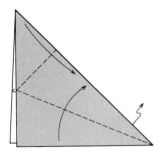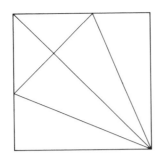

The mathemathics and art of origami, like those of fractal geometry, nature, or music, form a continuum, and there is no way to tell where discovery ends and creation begins. Somewhere in the accumulation of folds, absolute rigor gives way to beauty, and mathematical discovery yields to artistic creation.

TOWARD A VOCABULARY OF FORM

We have learned that the act of invention is many things. It is unconsciously playing with simple elements, rearranging them to form patterns, and choosing the patterns that are most efficient—*and* most beautiful. It is preparation, incubation, illumination, and verification. It is not one process but many, an infinite regress of iterative processes, a feedback loop that generates complex forms from simple forces. It is doing what nature does with human hands. It is artistic creation and scientific discovery and what happens between them. It is reductionism and holism, zooming in and stepping back. It is looking for the chance resemblance that will trigger inspiration. It is adult's work and child's play, and sometimes the hardest part is the play. And, above all, it is making patterns, beautiful patterns.

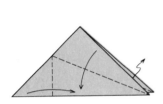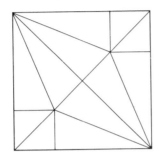

These ideas are clearer to me now than they were years ago, when I had reached a creative impasse and did not know how to go on. But even then the principles of invention were actively at work. They invaded my unconscious and guided me as I sorted through piles of crumpled paper in search of patterns. They told me that where there are patterns, there must be forces, the forces that created them. The rest was up to me. If I could apply the principles of invention to origami, I could harness the forces in the paper and produce new patterns. Forms no human being had ever seen would appear for the first time in my hands! The solution to my impasse lay within reach. Thus inspired, I returned to the familiar kite base, fish base, bird base, and frog base to uncover the patterns of origami.

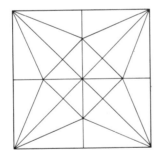

When I drew the folding patterns to the four fundamental bases, I came to a startling realization. Unfolding model after model, deciphering their intricate geometry, I recognized the same simple elements over and over. They formed a remarkable progression: Two modules made a kite base, four a fish base, eight a bird base, sixteen a frog base! Like a nuclear family, their resemblance was undeniable. Repeating the module on smaller and smaller scales leads inexorably from kite base to fish base, fish base to bird base, bird base to frog base. That was as far as the Japanese had taken it. But I saw no reason why the pattern should stop.

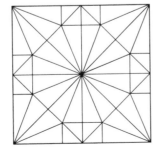

The operation for producing bases turns out to be a feedback loop. Take a square. Fold it in half, making a

**THE FOUR BLINTZED BASES AND THEIR
FOLDING PATTERNS**

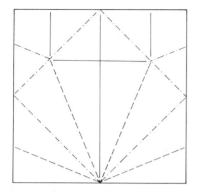 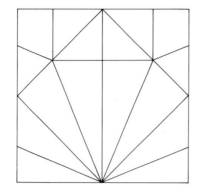 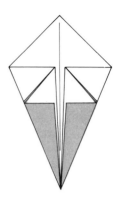

Blintzed kite base.

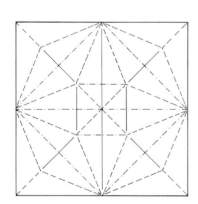 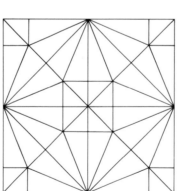 

Blintzed fish base.

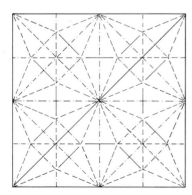 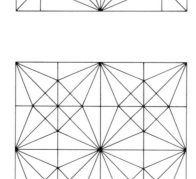 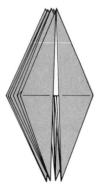

Blintzed bird base.

Blintzed frog base.

right triangle, and form the module. The result is the *kite* base. Take a square, fold it in half twice, and form the module. The result is the *fish* base. Take a square, fold it in half three times, and form the module. The result is the *bird* base. Take a square, fold it in half four times, and form the module. The result is the *frog* base. Repeat again, and again, and again . . .

When I continued this pattern beyond the frog base, I encountered unforeseen scales of complexity. One iteration beyond the frog base produced thirty-two modules. Two iterations beyond the frog base produced sixty-four modules. The operation could be continued ad infinitum, generating ever higher levels of complexity. Like the patterns of nature, the computer-generated fractal patterns, and the combinations of simple elements assembled by composers, artists, and architects, my new folding patterns were masterpieces of simple design. But a crucial question remained: Would these patterns correspond to three-dimensional origami bases, the configurations of paper that would generate actual models? Incredibly, they did!

Each new iteration conforms to a folding procedure called a *blintz*. To blintz a square of paper, valley-fold the four corners to the center, like so:

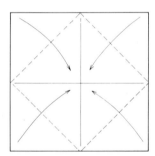 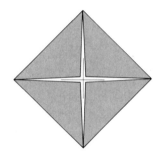

Valley-fold the four corners to the center.

The completed blintz fold.

The resulting figure, a smaller square rotated 45 degrees, is identical to the original square, but with the addition of four triangular flaps. The blintz fold, a twentieth-century invention, is named after a pastry:

blintze (blints), n. *Jewish Cookery,* a thin pancake folded around a filling, as of cheese or fruit. Also, **blintz** (blints). [<Yiddish *blintse* <Russ *blinets,* dim. of *blin* pancake]

The blintz was the only widespread innovation in origami since the invention of the frog base. I don't know who invented it, or who coined the name. Before my day, a number of folders had applied it to the bird base or the frog base, but none, to my knowledge, had explored its wider implications. I realized that blintz folding is an iterative process: It begins with a given geometric figure (the square), divides that figure in two (the four corner triangles make up half the area of the square), and produces a replica of the original. The resulting figure is, of course, self-similar.

The blintz fold can be performed on any base to double the number of potential flaps:

BASE	NUMBER OF MODULES	BASE	NUMBER OF MODULES
Kite	2	Blintzed kite	4
Fish	4	Blintzed fish	8
Bird	8	Blintzed bird	16
Frog	16	Blintzed frog	32

Nor must the progression stop there. Performing a blintz fold on a base that has already been blintzed produces a succession of nested squares, each rotated 45 degrees. In little time this process yields an astronomical number of modules, 64 for the *double-blintzed* frog base, 128 for the *triple-blintzed* frog base—more than a folder would ever need.

In the ideal, mathematical world, recursion can go on forever. But in the real world, it spans only a few orders of magnitude, limited by such absolutes as the minimum aperture of a blood vessel, the discrete size of a gene, or the smallest grouping of atoms that can form a crystal. In origami, it is constrained by the thickness of paper. When a model has only two or four long appendages, like the traditional whale or flapping bird, the flaps can be made from the corners of the square. The corners, of course, make the narrowest points: An appendage formed from an edge is twice as thick, from the middle, four times as thick. With each iteration, more and more of the flaps must come from the edges and middle of the paper. The principle here is the same as in a jigsaw puzzle. As the total number of pieces increases, the middle pieces increase in number much faster than the edge pieces, while the number of corner pieces always remains constant, at four. With each iteration, the flaps also move closer together. They grow simultaneously thicker and shorter, and the paper can no longer collapse compactly. Too many iterations and the model is doomed.

Inventing new patterns was, of course, only the beginning. A folding pattern is just a mute configuration of lines in a square, one of hundreds or thousands of patterns that promise much but may deliver nothing. Like a Rorschach blot or a computer-generated sequence of notes, the pattern is raw material to be rearranged, manipulated, transformed. As I worked and reworked the paper in my hands, my mind formed and selected patterns.

Working by sight and by feel, I raced through combinations of folds, bypassing individual mountain and valley folds and instead manipulating whole assemblies of reverse folds and squash folds and petal folds and bird bases. Like the chess player who glances at the board and instantly assembles a mating combination, I collapsed the paper into configurations that immediately suggested the shape of animals: the trunk of an elephant, the coils of a snake, the wings of a butterfly. But a configuration of folds is not yet a butterfly. It must be molded into a plastic form, the body shaped, the wings curved, the manifold subtleties that identify a butterfly gracefully and lovingly crafted. It might be weeks, months, or years before the completed model emerges.

The blintz fold opened the floodgates to new techniques. I blintzed a frog base and produced a scorpion and a squid. I double-blintzed a frog base and made an eight-pointed star, a knight on horseback, and a crab. I invented a new procedure for the crab—an *open double sink fold*—and realized that a sequence of these folds, lined up end to end, matched the segments of a centipede. Encouraged, I looked for new and different modules. I found that a rectangle with proportions $1 \times \sqrt{2}$ replicates itself: Divided in half widthwise, it becomes two smaller rectangles with exactly the same proportion. Folding the paper in half again and again produces an infinite succession of smaller rectangles:

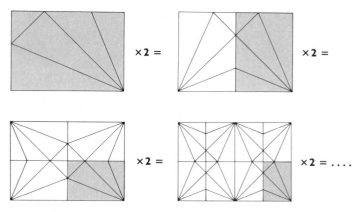

Replication of the $1 \times \sqrt{2}$ module into two copies.

The $1 \times \sqrt{2}$ rectangle proved to be the basis of an elephant and a tiger. Other iterative figures followed. A triangle with proportions $1 \times \sqrt{3}$ replicates itself in two different ways: Divide it one way, and *three* smaller triangles replicate the parent. Divide it a different way, and *four* smaller triangles replicate the parent. The $1 \times \sqrt{3}$ triangle generated a reindeer and a one-dollar crab. Like the other iterative processes, this one repeats ad infinitum.

I was on a roll. Combining different modules produced even more forms. In a process I call *grafting* (it reminds me eerily of biological implanting), I inserted a

REPLICATING MODULES

Replication of the I x I module into two copies.

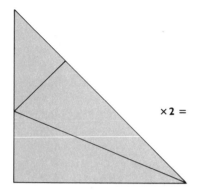 ×2 =

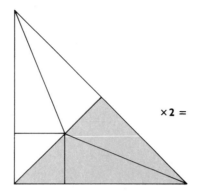 ×2 =

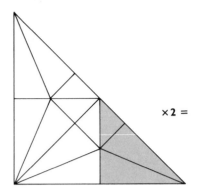 ×2 =

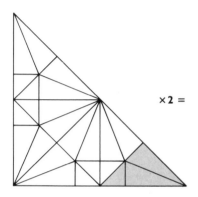 ×2 =

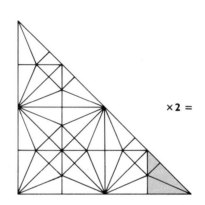 ×2 =

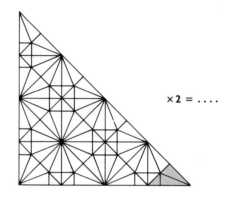 ×2 = ...

Replication of the I x $\sqrt{3}$ module into three copies.

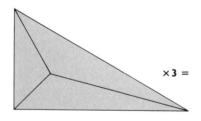 ×3 =

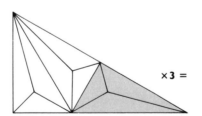 ×3 =

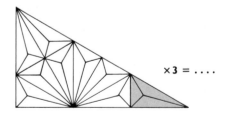 ×3 = ...

Replication of the I x $\sqrt{3}$ module into four copies.

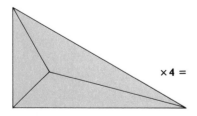 ×4 =

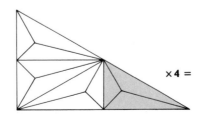 ×4 =

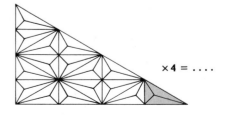 ×4 = ...

SIMPLE ANGLES AND PROPORTIONS GOVERN
THREE MODULES

Two triangles make up nearly all the models in this book. The triangles are combined in different ways to form three modules.

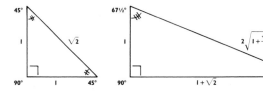

1 x 1 module

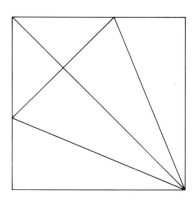

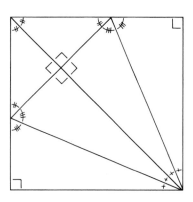

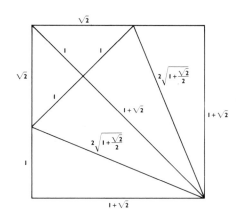

1 x √2 module

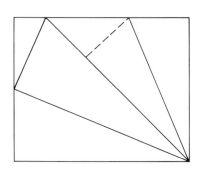

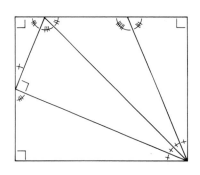

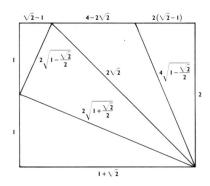

1 x (1 + √2)/2 module

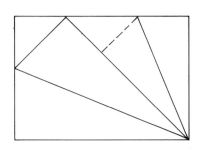

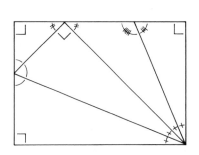

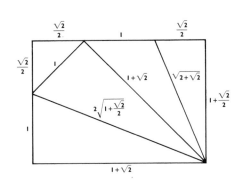

frog base into the center of a bird base to make a baby for my kangaroo. Repeating the procedure on a larger scale, I plugged four frog bases into a blintzed frog base to make the eyes and funnel of an octopus.

After grafting came *hybrid modules:* clusters of modules assembled into superclusters, ever larger and more complex forms. One hybrid consisted of a large square, a small square, and two $1 \times \sqrt{2}$ rectangles, all assembled to make a kind of supersquare. Even this hybrid module could be repeated. The first iteration is the simple bird base. The second, containing the two rectangles and two squares, became an alligator. And the third, utilizing a new rectangle of proportions $1 \times (1 + \sqrt{2})/2$, became my most challenging model to date, a butterfly.

As I continued the struggle to make new forms, the days of despair grew distant. I communicated with other folders and found that many had reached the same impasse; a few, like me, had found a way out. My models became better and more complex: the octopus, with eight tentacles and a head, required nine flaps, the knight on horseback eleven, the reindeer twelve, and the butterfly sixteen. I knew, at last, that origami would never exhaust the square. With the endless variety of life to inspire me, the only limit would be my own imagination.

The deeper I penetrated into the patterns of the paper, the more the creation of an origami model struck me as an analogue for life. Each new module contains the blueprint for its subsequent division and reproduction; each new base contains its entire life history. It is not hard to see in self-replication a host of biological processes: the duplication of DNA by RNA, the division of the fertilized egg during mitosis, the twinning of an amoeba, the budding of a hydra, the passing of chromosomes from generation to generation.

M. C. Escher had called crossing the divide a spiritual act. He, too, would have wondered, Is the model immanent in the paper, or is the square a blank slate to be written on by the creator? Does each model possess a set of phylogenetic rules governing its shape and structure? In the morphogenesis of the model, how do local (cellular) and global (organismic) structures meet? Like natural selection—or God—does the folder impose a teleology on a blind, mechanical process? The answers are remote and elusive—as elusive as the origin of life.

For two months after I saw a square of paper floating through space, I carried the image around in my head. Or perhaps it carried me. It hovered in the back of my unconscious, folding and refolding itself in a spectacle of complex patterns, stealing my attention. But life does not come to a halt for a piece of paper, especially not a floating square. And so I went about my activities and allowed the image to incubate. From time to time, I

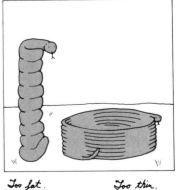

Too fat.   Too thin.

Grafting a frog base onto a bird base.

 + 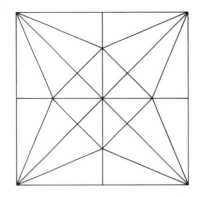 =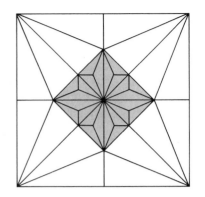

Grafting four frog bases onto a blintzed frog base.

 + 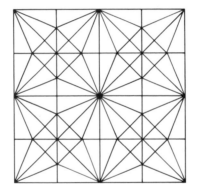 =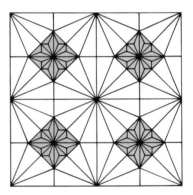

Replication of a hybrid module.

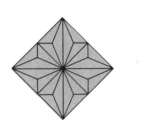 → 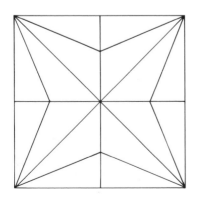 →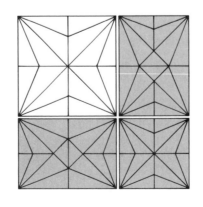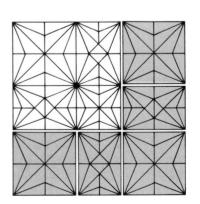

retrieved it from my unconscious to attack the problem anew. Without touching the paper, I began to isolate the hurdles that lay ahead.

First of all, I would have to capture the appearance of the snake's body. It would not be satisfactory merely to draw lines on the paper; I would have to form a series of tiny parallel pleats to give the body texture, creating the illusion of deep three-dimensionality. I would have to find a way of getting two flaps to protrude from the top and bottom of the coil, so that I could mold the head and tail. Because the coil would have a natural tendency to spring outward, I would have to devise a locking mechanism to hold it in place. Finally, the proportions of the animal would have to be anatomically correct, or nearly so; the crucial ratio would be the thickness of the body in relation to the diameter of the coil. Beyond this last hurdle lurked intangibles such as the character and aesthetic appearance of the finished model, but these lay far down the line.

Working out these problems with the paper consumed many waking hours, and even some sleeping ones, over the coming weeks. The process of invention was often laborious and dull, with extended lapses of productivity and stretches in which every move was either a false start or a dead end.

I believe, though, that chance favors the prepared mind, and that the many hours spent discarding useless combinations are far from worthless. In the end, I prevailed, and the snake took the form you see in this book. But often the problem confounds and must disappear, unsolved, into the inventor's mind, only to reemerge weeks, months, or years later, surging up within him, demanding a resolution. Only then, after a seemingly endless string of wrong turns, does the long-awaited moment of illumination occur, when from a meaningless jumble of angles and edges the pattern appears, the divide is crossed, and there sits the model, the theorem, the chess sequence, the melody, the painting, the poem. This is the exhilarating instant when that which was mute first speaks. And when it does, it utters the joyful, childlike cry that is the common language of all invention.

THE MODELS

ADDITIONAL PROCEDURES

Before folding the models, you will need to know the following procedures.

In a *crimp fold,* a pair of valley folds and mountain folds converge at a point. The creases on the front and rear layers form mirror images of each other.

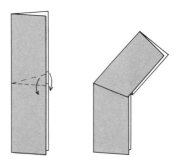

Valley-fold and mountain-fold the front and back.
The completed crimp fold.

In a *pleat fold,* a mountain and a valley fold are parallel. A pleat can be performed on any number of layers. They are folded together as one.

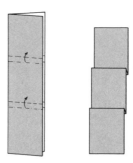

Valley-fold and mountain-fold the front and back.
The completed pleat fold.

In a *rabbit's ear fold,* the three angles of a triangular flap are bisected (divided in two) by valley folds. The triangle can be any shape. This example uses the bird base.

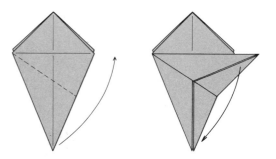

Bisect one angle with a valley fold.
Unfold.

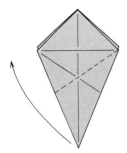 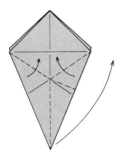

Bisect another angle with a valley fold. Unfold.

In a single motion, refold the two previous steps and bisect the loose third angle. Swing the loose angle to either side. A small mountain fold forms automatically. Flatten.

The completed open sink fold.

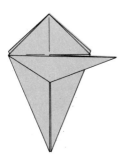

The completed rabbit's ear fold.

In a *closed sink,* the portion to be sunk remains closed and never lies flat. Instead, it "pops" from its convex form to its concave form. The operation is indicated by a filled arrow.

 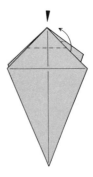

The *sink fold* is the last and hardest of the folding procedures. In a sink, a portion of the paper that is convex (that is, projects out) becomes concave (projects in). This fold comes in two types. In an *open sink,* the portion that is sunk passes through a stage when it is fully open and flat. The operation is indicated by a hollow arrow.

Crease firmly to form the line of the sink. Spread the paper, and push in at the top.

Continue pushing until the sunk portion forms a flat, open square and then collapses inside the paper. Flatten.

Crease firmly to form the line of the sink. Pinch the two left-hand flaps, and spread the two right-hand flaps.

The sunk portion forms a triangular pyramid that will not lie flat. Push in at the top until the pyramid collapses inside the paper.

Flatten.

The completed closed sink fold.

Now choose a model and get to work!

ANGELFISH

Use a sheet of paper colored brightly on one side, or a sheet with a different color on each side. A 10-inch square will produce a model 10 inches tall. Begin with the preliminary fold.

1 Unfold the side flaps.
2 Crimp the side flaps, and swing them downward.

3 The triangles projecting from the top and bottom will be the body fins, while the squares facing front and back will form the body. In a single motion, narrow the top body fin with valley folds and valley-fold the body as far as it will go. Repeat behind.
4 Repeat step 3 on the bottom body fin. Pull out the trapped paper and pinch it to form a rabbit's ear.
5 Unfold the white portion and press it flat.

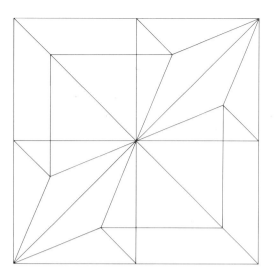

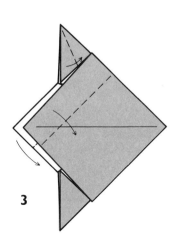

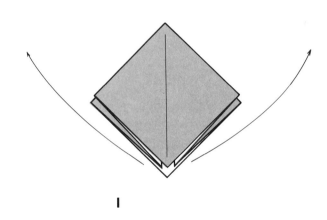

1

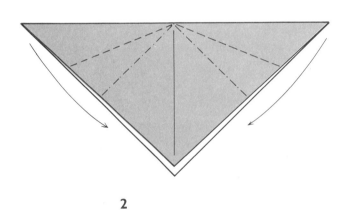

2

3

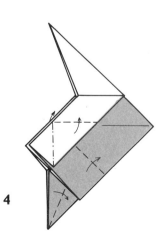

4

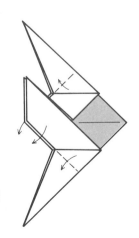

5

6 Following the existing creases, tuck the loose paper inside the body.

7 The shaded triangles projecting from the top will be the tail fins. Narrow them with valley folds and unfold.

8 Swing both fins down.

9 Valley-fold the fins in the other direction and unfold.

10 Swing the front fin upward.

11, 12 Following the existing creases, open-sink the front fin.

13 The sink is nearly completed. Sink the rear fin identically.

The completed ANGELFISH.

(1973)

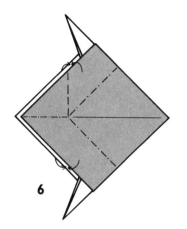

6

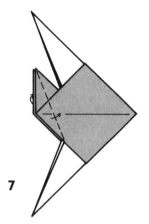

7

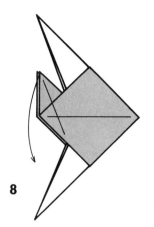

8

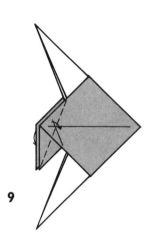

9

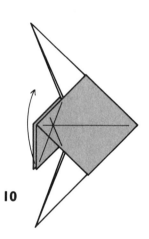

10

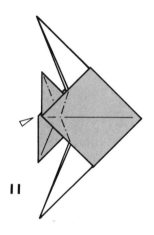

11

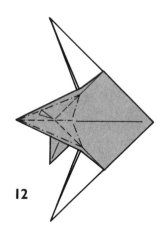

12

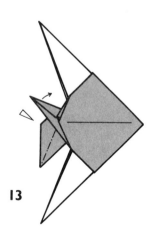

13

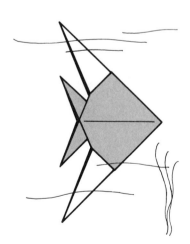

BUTTERFLY FISH

Use a sheet of paper colored brightly on one side. A 10-inch square will produce a model 6⅝ inches tall. Begin with the preliminary fold.

1 Lift the top flap and stretch. This is a petal fold.
2 Flatten.
3 The shaded side flaps will be the body fins. Swing them as high as they will go.

4 Narrow the body fins with valley folds.
5 The triangular flaps at the top and bottom will be the tail fins. Valley-fold the upper fin. Dotted lines in the next step show where the edge of the paper should fall.
6 Unfold.

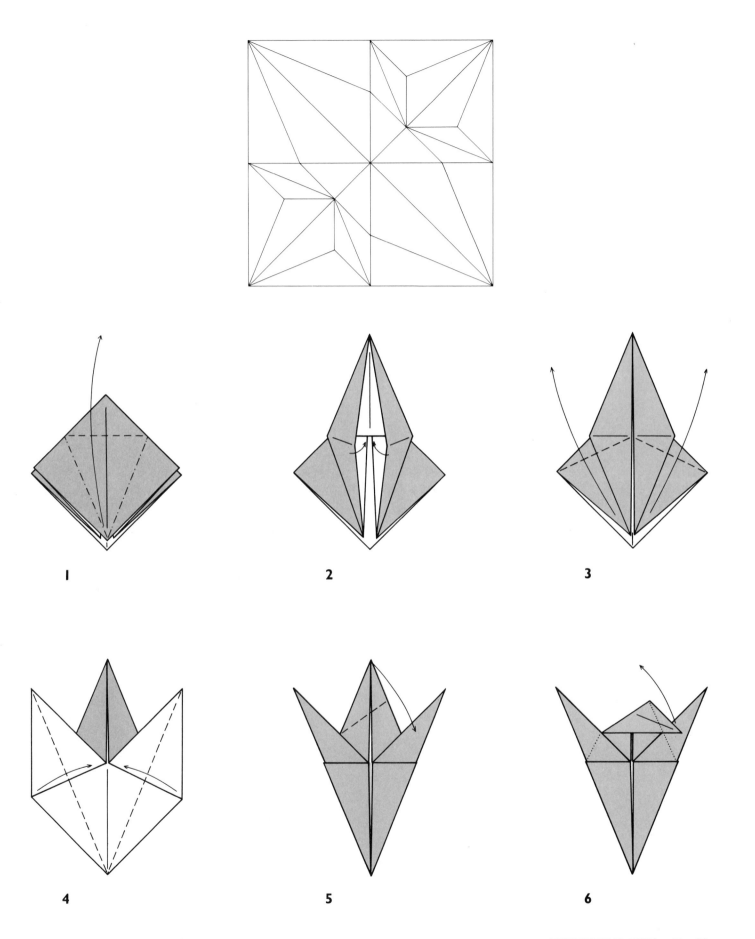

1

2

3

4

5

6

7 Repeat steps 5 and 6 on the right-hand side of the upper tail fin and on both sides of the lower tail fin. Then, following the existing creases, rabbit's ear both fins.

8 Valley-fold both tail fins. Make the crease perpendicular to the outer edge of each fin so that the edge lands on itself.

9 Valley-fold the upper fin along the centerline.

10 Unfold the entire upper fin to step 7.

11 Mountain-fold along the existing crease.

12 Rabbit's ear the full thickness along the existing creases.

13 Unwrap the upper tail fin and swing it to the left.

14 Fold the entire model in half, and tuck the protruding paper from the lower fin into the pocket in the upper fin to lock the body.

The completed BUTTERFLY FISH.

(1973)

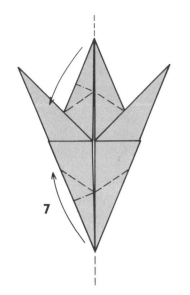

7

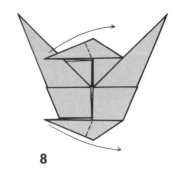

8

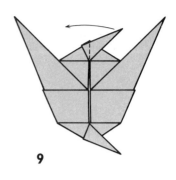

9

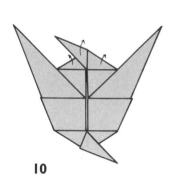

10

11

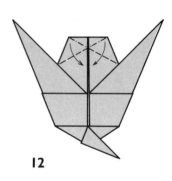

12

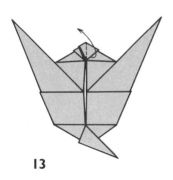

13

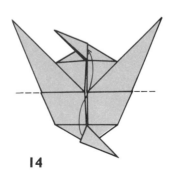

14

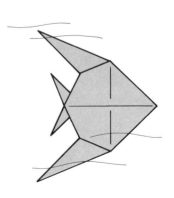

DISCUS FISH

Use a sheet of paper colored brightly on one side, or a sheet with a different color on each side. A 10-inch square will produce a model 6⅝ inches tall. Begin with the preliminary fold.

1 Valley-fold the front and back squares.
2 Valley-fold the four side flaps to the centerline.
3 Unfold the four side flaps.

4, 5 In a single motion, refold the four side flaps and mountain-fold the upper flaps to the centerpoint. Tuck the loose paper inside.
6 Separate the white flaps, and swivel the shaded flaps clockwise.

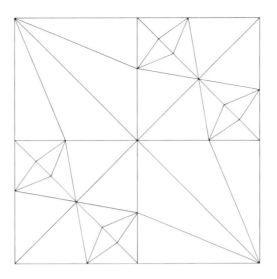

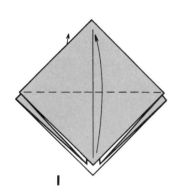

1

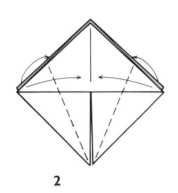

2

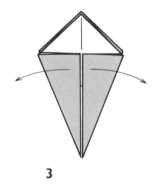

3

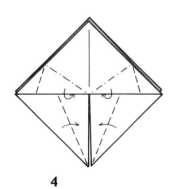

4

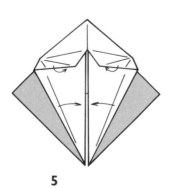

5

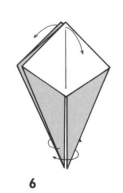

6

7 The tips of the shaded flaps will be the tail fins. Swing the front tip upward.

8 Repeat steps 5 through 9 of the BUTTERFLY FISH.

9 Steps 9 through 14 show how to change the color of the tail fins. (Alternatively, you can repeat steps 10 through 14 of the BUTTERFLY FISH, so that the shaded side will show.) Unfold both fins to step 8.

10 Spread the two sides of the upper fin. Squash the entire fin downward, forming a horizontal valley fold on the hidden layer at rear. Two new valley folds form automatically on the front layer, and two existing valley folds become mountain folds. Following the existing creases, turn the lower fin inside out.

11 Following the existing creases, valley-fold the upper and lower fins.

12 Form a tiny rabbit's ear.

13 Slide the tail fin upward without unfolding the rabbit's ear.

14 Fold the model in half. Tuck the protruding paper from the lower fin into the pocket of the upper fin to lock the body.

The completed DISCUS FISH.

(1973)

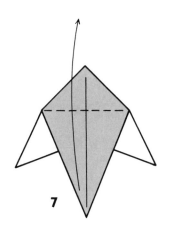

7

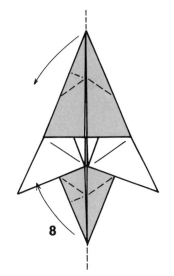

8

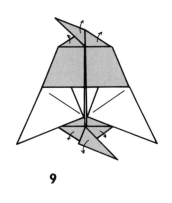

9

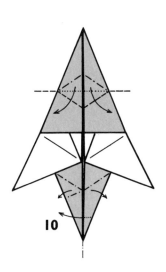

10

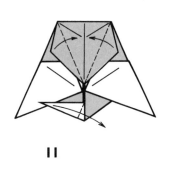

11

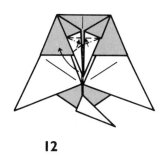

12

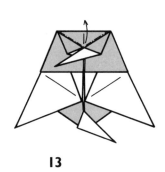

13

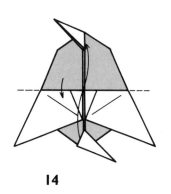

14

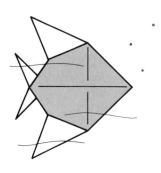

HUMMINGBIRD

Use a sheet of paper colored the same on both sides. A 10-inch square will produce a model with a 6-inch wing-span. Begin after step 2 of the ANGELFISH.

1 Swing the rear flap up to match the front.
2 Swing the front and rear flaps down.
3 The result is a bird base.

4 Stretch the two opposite flaps as far as possible. The flaps in the center will start to buckle.
5, 6 Collapse the center upward, and flatten. The result is called a *stretched bird base*. Note the location of the very center of the paper.

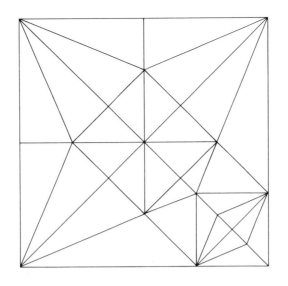

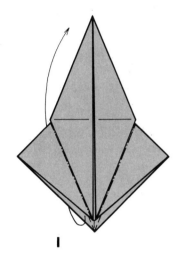

1

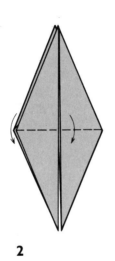

2

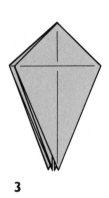

3

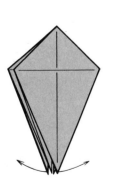

4

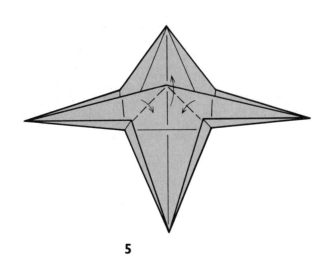

5

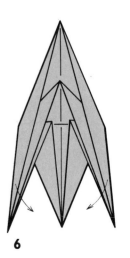

6

7 Grasp the flap at the lower left, and swing it counterclockwise until the cut edge of the paper (the edge of the original square) is horizontal and lies on top of the center of the model.

8 Pull out the loose paper, and flatten.

9 Valley-fold vertically the tiny flap at left along the existing crease. Mountain-fold the entire model in half. Then repeat steps 7 and 8 and the vertical valley fold behind.

10 Tuck the loose paper underneath with a mountain fold. Repeat behind.

11 Outside reverse–fold the flap at the extreme left so that the cut edge meets the center of the original square (visible in the next drawing). The flaps projecting from the top are the wings. Valley-fold them in half.

12 Valley-fold the flap at the extreme left where the crease falls naturally. Crease and close the wings in the same motion.

13 Tuck the excess paper into the model. Repeat behind.

14 Inside reverse–fold one layer only.

15 Inside reverse–fold to form the legs.

16 Pleat the front wing, and swivel it forward. The leg will follow. Some ungainly creases will appear. Flatten them as well as possible.

17 Repeat step 16 on the rear wing and leg.

18 Valley-fold the front edge of both wings. Swing the legs forward as far as they will go.

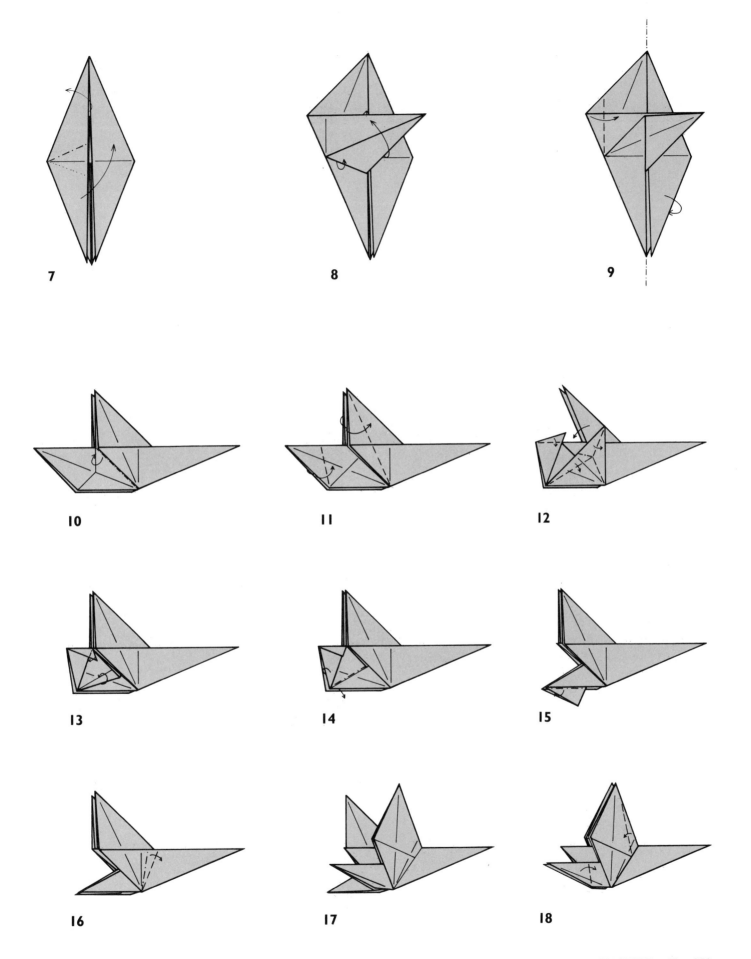

7

8

9

10

11

12

13

14

15

16

17

18

19 Squash the legs.
20 Petal-fold the legs. Inside reverse–fold the neck.
21 Swing the legs back down. Outside reverse–fold the neck to form the head.

22 Narrow the legs. Pull out the loose paper from beneath the head.
23 Crimp the wings and the tail. Inside reverse–fold the legs and the head. Narrow the nape of the neck. Crimp the head to form the beak.
24 Tuck the tiny flap into the belly. Curl the wings. Narrow the beak. Shape the neck and the body.

The completed HUMMINGBIRD.

(1979)

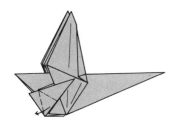

19

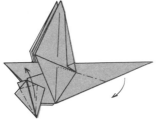

20

21

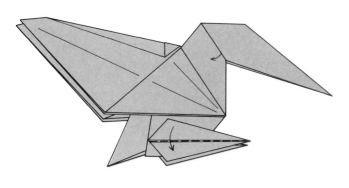

22

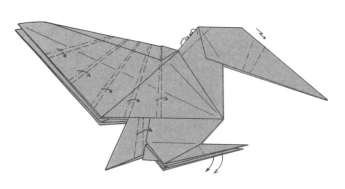

23

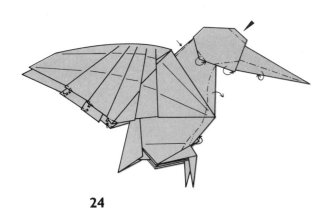

24

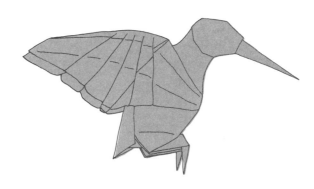

PENGUIN

Use a sheet of paper colored black on one side and white on the other. A 10-inch square will produce a model 6 inches tall.

1 Valley-fold one-sixth of the diagonal.
2 Narrow the upper edges with valley folds.

3 Pull out the loose paper and flatten.
4 Squash.

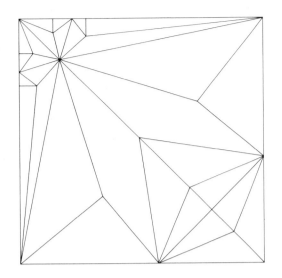

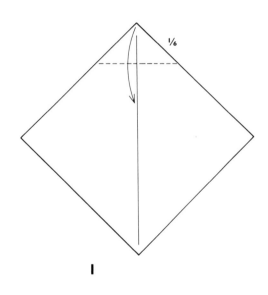

1

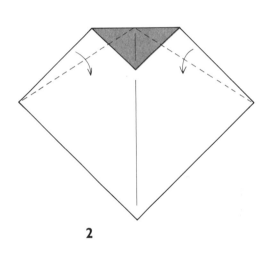

2

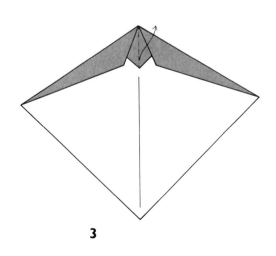

3

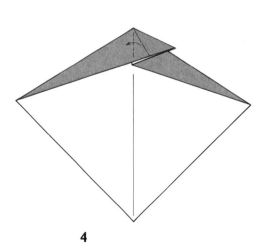

4

5 The shaded central flap contains the upper and lower parts of the beak. Narrow the lower part with a petal fold.

6 Crease the shaded side flaps and unfold.

7 Here through step 9 are details of the beak. Swing the lower part of the beak as far down as it will go.

8 Fold tip to tip.

9 Tuck the excess paper behind.

10 Valley-fold the long shaded flaps. Then make the remaining folds simultaneously.

11 Valley-fold the sides to the centerline and unfold.

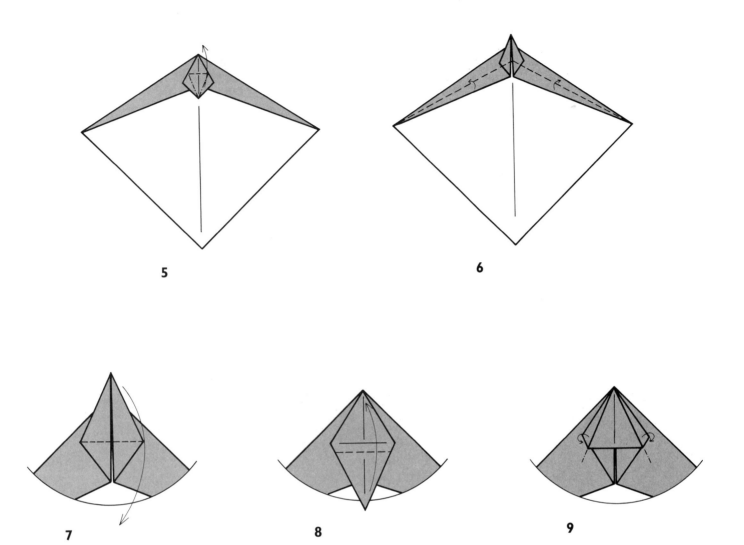

5

6

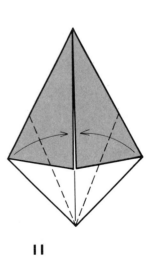

7

8

9

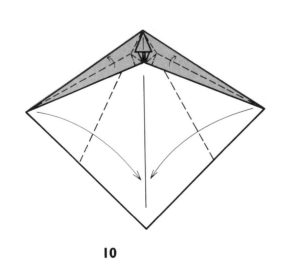

10

11

12 Valley-fold the sides to the existing creases and unfold.

13 Pinch to form mountain folds, and the valley folds will form automatically.

14 Valley-fold the shaded side flaps so that the cut edges meet the folded edges. Tuck the bottom triangle underneath. This will be the tail.

15 Swivel the top layer on each side until the cut edges cross the outside corners of the model. Flatten.

16 The shaded triangles projecting at either side are the wings. Valley-fold so that the upper cut edges meet the lower folded edges, then unfold.

17 In a single motion, narrow the bottom white triangle on each side and refold the wings.

18 Pull out the hidden beak, last seen in step 10. Mountain-fold the wings and tuck the loose paper into the pockets behind. Narrow the shaded flaps at the lower left and right to form the legs. Tuck the loose paper into the pockets behind. Turn the model over.

19 Rabbit's-ear the tail. Close the model with a valley fold.

20 Outside reverse–fold the head. Inside reverse–fold the body so that the hidden edge of the rabbit's ear meets the back edge of the body.

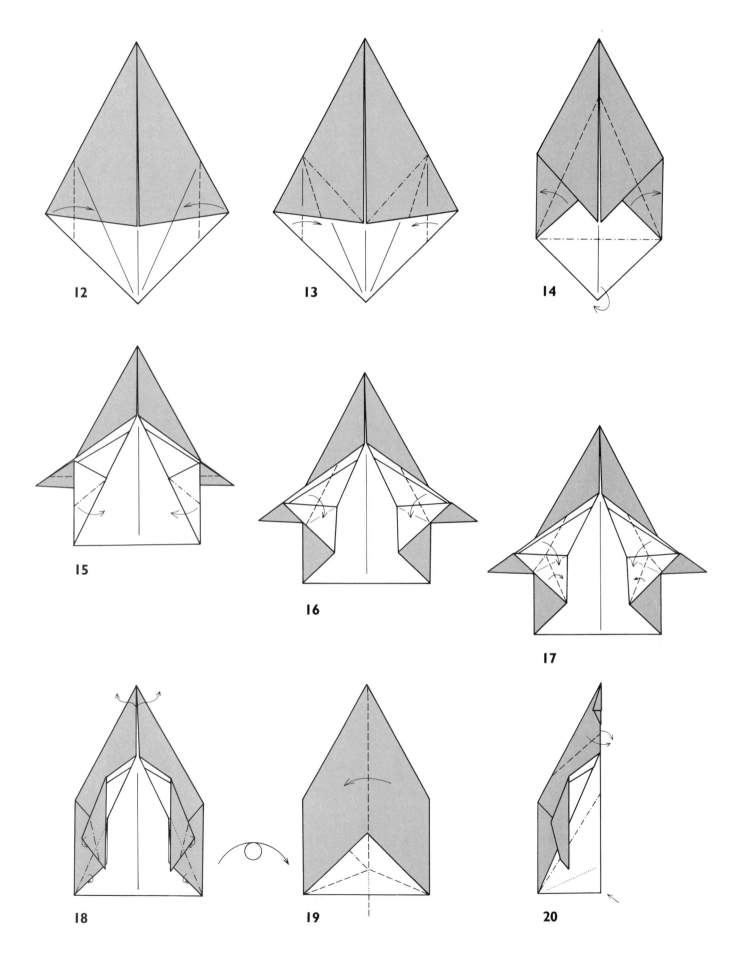

12

13

14

15

16

17

18

19

20

21 Crimp the head symmetrically, allowing the interior flaps to bunch neatly. Swivel the tail as far forward as it will go.

22 Inside reverse–fold the double beak. Tuck the white leg flap into the pocket behind it. Repeat on the other leg. Round the belly and spread the wings.

23 This is a detail of the head. Pull down the lower part of the beak. Shape the head with tiny mountain folds.

24 Here through step 28 are details of the legs. Inside reverse–fold each leg toward the rear.

25 Swing each foot forward, and both sides of the foot will narrow automatically.

26 Pull out the loose paper from both feet. Adjust the angle of the feet to make the penguin stand.

27 Valley-fold the white flap on each foot upward.

28 Tuck each white flap under the adjacent shaded flap.

The completed PENGUIN.

(1978–79)

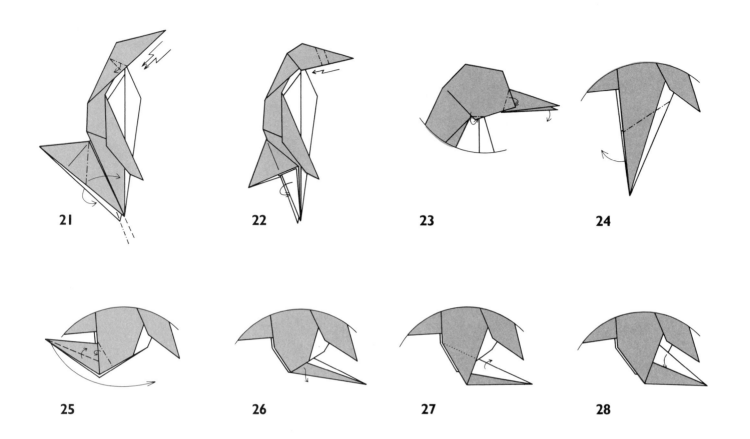

21   **22**   **23**   **24**

25   **26**   **27**   **28**

GIRAFFE

Use a sheet of paper colored on one side. A 10-inch square of paper will produce a model 4¾ inches tall. Begin with the bird base, white side out.

1 Open-sink the top halfway.
2 Swing the two triangular flaps to the sides.
3 Valley-fold tiny flaps front and rear.
4 Pull out the loose paper front and rear.

5, 6 In the same motion, swing the front face up and squash the side flaps.
7 Squash completed. The model should lie flat. Turn it over.
8 Valley-fold as shown, and the hidden mountain folds will form automatically.

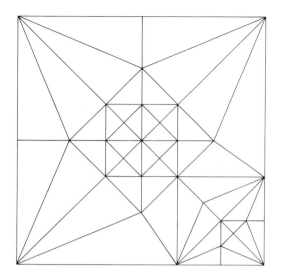

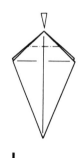

1

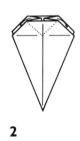

2

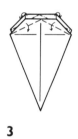

3

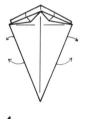

4

5

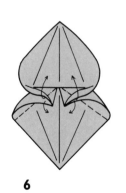

6

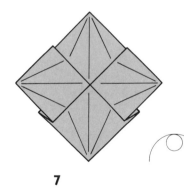

7

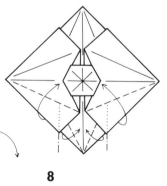

8

9 The shaded flaps at the left and right will be the front legs. Valley-fold and spread the left front leg.

10, 11 Fold in a single motion and flatten.

12 Separate the upper and lower layers of the left front leg, and squash them flat.

13 A small white flap remains exposed on the left front leg. Mountain-fold the loose paper underneath. Repeat steps 9 through 12 on the right front leg, and mountain-fold the loose paper underneath.

14 Valley-fold the two front legs in half.

15 Valley-fold the cut edges toward the center, and the front legs will spread. Crease and unfold the triangle at the very top. This will be the tail.

16 Squash and narrow the front legs. Crease and unfold the tail.

17 The shaded flaps near the top will be the hind legs. Narrow them slightly with mountain folds. Narrow the front legs with valley folds, and roll the loose paper toward the rear.

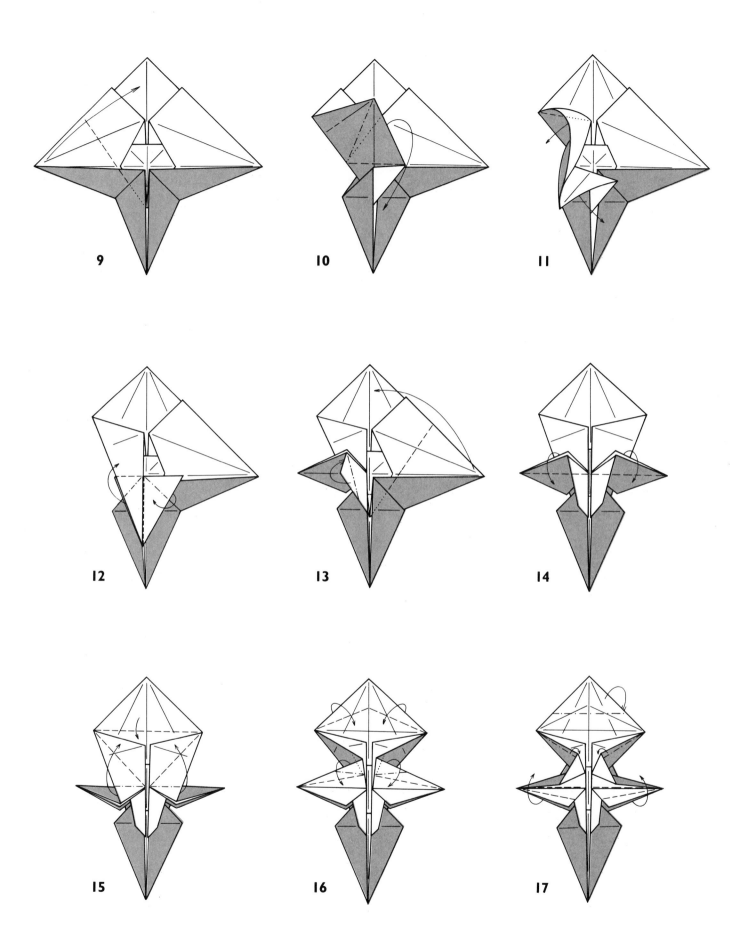

9

10

11

12

13

14

15

16

17

18 Narrow the hind legs with mountain folds. Narrow the front legs with valley folds, and tuck the loose paper into the adjacent white pockets. The flap at the bottom is the neck. Narrow it, but not to the very tip.

19 Turn the model over.

20 Refold the existing creases to form the tail.

21 Narrow the white flap with mountain folds, and swing it underneath.

22 Crimp the tail. Mountain-fold the entire model in half.

23 Divide the hind legs into thirds. Inside reverse–fold the neck to form the head.

24 Crimp the legs. Inside reverse–fold the head and the tail.

25 Tuck the exposed white paper into the hind legs. Crimp the neck. The valley fold should be perpendicular to the centerline of the neck.

The completed GIRAFFE.

(1976)

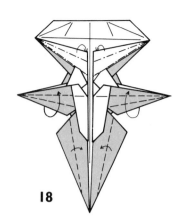

18

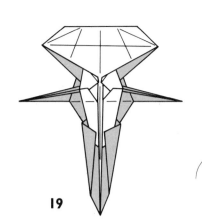

19

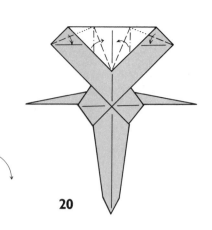

20

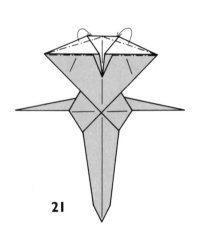

21

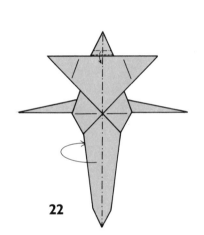

22

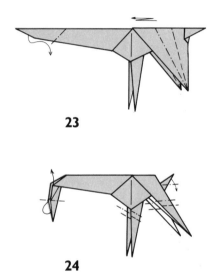

23

24

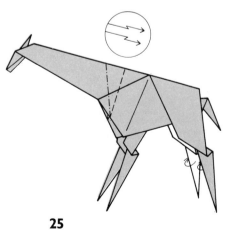

25

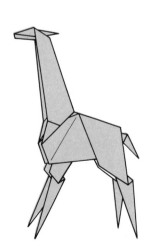

KANGAROO

Use a sheet of paper colored on one side. A 10-inch square will produce a model 3⅞ inches tall. Begin with the bird base.

1 Crease and unfold. Repeat behind.
2 Crease and unfold the double thickness.
3 Valley-fold where the two sets of creases meet. Unfold.
4 This step makes the model three-dimensional. Following the existing creases, spread the sides to form a pyramid that will project upward from the paper. This is the most difficult step in the model. Persevere!

5 The pyramid is completed, and the model is three-dimensional. This is a top view.
6 Form a rabbit's ear on each side of the pyramid, and squash it flat.
7 The model is now two-dimensional. The flattened tip of the pyramid (the very center of the paper) will be the head of the baby kangaroo. Rabbit's-ear the baby's head and mountain-fold the model simultaneously.
8 The two big flaps will be the hind legs of the big kangaroo. Rabbit's-ear both legs, and swing them to the left.

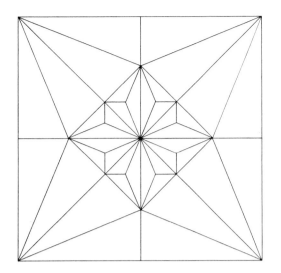

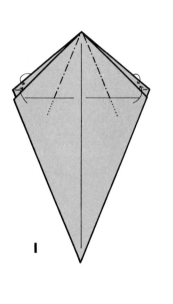

1

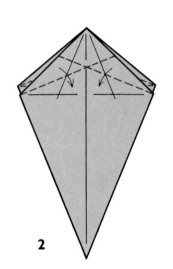

2

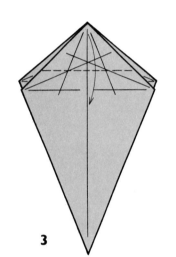

3

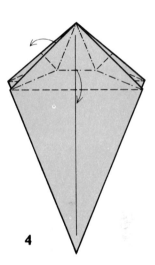

4

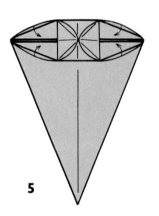

5

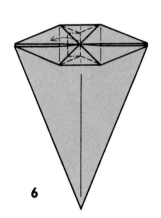

6

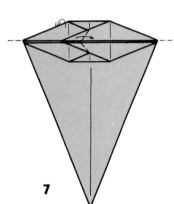

7

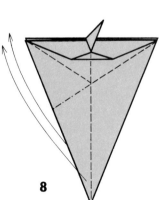

8

9 The two long flaps at the left will be the head (upper flap) and tail (lower flap) of the big kangaroo. Inside reverse–fold the head and the tail.

10 Narrow the tail with valley folds front and back. This step also forms the baby kangaroo's ears.

11 Open up the hind legs of the big kangaroo.

12 In a single motion, lift the baby's right ear and close the right hind leg. Repeat behind.

13 Crimp the tail. Valley-fold upward the loose paper covering the baby's right ear. Repeat behind.

14 Tuck the front half of the tail into the back half. Be careful not to tear the paper. Tuck the loose paper into the adjacent pockets in the baby's ears.

15 Slide the baby's ears forward slightly to free the big kangaroo's hind legs. Swing the hind legs downward.

16 Crimp the top layer of the hind legs, and pull out the loose paper from the bottom layer. Narrow the rear of the neck. Repeat behind.

17 Rabbit's-ear the hind legs. Tuck the loose paper into the neck to form the big kangaroo's front legs.

18 Mountain-fold the hind legs to form the feet and hips. Inside reverse–fold the neck. Swing down the front legs as far as they will go.

19 Outside reverse–fold the tail. Inside reverse–fold the neck. Narrow the front legs with valley folds. Pull out the loose paper from the top of the baby's head.

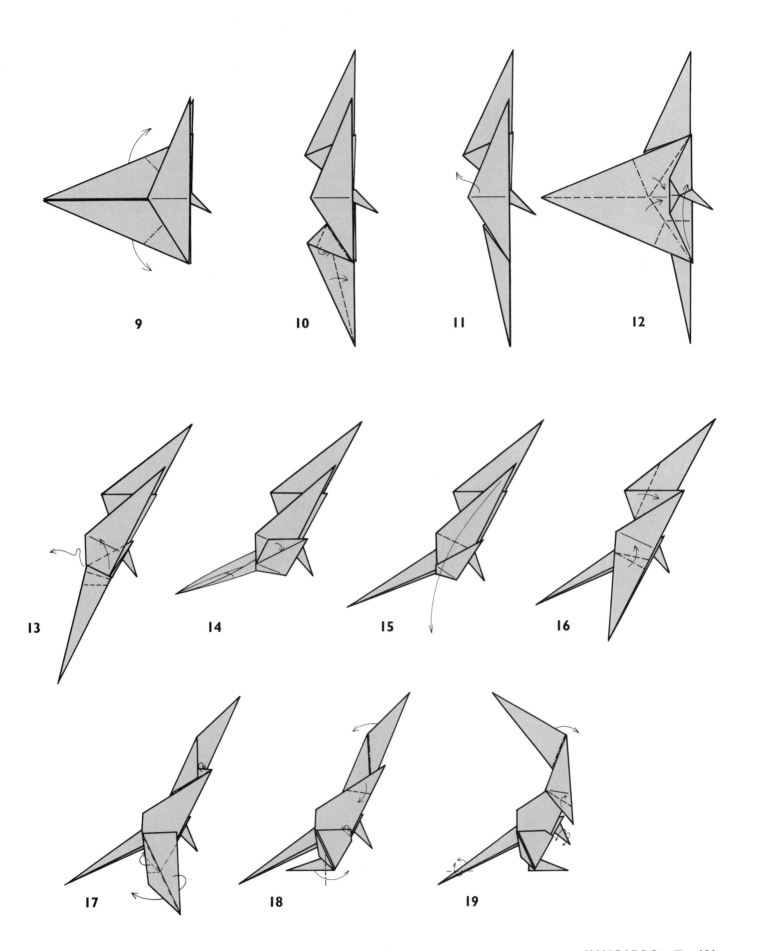

9

10

11

12

13

14

15

16

17

18

19

20 Here through step 24 are details of the upper body of the big kangaroo. Narrow the front legs with inside reverse folds. Outside reverse–fold the neck.

21 Narrow the front legs again. Crimp the neck to form the ears and the head.

22 Valley-fold the front legs to form the paws. Round the ears. Crimp the head to form the jaw.

23 Valley-fold the loose flap at the back of the neck to lock the body. Narrow the jaw, and roll back the tip of the nose.

24 The upper body of the big kangaroo is completed.

25 Here through step 27 are details of the baby's head. Narrow the head with mountain folds.

26 Crimp the head to form the jaw. Spread the ears. Roll back the tip of the nose.

27 The baby's head is completed.

The completed KANGAROO.

(1977)

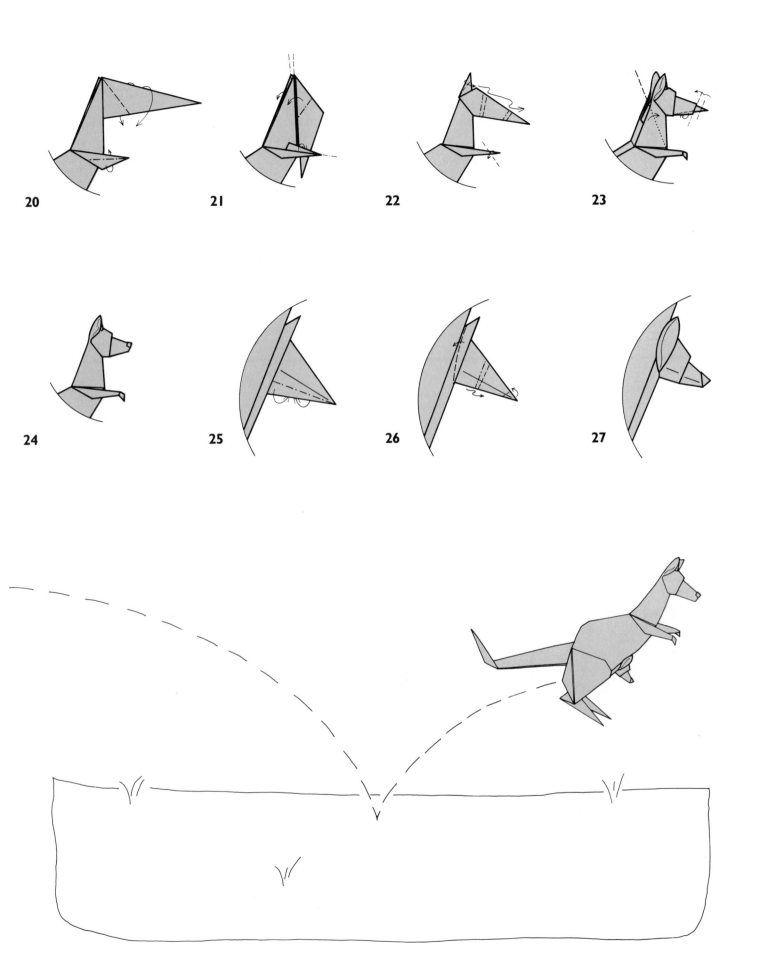

20

21

22

23

24

25

26

27

ONE-DOLLAR YACHT

This is the first of three models made from a one-dollar bill. For the budget version, use any sheet of paper in the proportions of a bill, 3 by 7. The side facing down will be the outside of the yacht. A one-dollar bill will produce a model 6 inches long.

1 Crease widthwise and unfold.
2 Crease lengthwise and unfold.

3 Valley-fold from the center of the paper to the corners.
4 Unfold to the previous step.

5 Following the existing creases, inside reverse–fold from the center of the paper through the corners.
6 Valley-fold the bottom point (the center of the bill) to the cut edge. Press firmly.

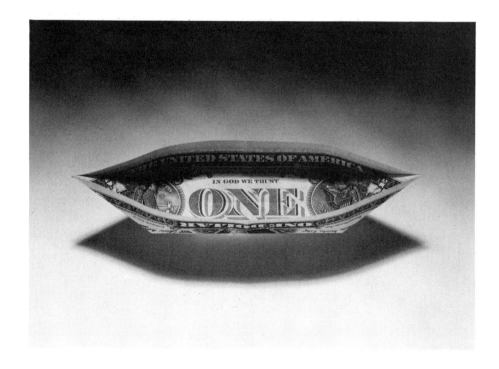

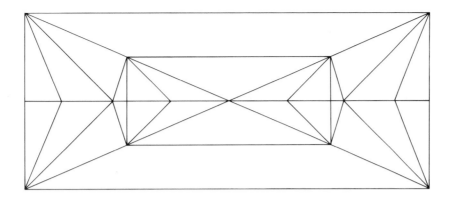

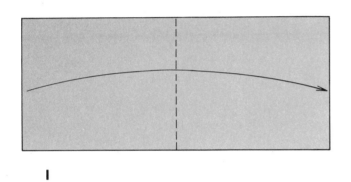

1

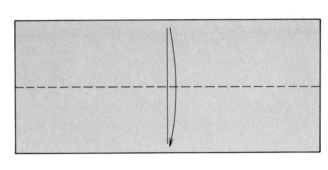

2

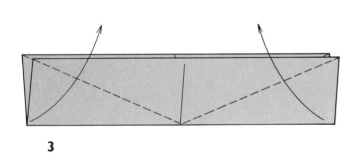

3

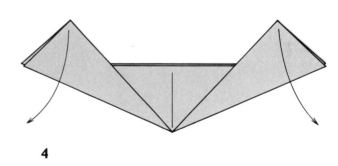

4

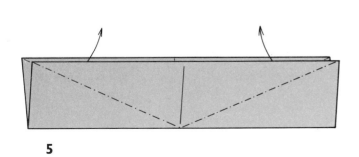

5

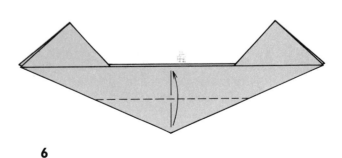

6

7 Unfold to the previous step.
8 Reaching underneath the model, place your thumbs between the two sides. In a single motion, spread the sides and squash the lower half of the hull through the existing creases. The paper will flatten automatically.

9 The model is now flat. Turn it over.
10 Mountain-fold the two projecting flaps.

11 Spread the sides of the hull to make the boat three-dimensional. Tuck the two projecting flaps underneath.
12 This is a top view with the sides of the hull spread open. Valley-fold the two projecting flaps to lock the hull.
13 Shape the hull as desired.

The completed ONE-DOLLAR YACHT.

(1975)

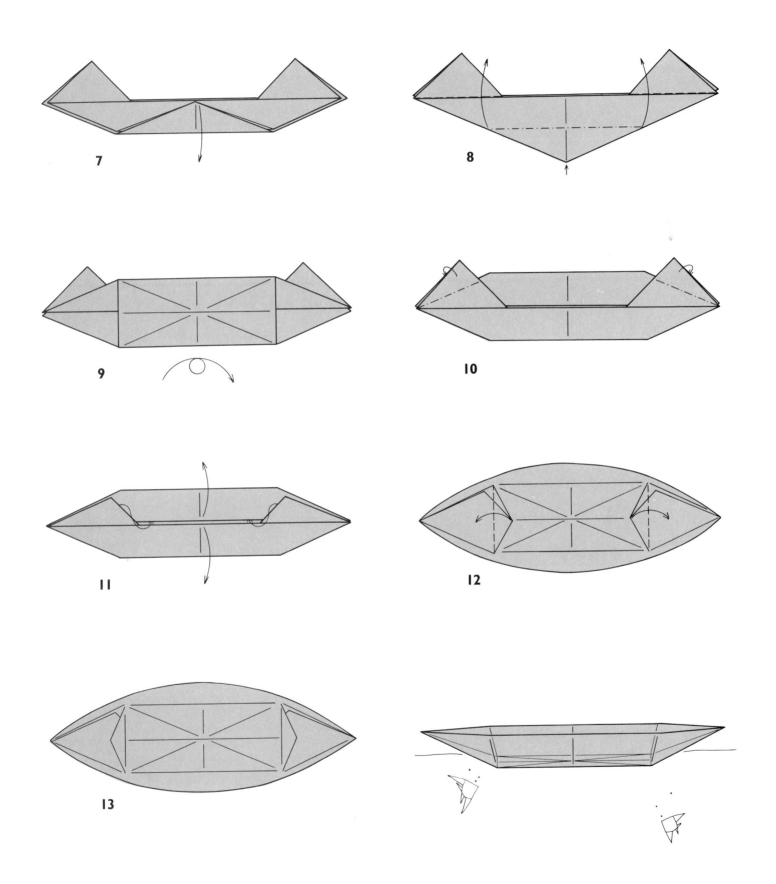

7

8

9

10

11

12

13

ONE-DOLLAR BOW TIE

A one-dollar bill will produce a model 5 inches long. Begin with the bill face down.

1 Crease lengthwise and unfold.
2 Crease widthwise and unfold. Turn the bill over.

3 Crease diagonally and unfold.
4 Crease diagonally in the opposite direction and unfold.

5, 6 Collapse the bill along the existing creases. The center square of the bill becomes a preliminary fold.

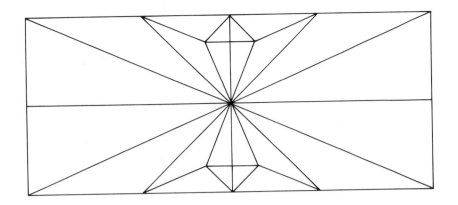

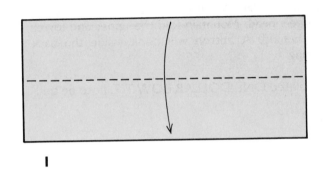

1

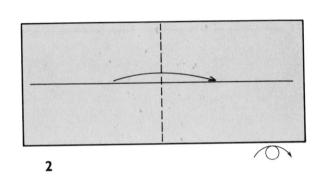

2

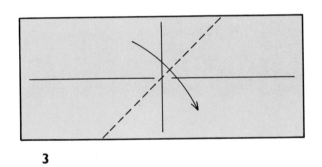

3

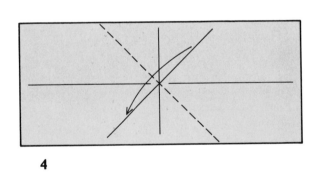

4

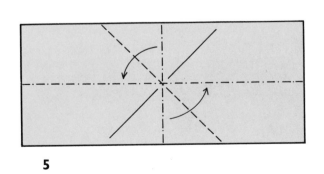

5

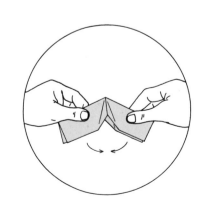

6

7 Squash through the centerpoint. Repeat behind.

8 Petal-fold. Repeat behind.

9 Inside reverse–fold the two side flaps from the centerpoint through the corners. Open up the petal folds to the previous step.

10 Tuck the tiny triangular flaps underneath.

11 Swivel the front and back flaps clockwise.

12 Lift the front flap as high as possible. The inside of the paper will stretch.

13 Turn the model over.

14 Valley-fold the tip halfway to the centerline. Press it firmly with tweezers. Then open the model entirely, and open-sink the octagonal region. If the bill is crisp, it will retain its shape while you massage the sink into place with the tweezers. Close the model.

15 Spread and flatten the octagonal region to reveal George's head. Mountain-fold the upper and lower flaps behind. A button will hook inside the back opening.

The completed ONE-DOLLAR BOW TIE, fit to be tied.

(1974)

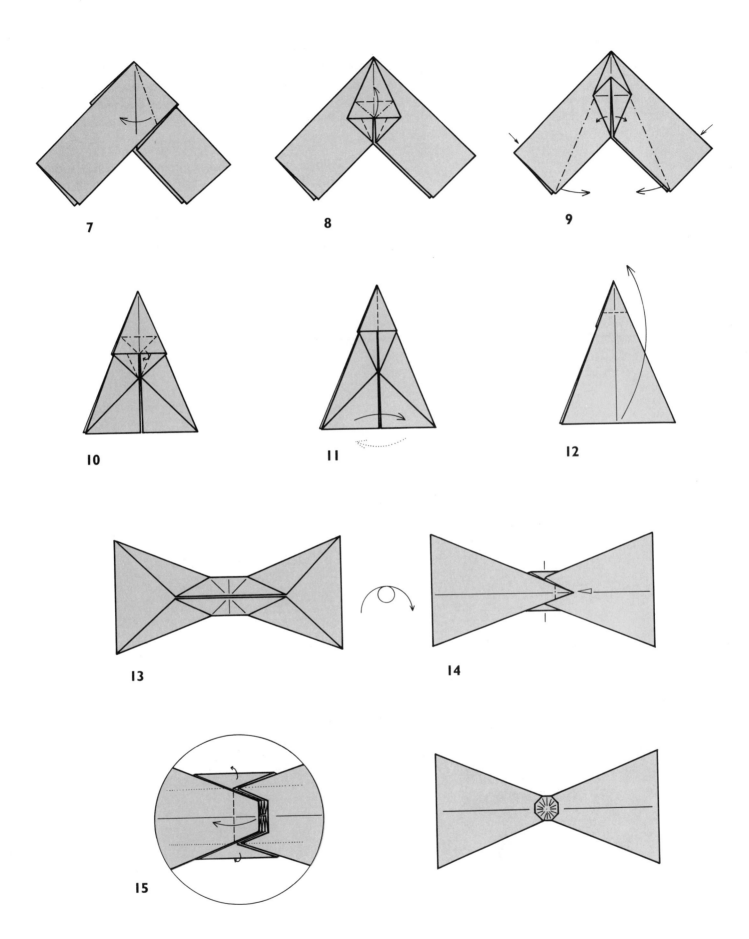

7

8

9

10

11

12

13

14

15

ONE-DOLLAR CRAB

A one-dollar bill will produce a model 1 inch wide. The side facing down will be the outside of the finished model. For your first attempt, use a sheet of paper measuring 6 by 14 inches or a larger one with the same proportion.

1 Fold in half lengthwise. Unfold. Fold in half widthwise. Fold each half in half and then in half again. Pleat like an accordion.
2 Make eight inside reverse folds.

3 Make eight more inside reverse folds.
4 Fold the uppermost flaps only, making the creases where they fall naturally. The little reverse folds behind will unfold.

5 Return to step 4.
6 Pull down the first of the four peaks.

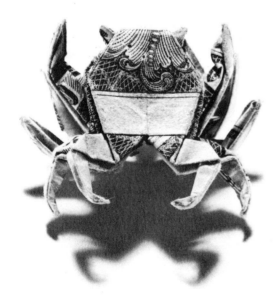

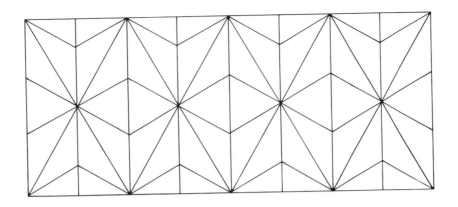

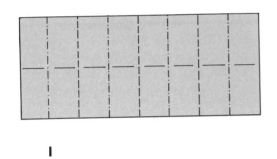

3

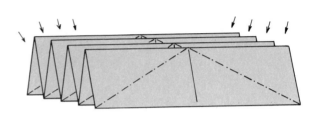

4

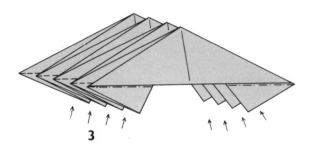

1

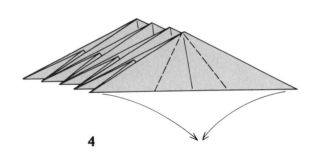

2

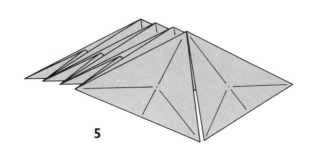

5

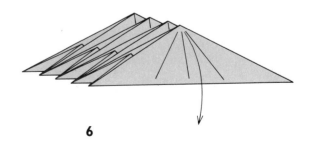

6

7 Rabbit's-ear the double thickness on each side of the model. Fold where the creases fall naturally.

8 Return to step 6. Pull down the second peak, and repeat step 7. Turn the paper over, and repeat all folds symmetrically on the reverse. Then unfold the entire model, but do not press the creases flat.

9 Push the four peaks inward. Turn the model over.

10 All the creases are now correct except three: the portions of the widthwise folds that bisect the three diamond shapes running along the centerline of the bill. Turn these mountain folds into valley folds. Bring the four peaks together, and collapse the paper along the existing creases. It should spring into shape automatically.

11 Flatten. If you are using a one-dollar bill, this may be a good time to press the model in a vise or under heavy books. From here on, it will only get thicker!

12 Mountain-fold the top flaps on either side. If you are using paper colored differently on each side, valley-fold instead. This will keep the front and back pairs of legs the same color as the rest of the crab.

13 Valley-fold one flap to the right.

14 Spread and squash the left-hand flap.

15 Mountain-fold the squashed flap behind, and swing it to the right.

16 Mountain-fold the next left-hand flap, and swing it to the right.

17 As you continue narrowing, the model may become too thick to allow accurate folding. If this is the case, undo each fold as soon as you have made it. Once all the creases have been made, you can put the folds back in place. Repeat steps 14 and 15 on the left-hand side of the model. On the next flap repeat step 16. Use the two narrowing procedures alternately all the way to the other end of the paper. When you reach the opposite face, repeat step 12. When you are all done, the model will be fully symmetrical. All told, you will perform steps 14 and 15 eight times, step 16 six times, and step 12 twice.

18 Undo the front face.

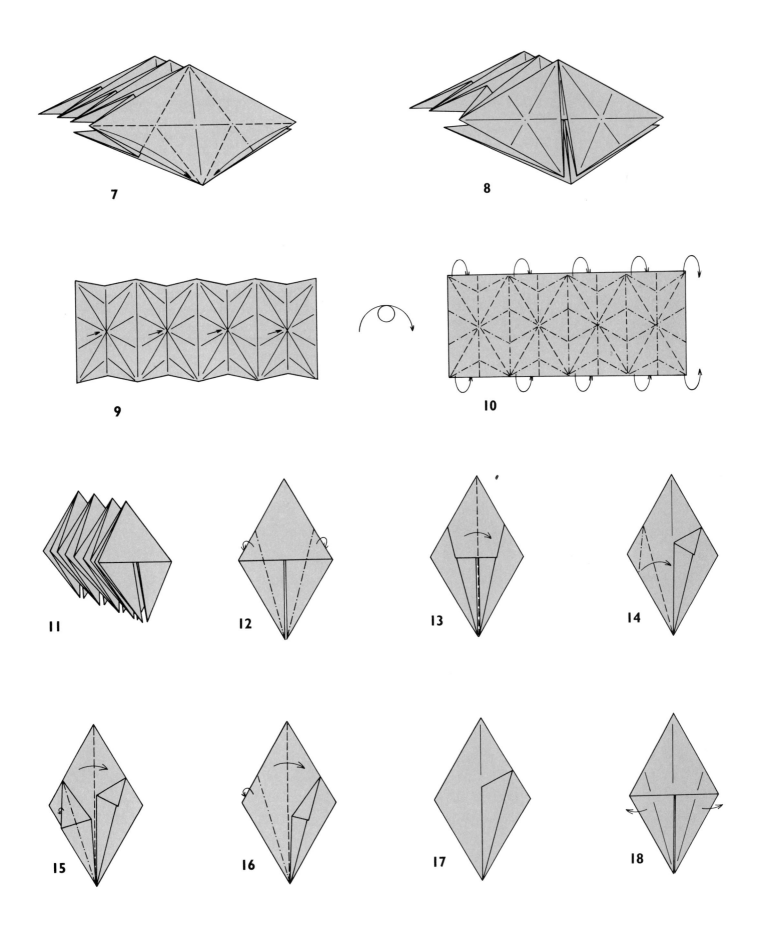

19, 20 Closed-sink the peak one-third of the way to the horizontal edge. As shown in the top view in step 20, the pleats that radiate toward the back of the model remain closed during the sinking.

21 Following the existing creases, closed-sink and rabbit's-ear the side flaps. On each side, the two edges of the sink in steps 19 and 20 come together.

22 The dotted lines show the location of the little pocket that will be used to lock the model. Put back the mountain and squash folds unfolded in step 18.

23 Pull down the edge of the sink and the peak behind it.

24 Divide the two exposed peaks into thirds from opposite sides. Rabbit's-ear the outer two-thirds of each peak. These will be the eyes.

25 Fold up the eye flap and the sunk flap. Turn the model over. This may be another good time to press the model flat.

26 Inside reverse–fold the five pairs of flaps as symmetrically as possible. The fourth pair from the top goes farthest forward to become the claws.

27 Form inside and outside reverse folds to shape the legs. Mountain-fold the remaining peak back between the eyes, and tuck it into the pocket below. (If the model is too thick, the lock will not work.) Outside reverse–fold each claw, and pull out the loose paper, as shown in the detail. Spread the eyes.

The completed ONE-DOLLAR CRAB.

(1977)

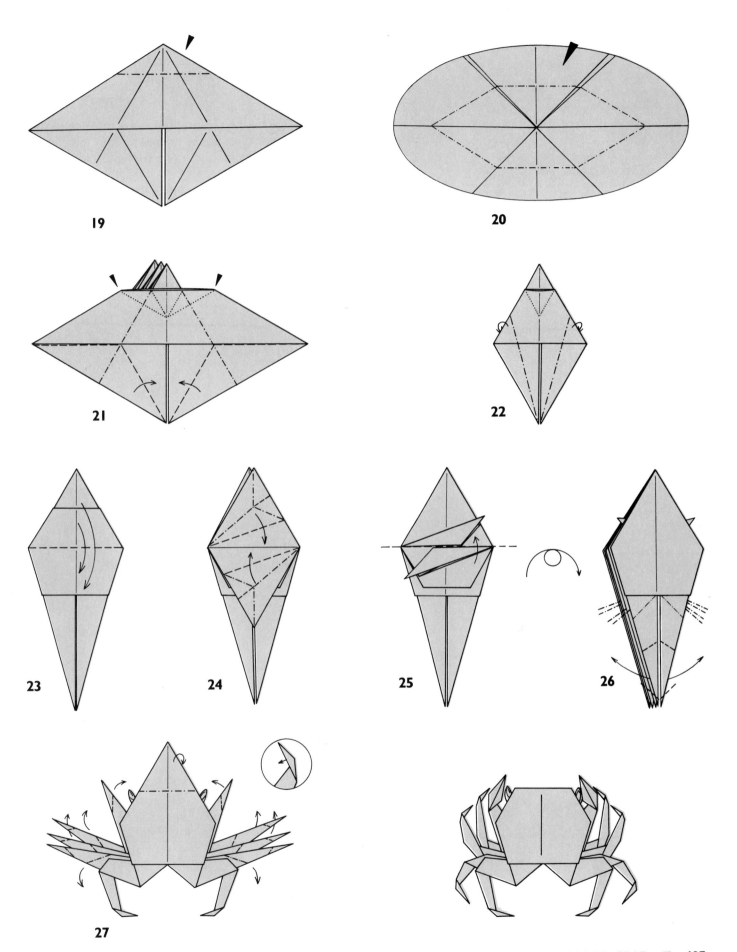

19

20

21

22

23

24

25

26

27

EIGHT-POINTED STAR

Use a sheet of paper colored brightly on one side. A 10-inch square will produce a model 7 inches in diameter. Begin with the preliminary fold.

1 Open-sink the top to the midpoint. Inside reverse—fold the four sides to the midpoint.
2 Collapse the front face upward. Repeat on each of the three other sides.
3 Pull down the four sides, and flatten the model.

4 Turn the model over.
5 From this step on, the upper and lower halves of the model are treated identically. Valley-fold the four white squares.
6 Crimp all four flaps by swiveling them from the centerpoint.

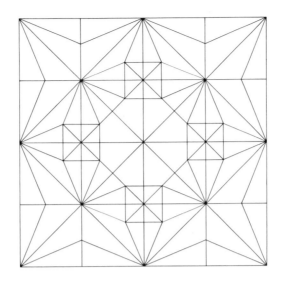

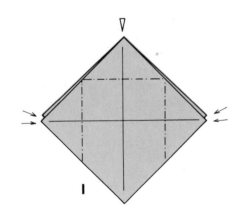

1

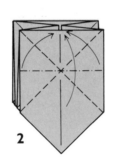

2

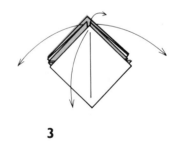

3

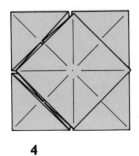

4

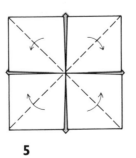

5

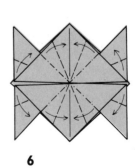

6

7 Form four valley folds.

8 Valley-fold the two tips toward the center. Then unfold the model to step 6.

9 Lift each single ply and stretch. A shape similar to a petal fold will form automatically.

10 Grasp the white corners of the upper half, and swing them upward and outward.

11, 12 The model is now three-dimensional. Continue stretching the paper, and the small triangular tip will pop inward automatically. Collapse the tip toward the outer edge of the model. This combination of creases is similar to a stretched bird base (see step 6 of the HUMMINGBIRD).

13 The model is now flat, and steps 10 through 12 have been repeated on the identical lower half. The dotted lines show the location of the hidden triangular tips. Valley-fold the tips back toward the center of the model, where they will remain hidden. Valley-fold two flaps in each quadrant.

14 Repeat steps 6 through 13 on the identical left and right sides.

15 Narrow the eight points with valley folds. When all the folds are in place, the model will not lie flat.

16 Four of the eight points should stand up. Spread and squash them, yielding to the existing creases. Tweezers may help.

17 There are eight loose flaps hidden from view. Tuck them into the adjacent pockets to lock the model. Turn the model over.

The completed EIGHT-POINTED STAR.

(1974)

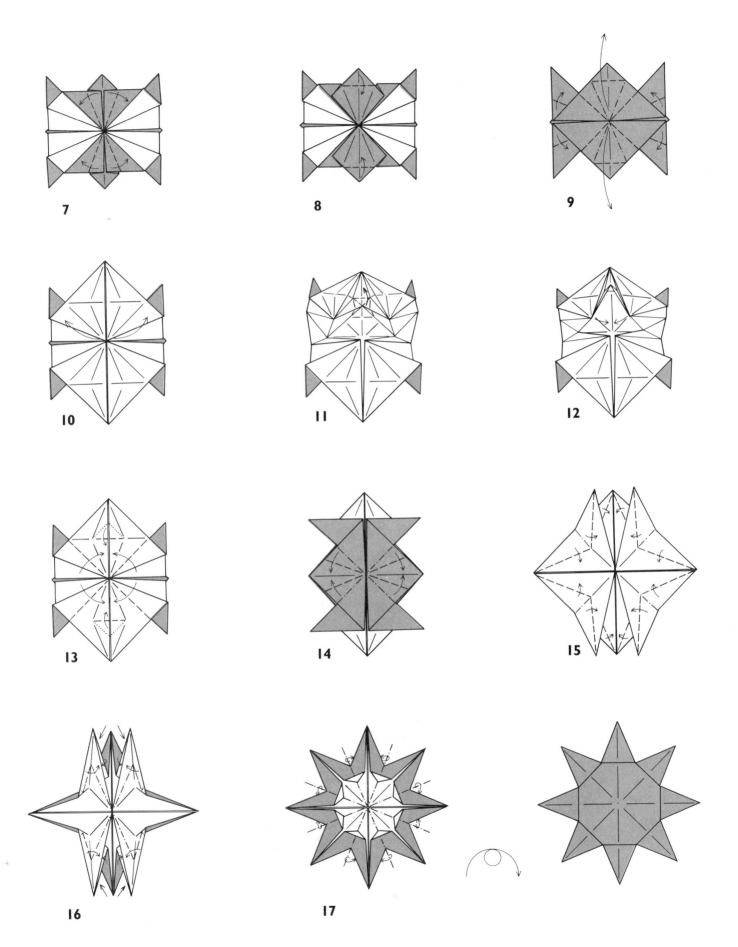

7

8

9

10

11

12

13

14

15

16

17

VALENTINE

Use a sheet of paper colored red on one side and white on the other. A 10-inch square will produce a model 5½ inches long.

1 Form a preliminary fold.
2 Open-sink the top to the midpoint. Inside reverse—fold the four sides to the midpoint.
3 Valley-fold to the centerline front and back.
4 Form two tiny inside reverse folds on the innermost-layers.

5 Pull out the loose paper from each side.
6 Undo the valley folds from step 3.
7 Pull down the small triangle in the middle, and the side flaps will valley-fold inward automatically. Repeat behind.
8 Unfold to step 7.

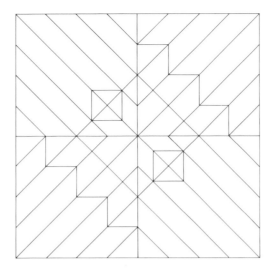

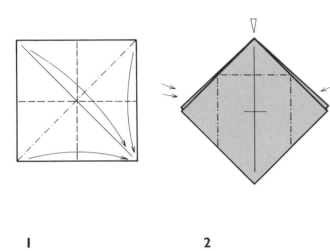

1

2

3

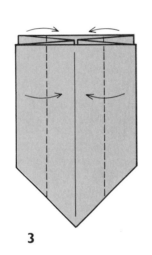

4

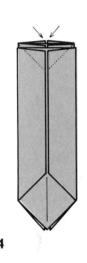

5

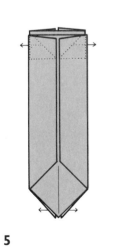

6

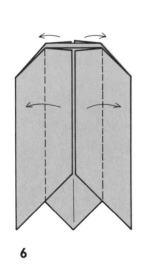

7

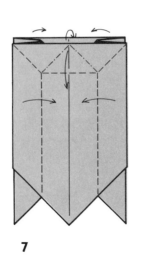

8

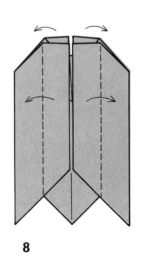

9 Valley-fold the sides to the centerline again, this time keeping the small triangle up.

10 Tuck the small triangles into the pockets behind. Tweezers may help.

11 Rabbit's-ear the hidden flaps front and back, and pull them through the slots.

12 The model is now three-dimensional. The white flaps will form the shaft of the arrow. Open-sink the shaft front and back.

13 Squash the shaft front and back.

14 Narrow the shaft front and back, and swing both halves upward.

15 Pinch the front of the shaft, and tuck its base under the adjacent shaded flaps. Repeat behind.

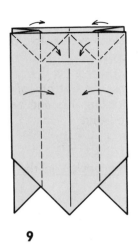

9

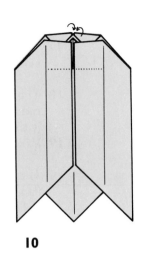

10

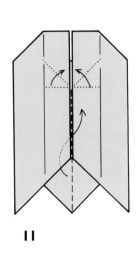

11

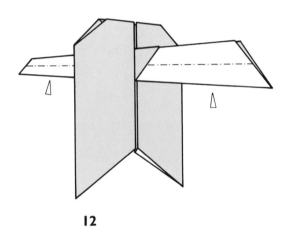

12

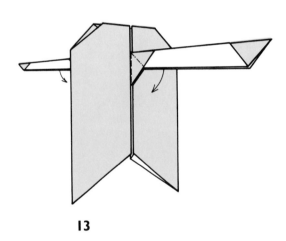

13

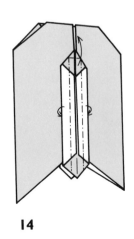

14

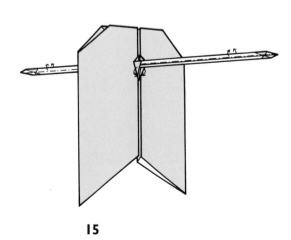

15

16 The shaft is completed.
17 This view is from head-on. Inside reverse–fold both sides of the heart. They will cross.

18 The two white flaps will lock the bottom of the model. Valley-fold the back locking flap, and swing it through the slot toward the front.
19 Valley-fold both flaps together.

20 Tuck the bottom flap into the pocket in the top flap.
21 Valley-fold both flaps together. Tuck them into the pocket at left to lock the bottom of the model. Then spread the layers at the top of the model.

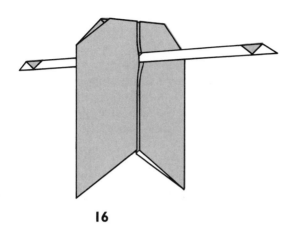

16

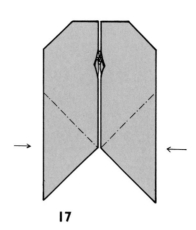

17

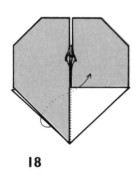

18

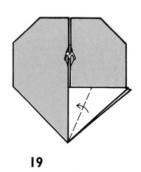

19

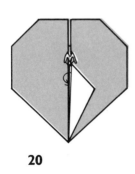

20

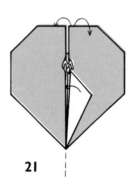

21

22 Here through step 24 are top views. Valley-fold the upper and lower halves one-third of the way toward the center.

23 Valley-fold the loose paper in the upper half to form locking flaps. Tuck the loose paper in the lower half into the pockets behind. Use tweezers if necessary.

24 Tuck the upper locking flaps into the lower pockets. This step locks the top of the model.

25 Here through step 30 are details of the shaft. The head is the upper half, the tail the lower half. Head: Spread the paper, and form a rabbit's ear one-third of the way into the shaded square. Tail: Spread the paper, and valley-fold through the diagonal of the shaded square.

26 Head: Pleat, and turn over. Tail: Crease the diagonal lightly and unfold.

27 Head: Narrow the shaft. Tail: Pleat.

28 Head: Form a rabbit's ear, and turn over. Tail: Mountain-fold the sides.

29 Head: Pinch the shaft, and turn over. Tail: Form two tiny inside reverse folds.

30 Head: Open out, and form the point. Tail: Shape the tip with an inside reverse fold, and mountain-fold the excess paper inside. Pinch the shaft, and turn over.

31 Curl the shaft, and twist it 90 degrees so the head and tail align. Round the heart to make it three-dimensional.

The completed VALENTINE.

(1984)

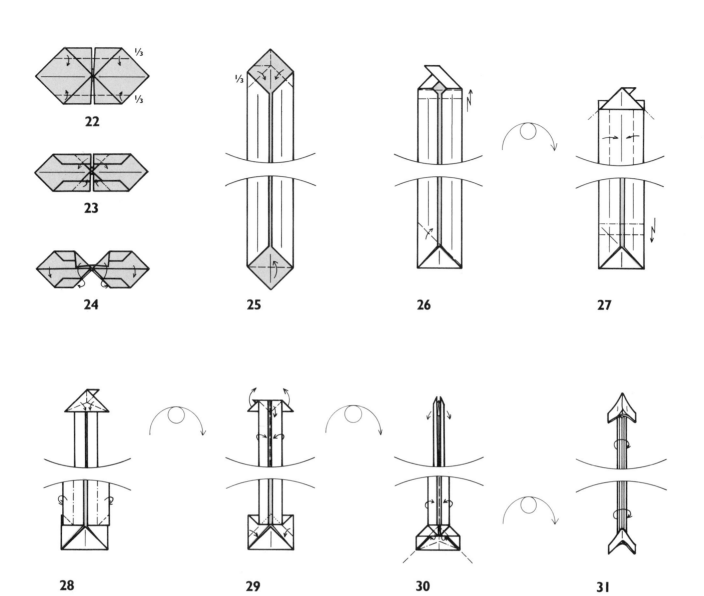

22

23

24

25

26

27

28

29

30

31

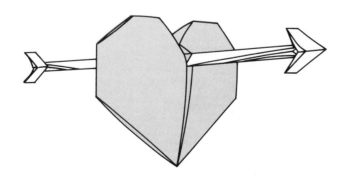

CRAB

Use a sheet of paper colored on one side. A 10-inch square will produce a model 2¼ inches wide.

1 Blintz and unfold.
2 Mountain- and valley-fold.
3 Fold the entire thickness.

4 Crease the entire thickness in thirds, and unfold to step 3.
5 Fold the entire thickness. This is an *open double sink*.
6 Pull out the two hidden flaps, each a single thickness.

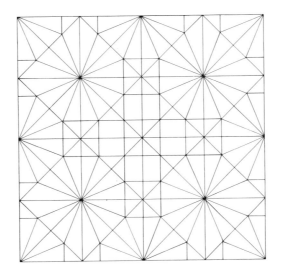

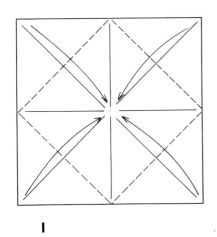

1

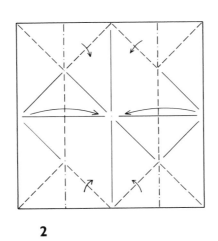

2

3

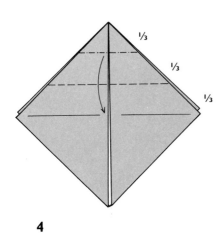

4

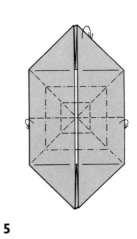

5

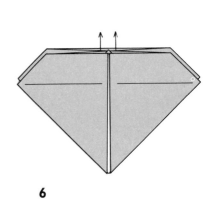

6

1/3
1/3
1/3

7 Form a preliminary fold on the front face.
8 Form a preliminary fold on the back face.
9 Petal-fold front and back, making sure to lift the two hidden flaps along with the petal fold. Then fold back down. Repeat on the remaining flaps.

10 Pinch the front and back flaps, and spread them as far apart as possible.
11 Pull down both layers of the little triangle on each side, and return the model to step 10.

12 Open-sink the two peaks halfway.
13 Open the model slightly, and disengage the two triangles from step 11. Swing them upward.

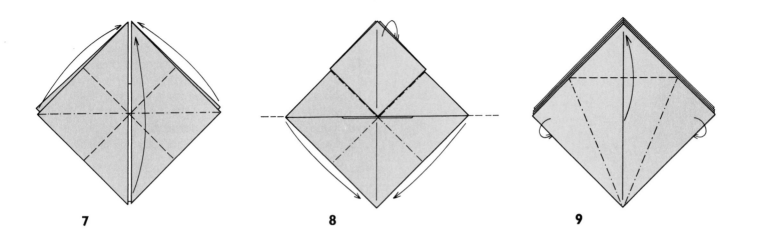

7

8

9

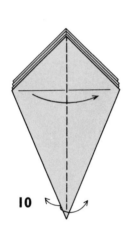

10

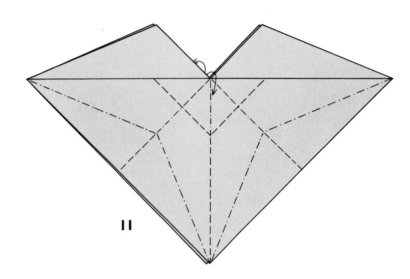

11

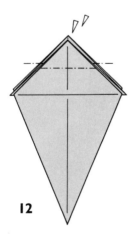

12

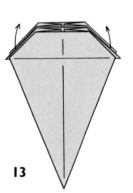

13

14 Open the model slightly, and outside reverse–fold the two triangles to form the eyes.
15 Pull out one ply from the front face.
16 Valley-fold to the existing horizontal crease.

17 Narrow the tip with mountain and valley folds. This will be a locking flap.
18 Tuck the locking flap underneath.
19 Swing two flaps upward. The body will close around them.

20 Upper half: Inside reverse–fold the two upper flaps to form legs. They will cross. Lower half: Inside reverse–fold the top three flaps on each side to form more legs. The third pair from the top goes farthest forward, to become the claws.
21 Narrow the legs symmetrically. Outside reverse–fold the claws.

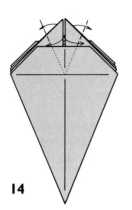

14

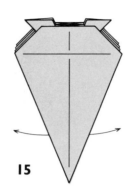

15

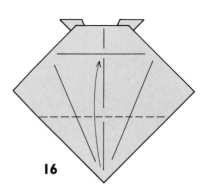

16

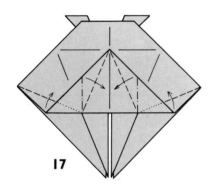

17

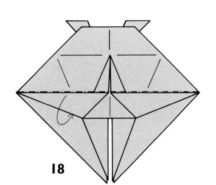

18

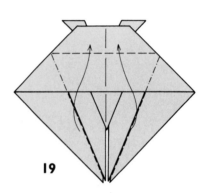

19

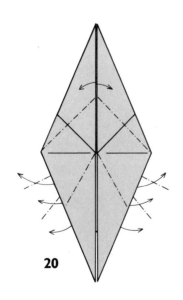

20

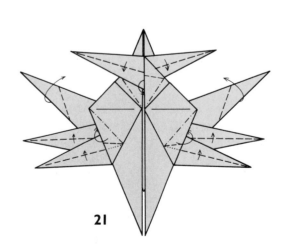

21

22 Uncross the two top legs, and swing the entire assembly down. To make the two remaining legs and the remaining locking flap, repeat steps 15 through 22 on the back face. (It may be necessary to unfold the claws to free some trapped paper.) Shift this pair of legs upward slightly, so that they will not be hidden from view.

23 Shape the eight legs with inside and outside reverse folds. Pull out the loose paper from inside the claws. Use tweezers to narrow the thicknesses inside the body.

24 Pull out the loose paper from the claws and the rear legs. Narrow the eyes with mountain folds.

25 Pinch the claws. Shape the eyes and the carapace. Roll the two locking flaps together, and tuck them into the pocket beneath.

The completed CRAB.

(1976)

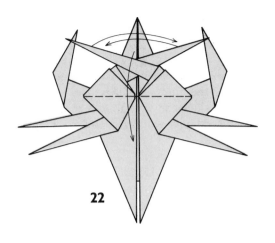

22

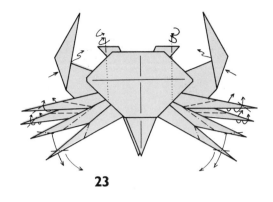

23

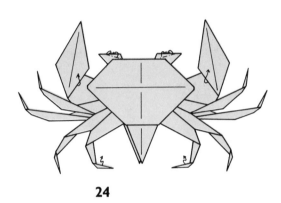

24

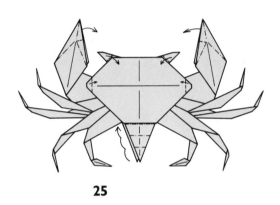

25

CENTIPEDE

Use a sheet of paper colored on one side. A 10-by-40-inch sheet will produce a model 13½ inches long. Alternatively, you can use any rectangle of integral proportions: 1 by 1, 1 by 2, 1 by 3, 1 by 100, and so on. (But not, for example, 1 by 2½.) The longer the rectangle, the greater the number of legs. The 1 by 4 rectangle shown here produces an animal with thirty legs. In general, a 1 by n rectangle will produce $8n - 2$ legs.

1 Crease lengthwise. Divide widthwise into eight strips. (If you use a rectangle longer or shorter than 1 by 4, divide widthwise into $2n$ strips.) Pleat like an accordion.
2 Form eight inside reverse folds.
3 Unfold to step 2.

4 Form four valley folds and six inside reverse folds.
5 Unfold to step 2.

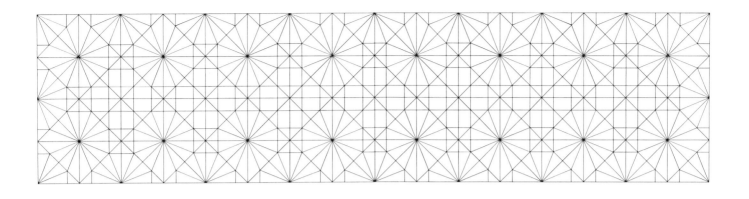

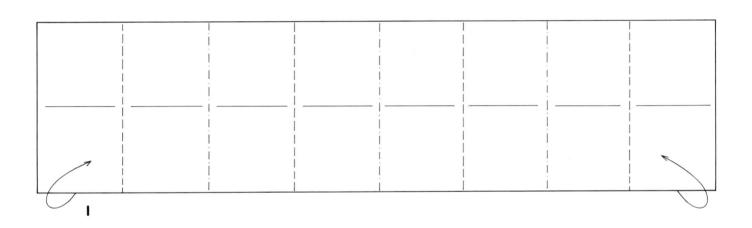

1

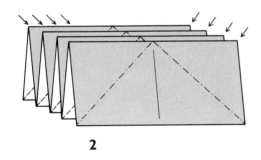

2

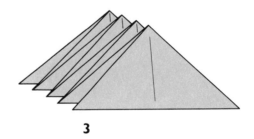

3

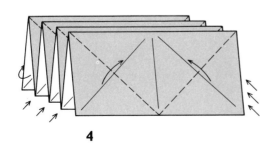

4

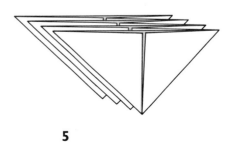

5

6 Divide into sixteenths.

7 Unfold completely.

8 Mountain- and valley-fold. Note the similarity in this and the following steps to the early stages of the CRAB.

9 Fold the entire thickness.

10 There are seven peaks. Crease each peak in thirds, then open double–sink as in step 5 of the CRAB.

11 Pull out the hidden flaps, each a single thickness. There are seven on each side.

12 Swing the front face upward. The double-sunk square portion will stretch and lie flat.

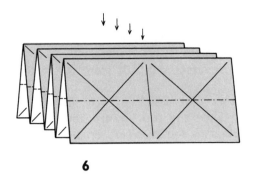

6

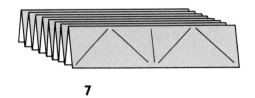

7

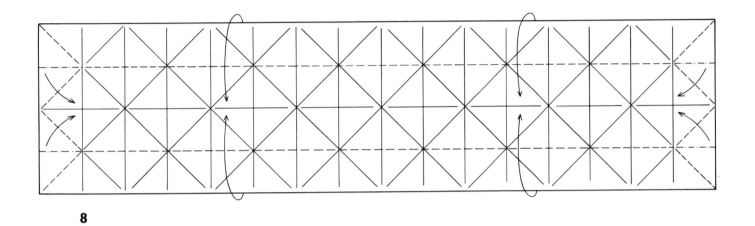

8

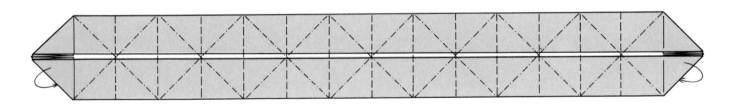

9

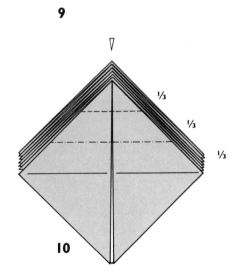

10

⅓
⅓
⅓

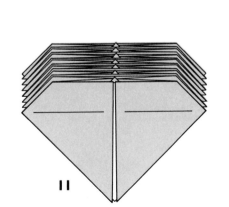

11

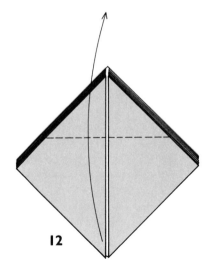

12

13 Inside reverse—fold, keeping the three top flaps together.

14 Slide the top upward and stretch the next double-sunk square.

15 Inside reverse—fold, as in step 13.

16 Inside reverse—fold the two triangular flaps at the sides. Slide the top upward and stretch the next double-sunk square, as in step 14.

17 Inside reverse—fold, as in step 13.

18 Inside reverse—fold the two triangular flaps at the sides, as in step 16. Slide the top upward and stretch the next double-sunk square, as in step 14. Repeat this two-step pattern throughout the rest of the model.

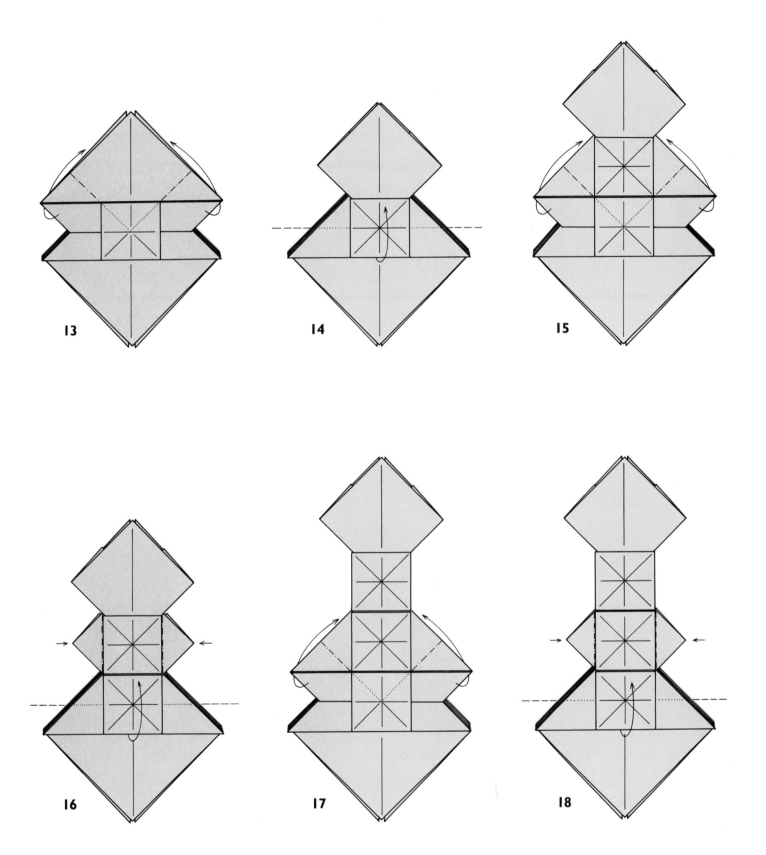

13

14

15

16

17

18

19 Turn the model over.

20 There are two types of flaps, marked A and B. Inside reverse–fold the flaps in set A. (There are twelve in this version.)

21 This is the assembly line, a sequence of folds that can be repeated ad infinitum to produce legs. Valley-fold the legs in set B.

22 Pinch and narrow the legs in set B.

23 Tuck the loose paper into the pockets of the legs in set B. Valley-fold the legs in set A.

24 Pull out more loose paper from the legs in set B. Narrow the legs in set A.

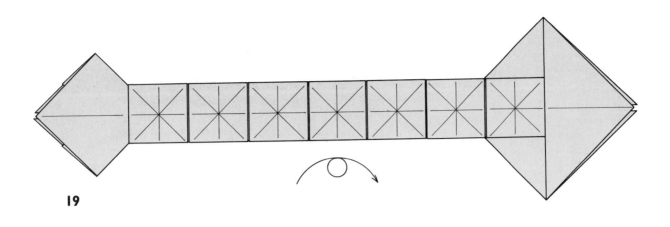

19

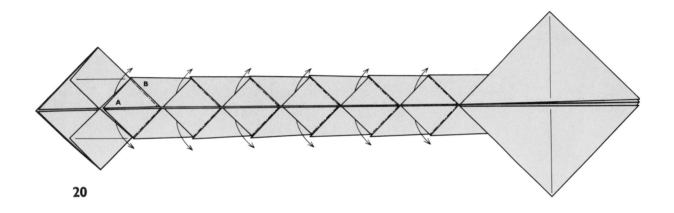

20

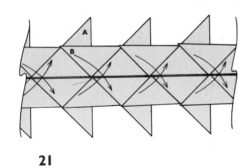

21

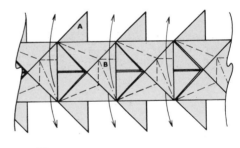

22

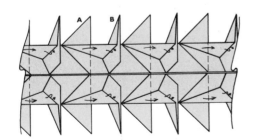

23

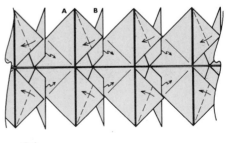

24

25 In a single motion, valley-fold the legs in set A and swing open the legs in set B. Stretch and flatten the loose paper that appears.

26 Valley-fold the legs in set A. Mountain-fold the legs in set B. From the bottom, the two sets of legs should now appear identical.

27 Here through step 34 are details of the head, similar to the previous details of the legs. Valley-fold, as in step 13, so that loose paper comes into view. (In step 13 the procedure was a mountain fold, but this is the opposite side of the model.)

28 Inside reverse—fold the two triangular flaps at the sides, as in step 16.

29 The left-hand folds are identical to those in step 25. The right-hand folds are the mirror images of those in step 21.

30 Left-hand side: Tuck the loose paper into the pockets behind. Right-hand side: Pinch and narrow, as in step 22.

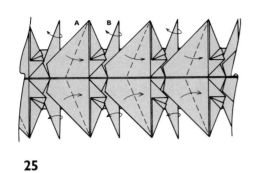

25

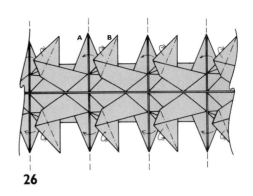

26

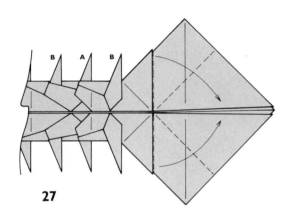

27

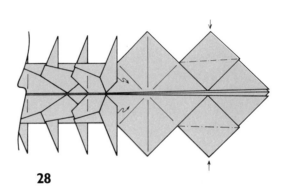

28

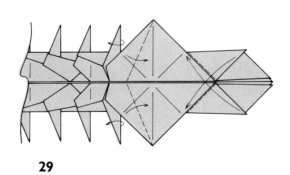

29

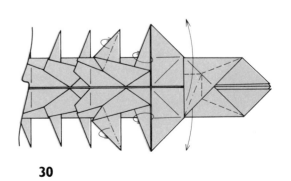

30

31 Tuck the loose paper into the pockets contained at the right-hand side of each leg. Pull out the loose paper from the left-hand side of each leg.

32 The folds at the left are the mirror image of those in step 25. Inside reverse—fold the two flaps at the extreme right of the model. These will be the antennae.

33 Left-hand side: Tuck the loose paper into the pockets behind. These folds are the mirror image of those in step 30. Right-hand side: Grasp the antennae at either side of the slot, and pull them apart. A hidden flap will pop through the slot. Collapse the paper so that the flap remains exposed.

34 Pull out the loose paper from the exposed triangle. Crimp the entire model as a way of narrowing the pair of legs second from the front. Then uncrimp, to continue work on the tail. For the results of the crimp, see step 39.

35 Here through step 38 are details of the tail. Repeat the relevant parts of steps 28 through 33 in mirror image.

36 Pull out the loose paper from the exposed triangle.

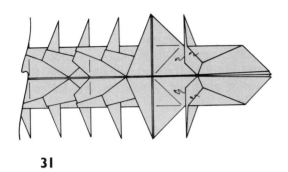

31

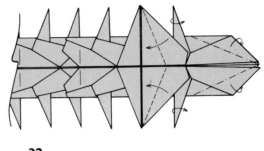

32

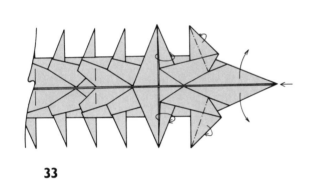

33

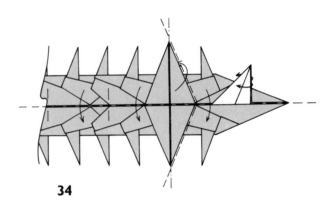

34

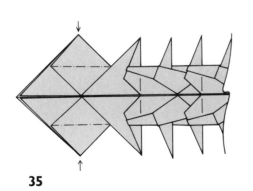

35

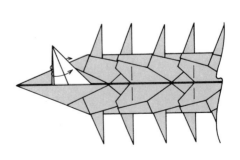

36

37 Fold the exposed triangle over, and tuck it under the adjacent flap.

38 Valley-fold the entire model.

39 Pinch the two tail flaps, and curl them outward. Crimp and round the body. Pinch the legs. Pinch and spread the antennae. Inside reverse—fold the tip of the head.

The completed CENTIPEDE.

(1976, revised 1987)

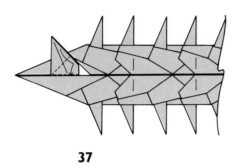

37

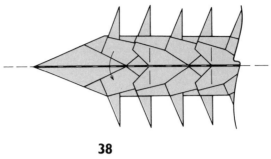

38

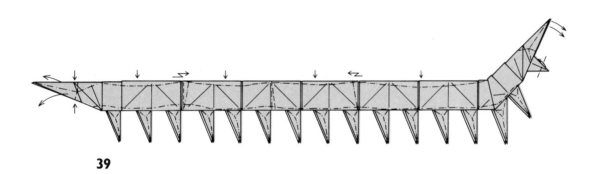

39

OCTOPUS

Use a sheet of paper colored on one side. A 10-inch square will produce a model 3½ inches long. For your first attempt, use a square measuring at least 18 inches to a side.

1 Blintz-fold the four corners.
2 Form a preliminary fold on the double thickness.
3 Squash one flap.

4 Petal-fold.
5 Unfold the model slightly, and pull out the loose paper.
6 Following the existing creases, flatten the shaded flap.

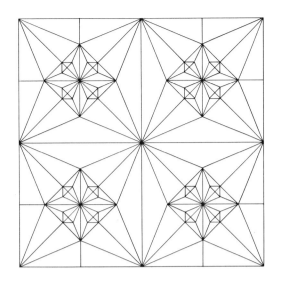

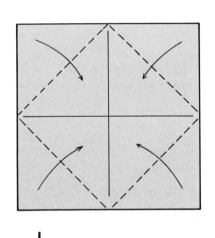

1

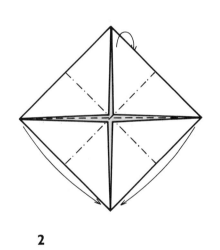

2

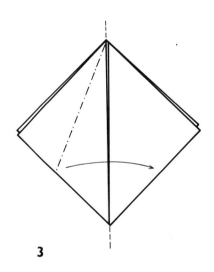

3

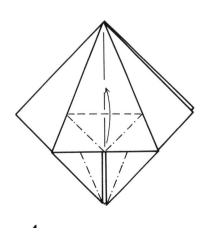

4

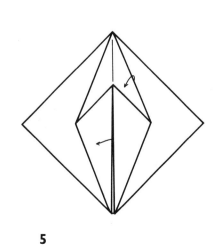

5

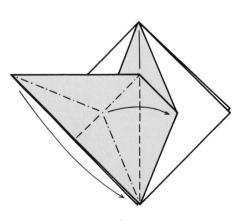

6

7 The following steps resemble the early stages of the KANGAROO. Crease as in steps I through 3 of the KANGAROO. Then collapse the central triangle (it is not yet a pyramid) as shown.

8 Valley-fold the tip downward so it meets the intersection of the folds formed in step 7. Then unfold to step 7.

9 Following the existing creases, open up the paper and open-sink the tiny central square.

10 Spread the sides, as in step 4 of the KANGAROO, to form a pyramid with a hollow top.

11 This is a top view. The model is now three-dimensional. Fold in the sides of the pyramid.

12 Form tiny rabbit's ears on the left and right of the pyramid, and flatten it. (Note that the pyramid flattens in a different direction from the one in the KANGAROO.)

13 The model is now flat. Open the model slightly, and tuck the upper and lower portions of the flattened pyramid into the adjacent pockets. (This procedure is a form of sink. Part of the paper is turned inside out.) The tip of the pyramid remains in view. This is an eye.

14 Valley-fold the lower shaded triangle upward.

15 Narrow each of four quadrants into thirds with valley folds. Unfold.

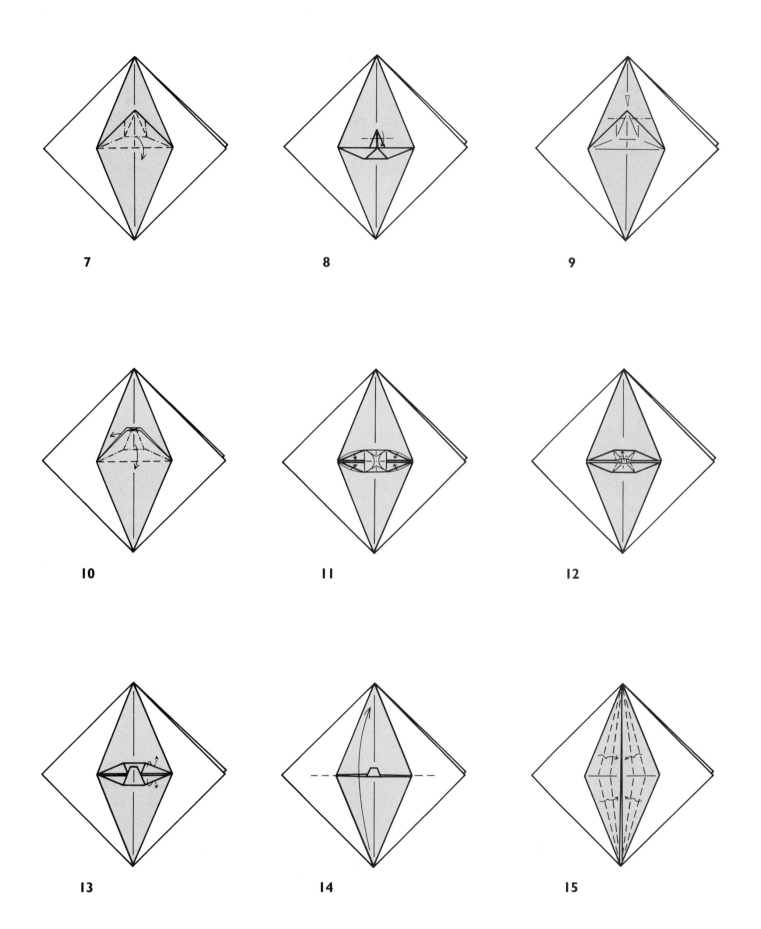

7

8

9

10

11

12

13

14

15

16 With the left-hand flap, form a long, thin rabbit's ear that crosses the centerline.

17 Tuck the tiny, protruding corner underneath, as shown in the detail. Then mountain-fold the long, thin flap in half, and tuck the loose paper underneath. Repeat this and step 16 on the right-hand flap.

18 Mountain-fold the two shaded flaps in thirds.

19 This completes one-quarter of the octopus. There are three more white flaps identical to the one squash folded in step 3. Swing one of these white flaps to the left.

20 Repeat steps 3 through 18 on the left-hand side.

21 Valley-fold one flap to the right, then turn the model over.

22 Two white flaps remain. They will be treated slightly differently from the previous ones. Repeat steps 3 through 7 on the left-hand side.

23 Repeat steps 10 through 13 without sinking the tip.

24 Mountain-fold the tip in half.

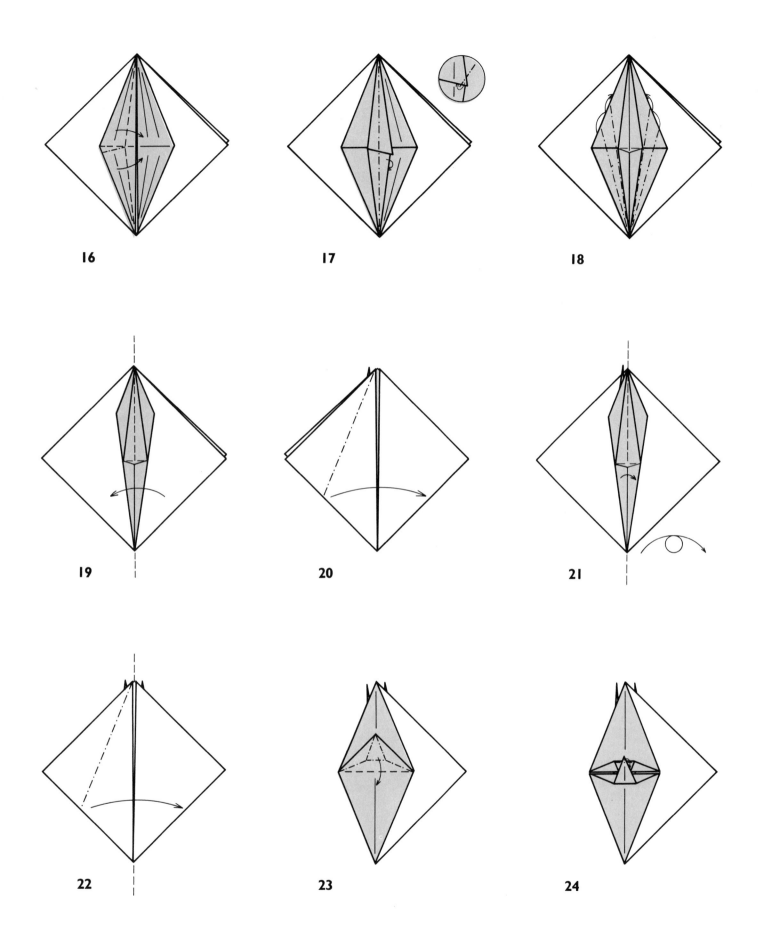

16

17

18

19

20

21

22

23

24

25 Open the model slightly, and tuck the upper and lower portions of the flattened pyramid into the adjacent pockets, as in step 13. The entire pyramid disappears from view.

26 Repeat steps 14 through 18.

27 Repeat steps 3 through 7 on the remaining white flap.

28 Valley-fold the tip half as far as in step 8. Repeat steps 9 through 12.

29 Repeat steps 14 through 18 to complete the last of the eight legs. Then swing the central leg down. The pyramid will reemerge and become three-dimensional.

30 This is a top view of the pyramid. In a single motion, pull the tip of the pyramid toward you and flatten the model.

31 The model is now two-dimensional.

32 Here through step 34 are details of the funnel, a device used by the octopus for jet propulsion and for shooting ink at predators. Crimp the funnel symmetrically.

33 Narrow the sides of the funnel with mountain folds. Use tweezers.

34 The funnel is completed.

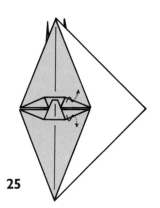

25

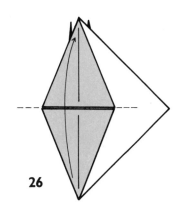

26

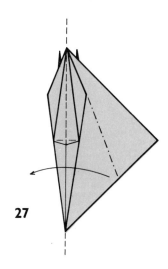

27

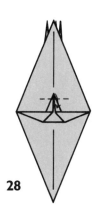

28

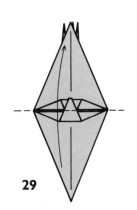

29

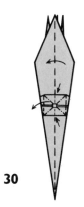

30

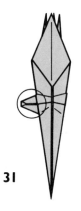

31

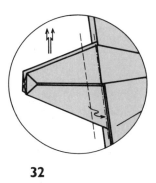

32

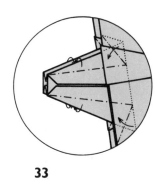

33

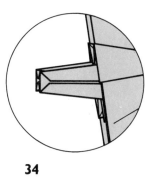

34

35 Inside reverse—fold three legs to the right. Reposition the head so that the eyes are located symmetrically on either side and the funnel below.

36 In a single motion, crimp the bottom of the head and flatten the top of the head. The model will become three-dimensional.

37 Swing the front and back legs toward the head.
38 Squash the front and back legs.

39 Narrow the front and back legs with valley folds.
40 Round the head. Curl the legs. Spread the eyes and the tip of the funnel.

The completed OCTOPUS.

(1974, revised 1986)

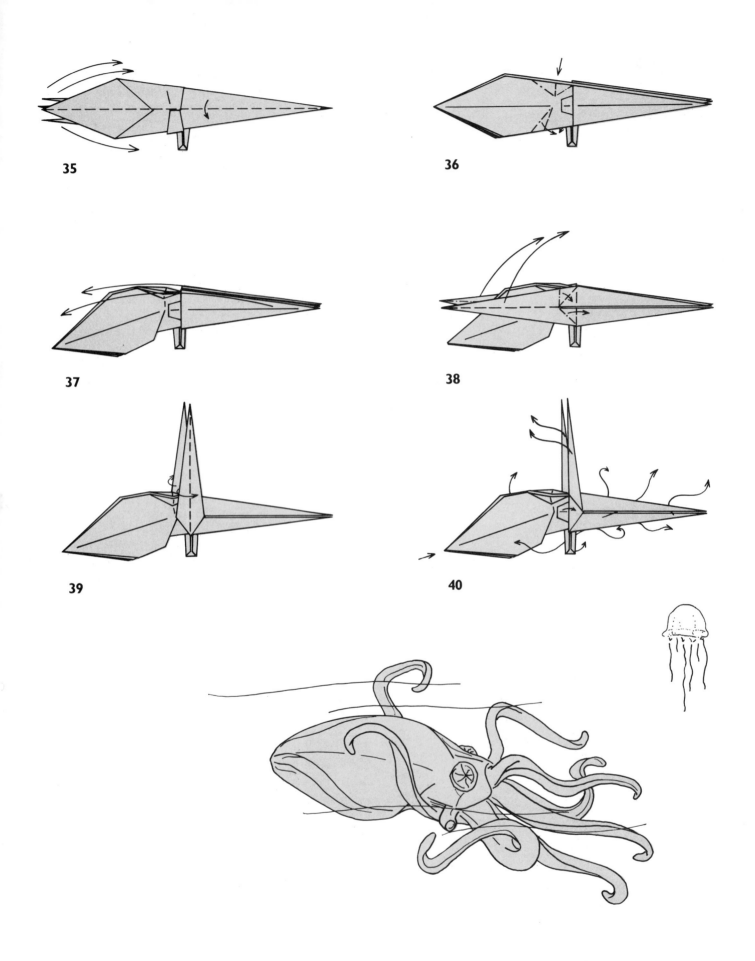

35

36

37

38

39

40

SQUID

Use a sheet of paper colored on one side. A 10-inch square will produce a model 6⅜ inches long. For your first attempt, use a square measuring at least 18 inches to a side.

1 Mountain-fold the upper corners to the center. Valley-fold the bottom corners to the center and unfold.
2 Rabbit's-ear the bottom two corners.
3 Squash the tiny triangles.
4 Petal-fold the tiny triangles.

5 Open the petal folds.
6 Valley-fold diagonally at the intersection of the existing creases.
7 Following the existing creases, pull the top and sides down. This is a form of preliminary fold.
8 Spread and squash the white flap on the left.

9 Petal-fold.
10 Unfold the model slightly, and pull out the loose paper, as in step 5 of the OCTOPUS.
11 Following the existing creases, flatten the shaded flap, as in step 6 of the OCTOPUS.

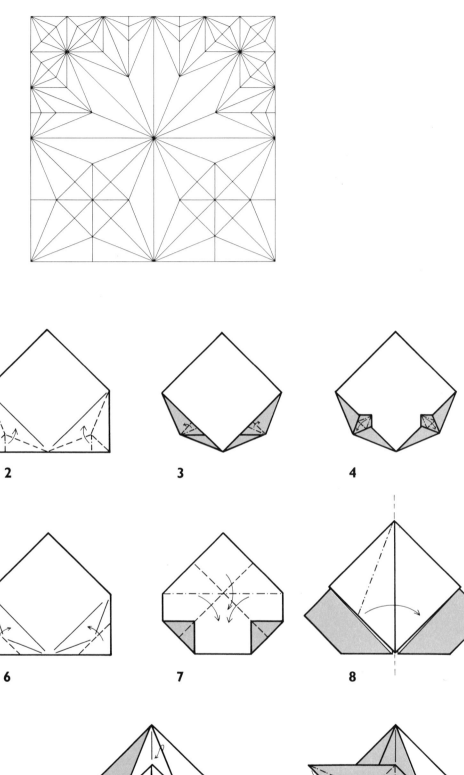

12 Grasp the shaded lower tip, and stretch it downward.
13 Valley-fold the shaded flap to the left.
14 Repeat steps 8 through 13 on the white flap on the right.

15 Crimp. The valley fold falls naturally. The mountain fold falls about a quarter of the way between the valley fold and the tip.
16 Like its cousin the octopus, the squid has a funnel. This is it. Narrow the sides of the funnel with mountain folds, and inside reverse–fold the tip.
17 Grasp the two sides, and pull them apart slightly. The funnel will pop up. Do not flatten it.

18 Still holding the sides apart, tuck the funnel into the body. If you follow the existing creases, the funnel should fit naturally. Close the sides.
19 The funnel is completed. The model should lie flat. Turn the model over.
20 Spread and squash the shaded flap on the left.

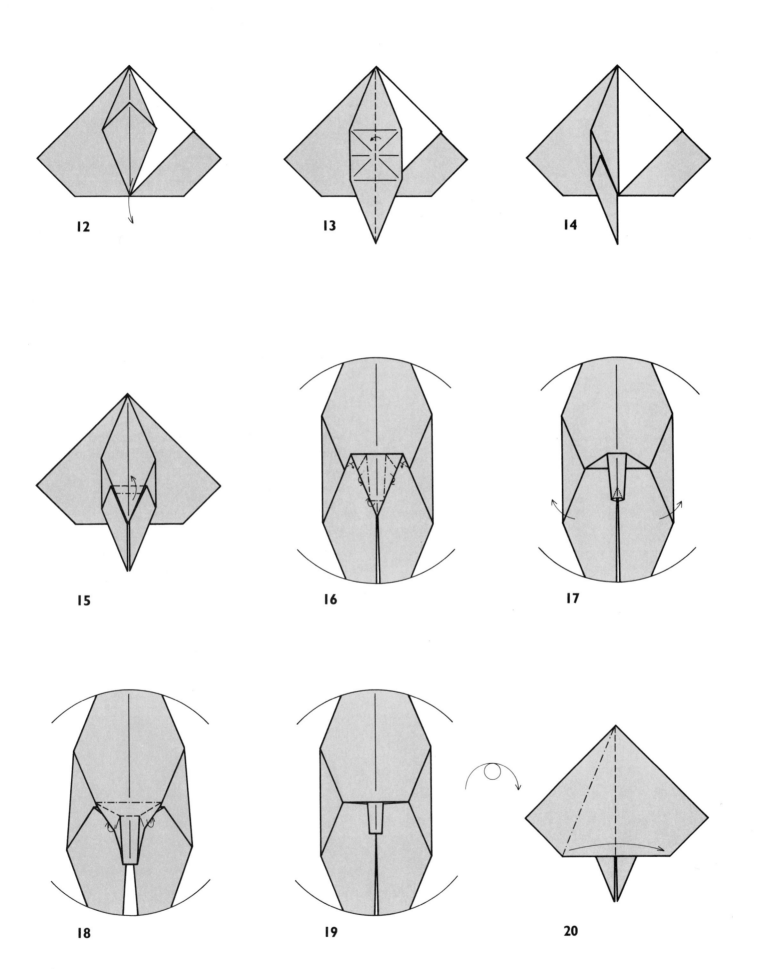

12

13

14

15

16

17

18

19

20

21 Valley-fold the lower-left-hand corner to the right-hand folded edge.

22 Valley-fold edge to edge.

23 Inside reverse–fold down the centerline.

24 Inside reverse–fold to the centerline.

25 Repeat steps 20 through 24 on the right-hand side. Then return both sides to their positions in step 21.

26 Following the existing creases, collapse both sides symmetrically.

27 Fold the tip up, and pull out the hidden paper from inside it.

28 Following the existing creases, collapse the loose paper symmetrically.

29 Petal-fold the front face of the loose paper.

30 There are two tiny flaps hanging below the front face. Tuck them underneath with tweezers. The loose paper at either side will close automatically.

31 Behind the front face is a thicker flap. Valley-fold the front face back down, but leave the thicker flap where it is.

32 Valley-fold the thicker flap about one-quarter of the way from the tip to the crease that separates the thicker flap from the front face. Press firmly and unfold.

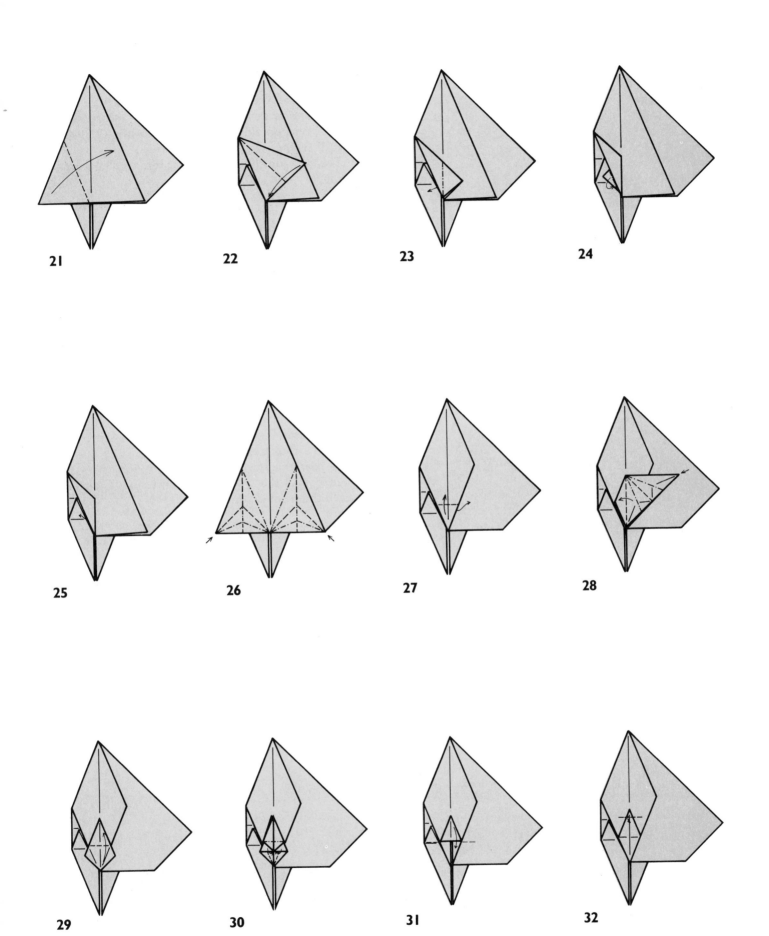

21

22

23

24

25

26

27

28

29

30

31

32

33, 34 Here through step 36 are details of the tip. Open-sink it through the existing crease, as in step 14 of the ONE-DOLLAR BOW TIE.

35 The sink is completed. Pull down and spread the octagonal portion, as in step 15 of the ONE-DOL-LAR BOW TIE.

36 The octagon should lie flat. Later, it will become an eye.

37 Valley-fold one flap to the left.

38 Repeat steps 20 through 37 on the right-hand side.

39 The flap at the center will be the front of the mantle. Place your thumbs inside the front, and stretch it upward.

40 The model is now three-dimensional. Squash the front of the mantle flat.

41 Petal-fold.

42 Valley-fold the small triangle in half. Press it firmly. Then spread the two small side flaps, and open the entire front assembly. Do not flatten.

43 Holding the front assembly open, tuck the small triangle up and into the assembly, following the existing creases. Then collapse the front assembly as in the previous step.

44 Narrow the front of the mantle with valley folds, but not all the way to the centerline. Then valley-fold the front downward.

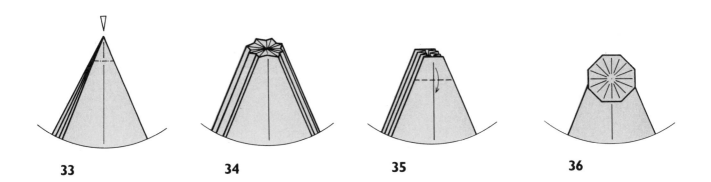

33　　　　**34**　　　　**35**　　　　**36**

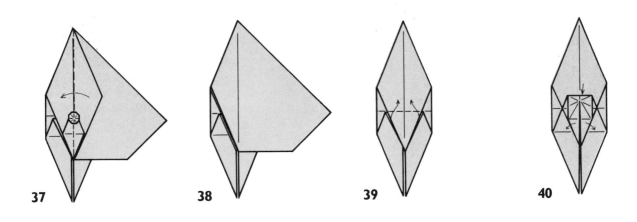

37　　　　**38**　　　　**39**　　　　**40**

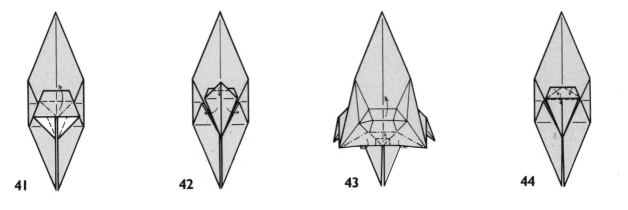

41　　　　**42**　　　　**43**　　　　**44**

45 The front of the mantle is completed. Turn the model over.

46 The two flaps at the bottom will be the long tentacles. Mountain-fold one-third of the front of the tentacles. Valley-fold the back to match.

47 Inside reverse–fold the tentacles.

48 Valley-fold the tentacles in half.

49 Tuck the loose paper inside.

50 Inside reverse–fold the tentacles as far as they will go. They will cross.

51 Pinch the tentacles, and swing them apart from each other.

52 Turn the model over.

53 Swing two flaps to the right.

54 Valley-fold the sides approximately in thirds. The creases should not reach the tip.

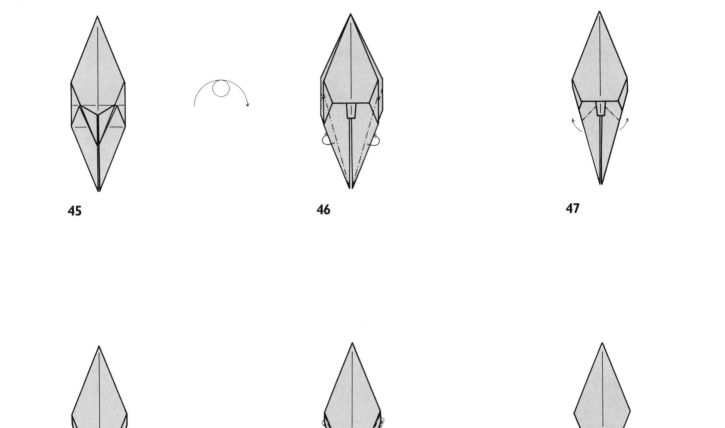

45

46

47

48

49

50

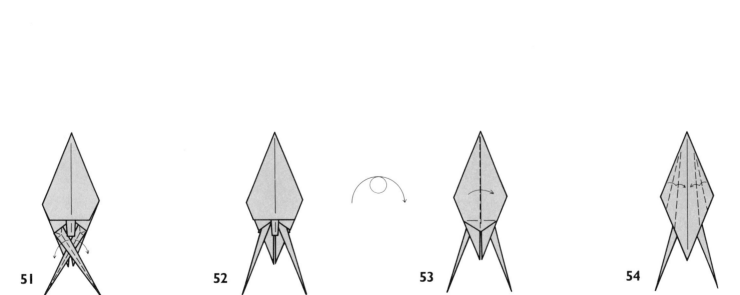

51

52

53

54

55 Valley-fold one flap to the left.

56, 57 In a single motion, pull down the eye and close the model, as shown in the detail. Repeat steps 53 through 57 on the other side.

58 This detail shows the completed eyes and the eight little tentacles.

59 Pinch the top two little tentacles on each side. Curve the front of the mantle. Crimp the body to form fins. Repeat behind. Turn the model over.

60 Pinch the remaining little tentacles. Mountain-fold the fins on the front face only, and tuck them into the mantle. They form pockets running the length of the mantle.

61 Tuck the edges of the remaining fins into the pockets, as shown in cross section in the detail. Round the mantle carefully, making sure not to unlock the fins. Pinch the funnel to make it three-dimensional. Curve the long tentacles, and form pads at the ends.

The completed SQUID.

(1983–84)

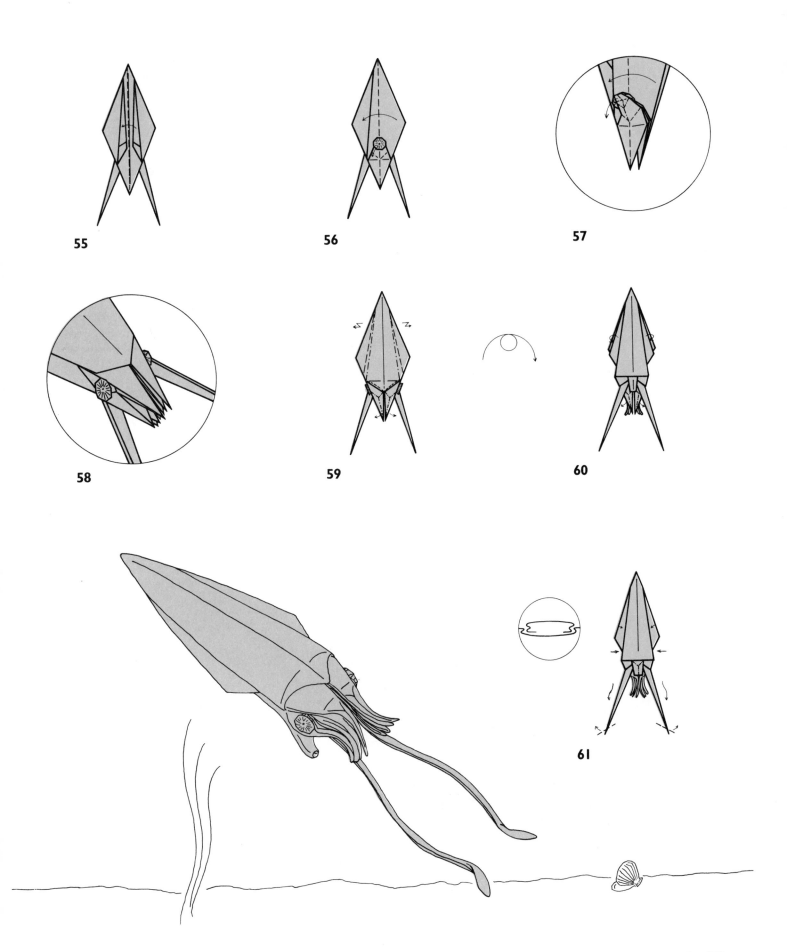

55

56

57

58

59

60

61

SCORPION

Use a sheet of paper colored on one side. A 10-inch square of paper will produce a model 2⅛ inches long. For your first attempt, use a square measuring at least 18 inches to a side.

1 Blintz and unfold.
2 Form rabbit's ears on the four corners.
3 Squash the four tiny triangles.
4 Petal-fold the four triangles.

5 Unfold the lower two corners.
6 Valley-fold diagonally at the intersection of the existing creases.
7 Pull the top and sides down. This is a form of preliminary fold.
8 Inside reverse–fold the four sides.

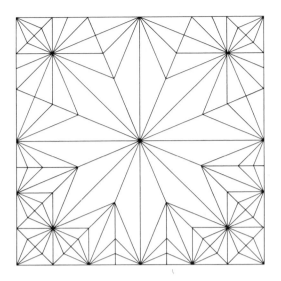

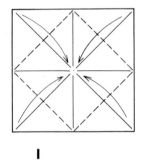

1

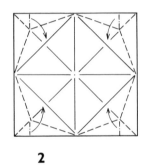

2

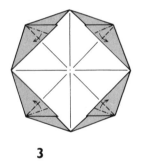

3

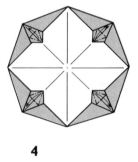

4

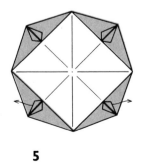

5

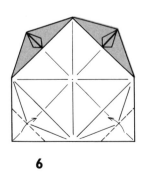

6

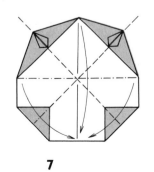

7

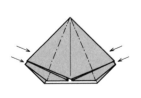

8

9 Valley-fold the left-hand flap so the existing crease meets the centerline.

10 Valley-fold down the centerline.

11 Valley-fold the right-hand flap so the existing crease meets the centerline.

12 Valley-fold down the centerline.

13 Unfold to step 9.

14 Following the existing creases, collapse the left- and right-hand flaps symmetrically.

15 Repeat steps 9 through 14 on the second layer.

16 Two layers are completed. Turn the model over.

17 Valley-fold so that the lower-left-hand corner meets the folded edge.

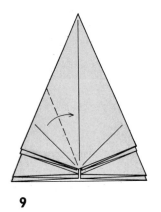

9

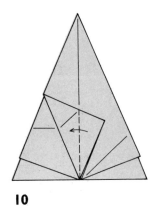

10

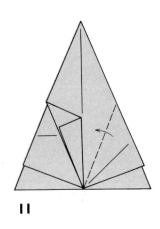

11

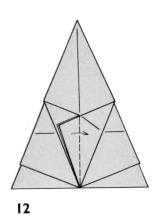

12

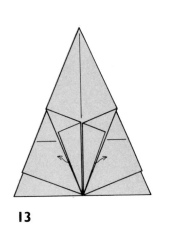

13

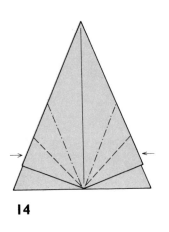

14

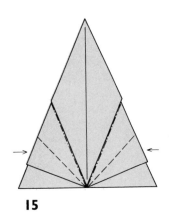

15

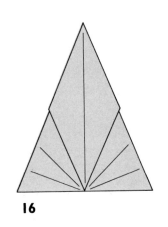

16

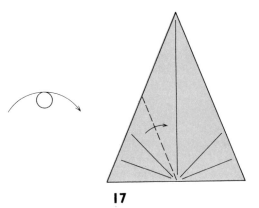

17

18 Valley-fold edge to edge.

19 Inside reverse–fold down the centerline.

20 Inside reverse–fold to the centerline.

21 Valley-fold so that the lower-right-hand corner meets the folded edge.

22 Repeat steps 18 through 20 on the right-hand flap.

23 Unfold to step 17.

24 Folding along the existing creases, collapse the left- and right-hand flaps symmetrically.

25 Repeat steps 17 through 24 on the second layer.

26 All four layers are completed. Swing one flap to the right.

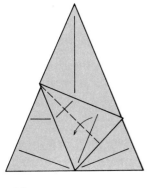

18

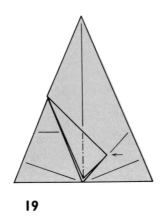

19

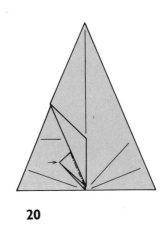

20

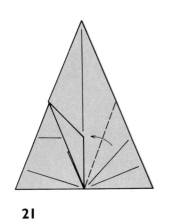

21

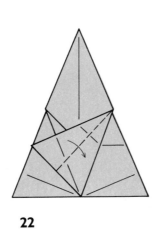

22

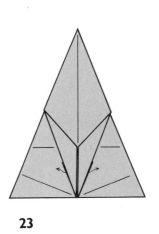

23

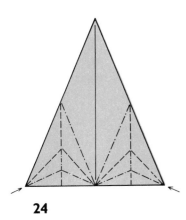

24

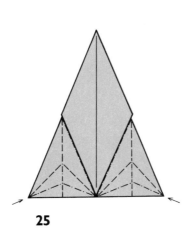

25

26

27 Fold the tip up, and pull out the hidden paper from inside it.

28 Following the existing creases, collapse the loose paper symmetrically.

29 Inside reverse—fold the two sides to the centerline.

30 Petal-fold the front face of the loose paper.

31 There are two tiny flaps hanging below the front face. Tuck the right-hand flap underneath with tweezers, as in step 30 of the SQUID. The loose paper at its side will close automatically.

32 Behind the front face is a thicker flap. Grasp the tip of the front face, and stretch it to the right, but leave the thicker flap where it is. Do not flatten.

33 The model is now three-dimensional. Tuck the tiny left-hand flap inside.

34 Swing the tip back down, and close the model.

35 Valley-fold one small flap to the right.

36 Valley-fold the thicker flap down.

37 Valley-fold two big flaps to the left.

38 Repeat steps 27 through 37 in mirror image. In repeating step 31, remember that it is the mirror-image *left*-hand flap that must be tucked underneath. When you repeat step 37, valley-fold only one big flap to the right. When all the folds are in place, turn the model over.

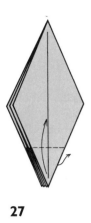

27

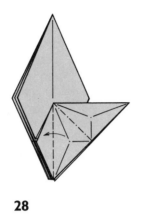

28

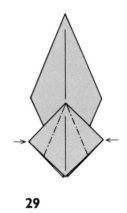

29

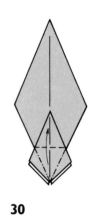

30

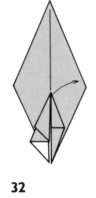

31

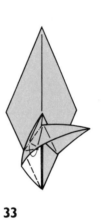

32

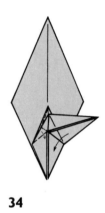

33

34

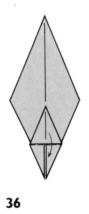

35

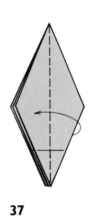

36

37

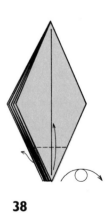

38

39 There are two hidden layers on each side. Curl the top layer on each side with mountain folds. Divide evenly into thirds. Tweezers may help.

40 Curl the second layer on each side with valley folds. Divide evenly into thirds.

41 Narrow the body by rolling it into thirds. Do not crease all the way to the tip. The first and third flaps receive mountain folds. The second and fourth flaps receive valley folds. The result is symmetrical.

42 The triangle below the valley fold conceals many thicknesses. The first four pairs of flaps will be the legs. Swing them upward, toward the rear of the model.

43, 44 The next pair of flaps will be the mandibles. Reach into the slot between them, and poke a single ply of each mandible from the inside out. In the same motion, slide each mandible toward the rear of the model. New creases will form. Flatten them.

45 Shift the eight legs farther toward the rear. The loose paper will stretch and flatten.

46 Narrow the mandibles with valley folds. The hidden paper will stretch.

47 Tuck the loose paper into the pockets beneath.

48 Following the existing crease, return the eight legs to their position in step 43. Open the top layer of the body to its position in step 41.

49 Place your thumbs under the top layer at the openings marked *x*. Lift the top layer, and shift the legs toward the rear. Collapse the entire assembly, making new creases as shown.

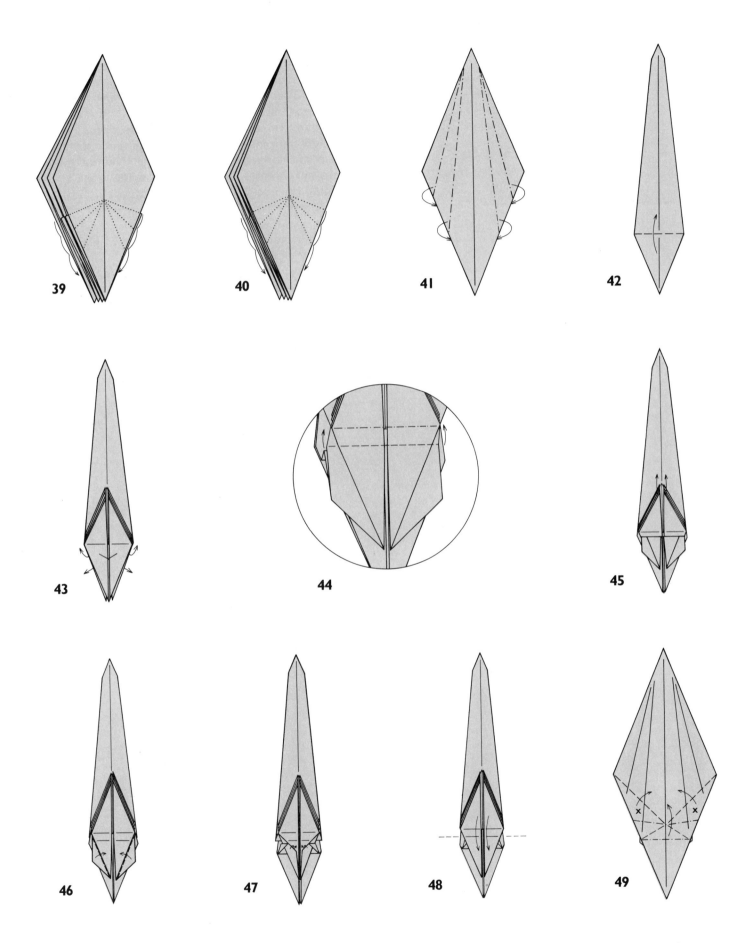

39

40

41

42

43

44

45

46

47

48

49

50 Valley-fold the layer concealing the legs, and tuck its tip into the adjacent pocket. Holding the tip in place, put mountain folds back into the top layer of the body. The body is now locked, and the eight legs will stand up.

51 The two remaining flaps at the front are the pincers. Open the pincers slightly, and pull out the hidden paper. Use tweezers if necessary. Without making any new creases, swing the legs to the rear.

52 Inside reverse–fold the top pair of legs and the pincers.

53 Inside reverse–fold the second pair of legs. Inside reverse–fold the pincers again.

54 Inside reverse–fold the third pair of legs. Outside reverse–fold the pincers.

55 Inside reverse–fold the last pair of legs.

56 Narrow all eight legs with mountain folds.

57 The legs have been narrowed. Turn the model over.

58 Valley-fold the top flap as far as it will go.

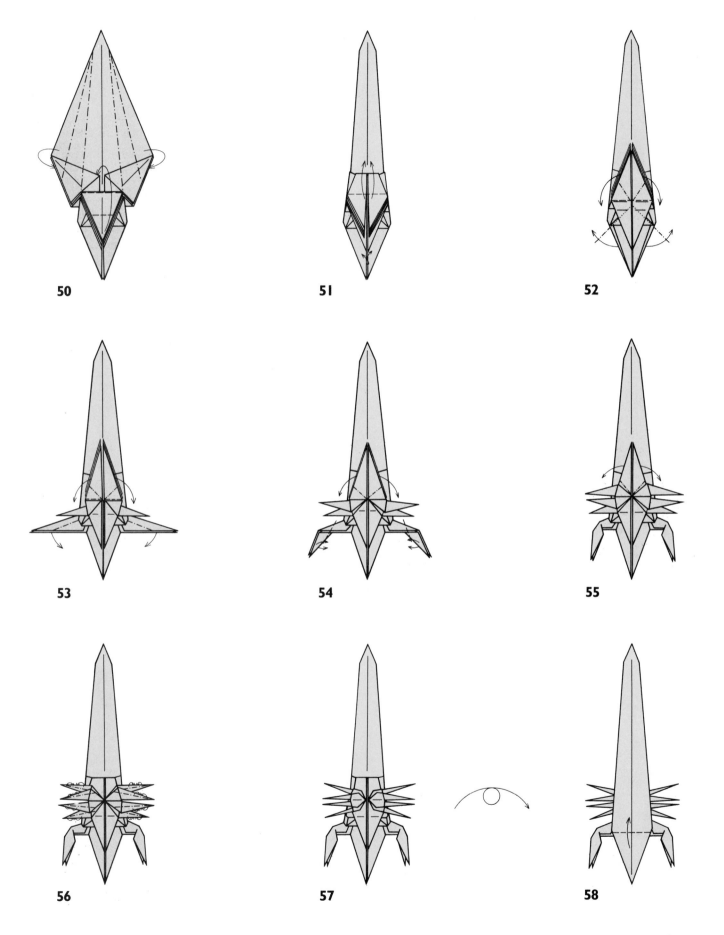

50

51

52

53

54

55

56

57

58

59 Here through step 67 are details of the head. Rabbit's-ear the head.

60 Pull out the loose paper.

61 Squash.

62 Pull out the loose paper.

63 Pinch at the centerline, and a rabbit's ear will appear.

64 Squash.

65 Petal-fold the tiny flap at the center. Carefully disengage the loose paper at the sides, and mountain-fold it out of view. Tweezers may be necessary.

66 Valley-fold the loose triangle over and over toward the head. Unfold the top layer of the body.

67 Narrow the edges of the top layer with mountain folds (A), then return the top layer to its previous position (B). Inside reverse–fold the head. Pinch the mandibles.

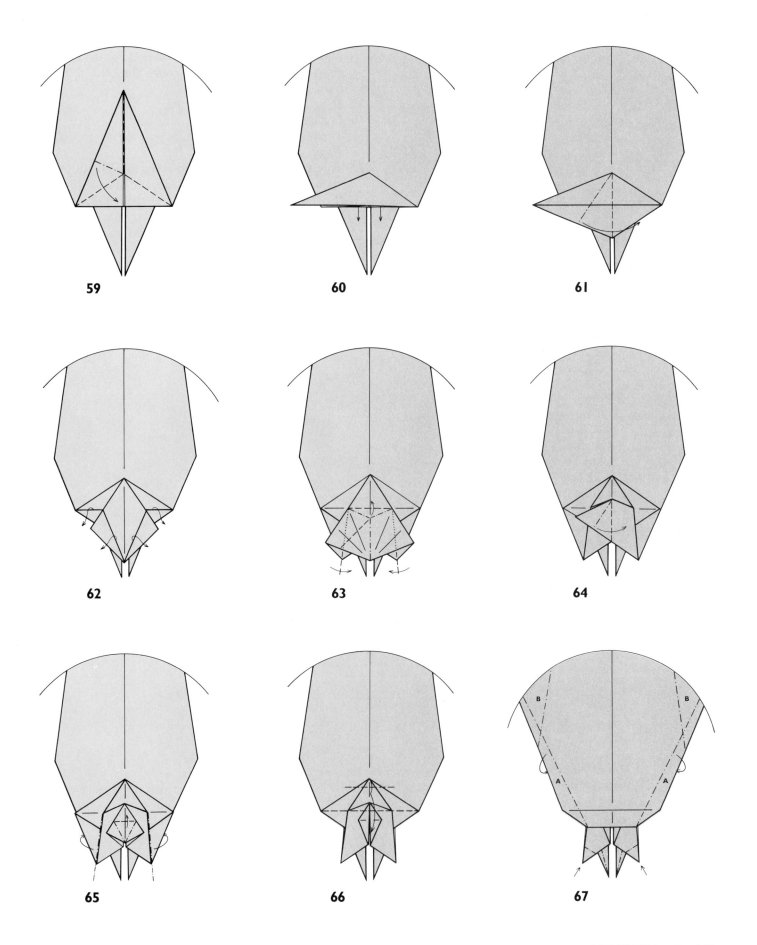

59

60

61

62

63

64

65

66

67

68 Here through step 71 are details of the pincers. Narrow the "arm" with mountain folds, and inside reverse–fold the pincers through the double thickness.

69 Shift the inner pincer forward.

70 Outside reverse–fold the outer pincer.

71 The pincers are completed. Repeat steps 68 through 70 on the other side.

72 This is the most difficult step in the model. In a single motion, roll the tail into a tube and arch it toward the head. Creases will form automatically as the tube deforms. Study the drawing to determine where the creases should fall, then unroll the tail and score the creases with tweezers. Roll the tail again, and massage the creases into place. If the paper is too bulky, you may have to settle for an approximation of the final drawing. Mountain- and valley-fold the legs to lift the body off the ground. Round the back and the pincers. Pinch the tip of the tail to form the stinger.

The completed SCORPION.

(1986)

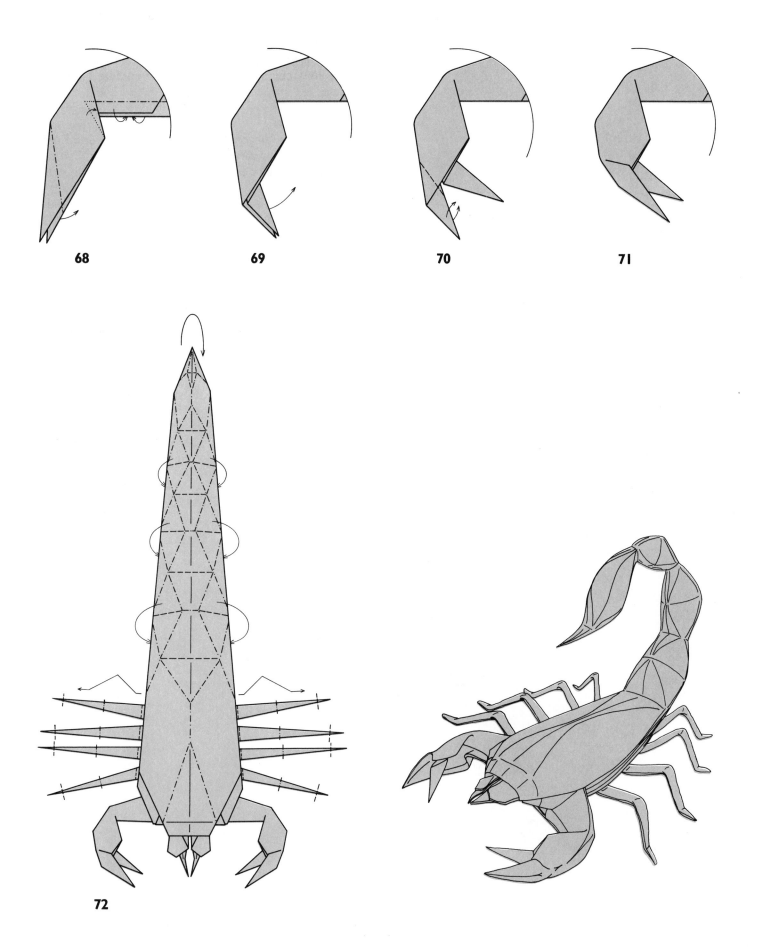

68

69

70

71

72

RATTLESNAKE

Use a sheet of paper colored on one side. A 10-inch square will produce a model 2¼ inches in diameter. If you could uncoil the snake's body, it would be 40 inches long.

1 Crease one diagonal heavily. The remainder of the creases in this step should be made lightly. Crease the other diagonal to mark the center of the square, and pinch the left and right corners. Fold the upper corner to the center to mark the one-quarter point of the diagonal. Fold the corner to the one-quarter point to mark the one-eighth point of the diagonal. Fold the corner to the one-eighth point to mark the one-sixteenth point of the diagonal.

2 Here through step 3 are details of the upper corner. Creasing lightly, valley-fold the cut edge to the sixteenth point of the diagonal and unfold. Note where the valley fold crosses the centerline. Repeat on the bottom corner.

3 Fold all four corners and edges identically.

4, 5 Pleat firmly. The details in steps 5 and 6 show the model turned over. Note that the valley folds in step 5 meet the edge of the model at the one-sixteenth point of the diagonal.

6 Unfold to step 4, but do not turn over.

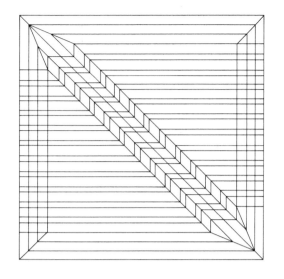

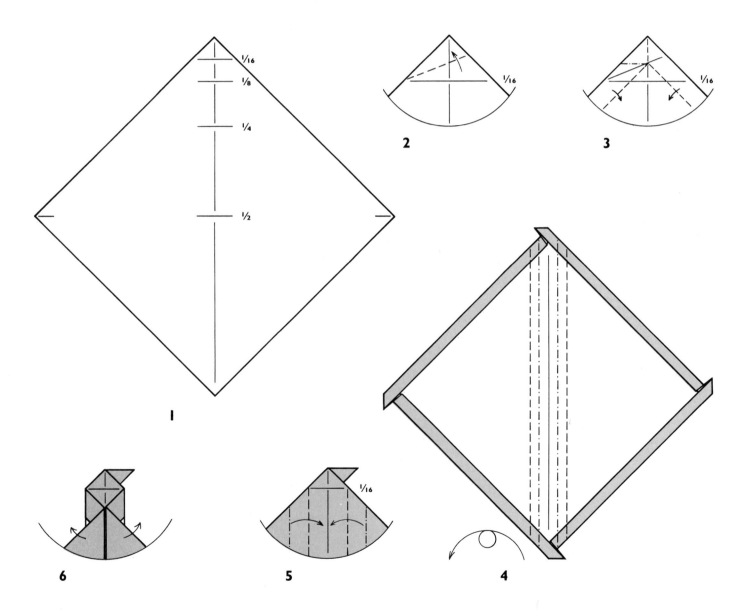

7 Valley-fold the edge to the centerline.

8 Inside reverse—fold.

9 Inside reverse—fold and squash the same flap.

10 Repeat steps 7 through 9 on the left-hand flap and on the two top edges.

11 Pull out and pinch in half the loose paper at the left- and right-hand corners. Swivel the top and bottom corners clockwise. (If you swivel them counter-clockwise, the coil will spiral in the opposite direction.)

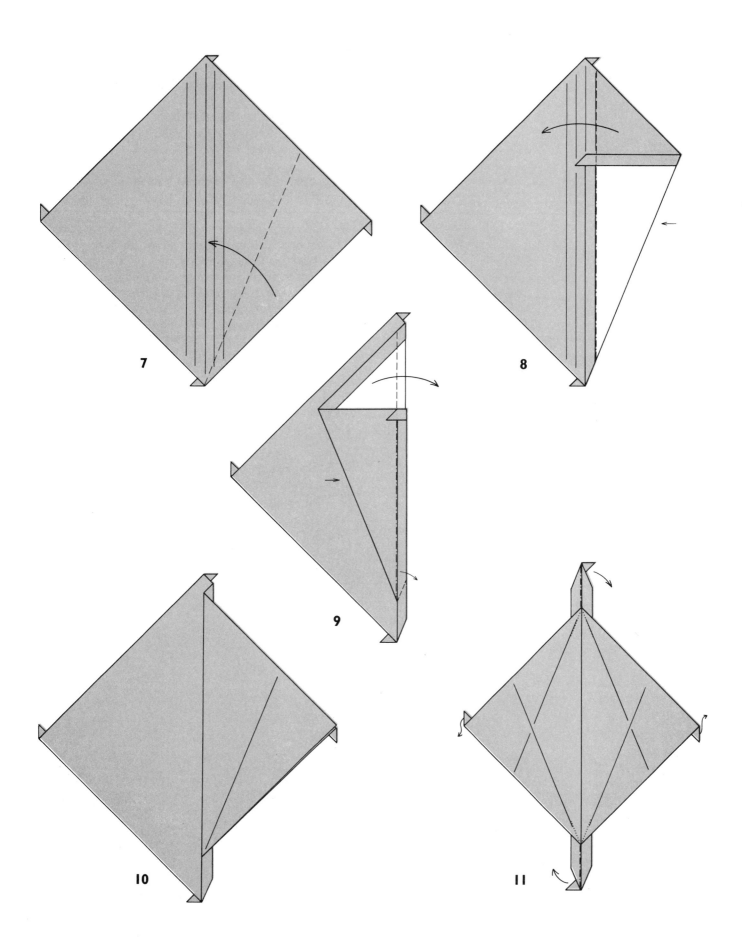

7

8

9

10

11

12 Valley-fold the flaps at the lower left and right. Both flaps will stand up.

13 Valley-fold. The model will not lie flat.

14 Closed-sink to the edge of the model.

15 The model is now flat. Valley-fold. Both flaps will stand up again.

16 Closed-sink the lower-left-hand flap. Unroll the right-hand edge, and pull out the loose paper from the lower-right-hand corner. Turn the model over.

17, 18 Here through step 20 are details of the two bottom corners. Crimp the entire bottom edge of the model by simultaneously tucking the loose paper into the left-hand corner and pulling out the loose paper from the right-hand corner.

19, 20 Tuck the tiny triangular protrusion at the left-hand corner into the pocket behind. Use tweezers if necessary. Unfold the double thickness at the right-hand edge with a valley fold. (Do not repeat this fold on the other side.) Then repeat steps 12 through 20 on the upper edge of the model. When you have finished, the model will lie flat.

21 The model is now in the form of a square with a head (upper right) and a tail (lower left). Fold the entire square in quarters. Make creases here through step 24 heavy (H) or light (L) as indicated.

22 Fold in eighths.

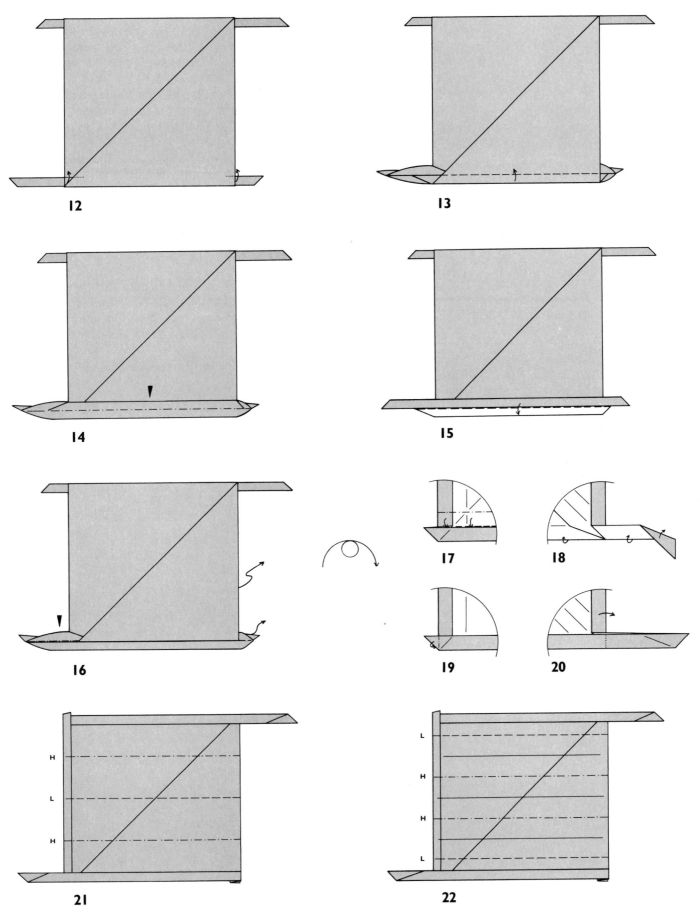

12

13

14

15

16

17

18

19

20

21

22

23 Fold in sixteenths.

24 Make ten crimps as shown. Solid lines show existing creases that are used only for reference. New creases made in this step are marked with *x*'s.

25 Roll into a cylinder. It may help to roll the paper around a cardboard tube. Press firmly.

26 Unroll and open up to step 24, but do not flatten.

27 This is the most difficult step in the model. Roll the paper once again, and interlock the two edges. Making sure to hold the edges in place, align the horizontal strips so that like creases slide into like creases. Then re-form the creases from step 24 all around the model. (This takes patience and several pairs of hands.) The horizontal strips form one long, continuous spiral.

28 Here through step 36 are details of the head. (Note that the head and tail are no longer identical. Make sure this is the correct flap.) Outside reverse–fold the head flap. Tuck the loose paper into the base of the "neck."

29 Closed-sink to form the head.

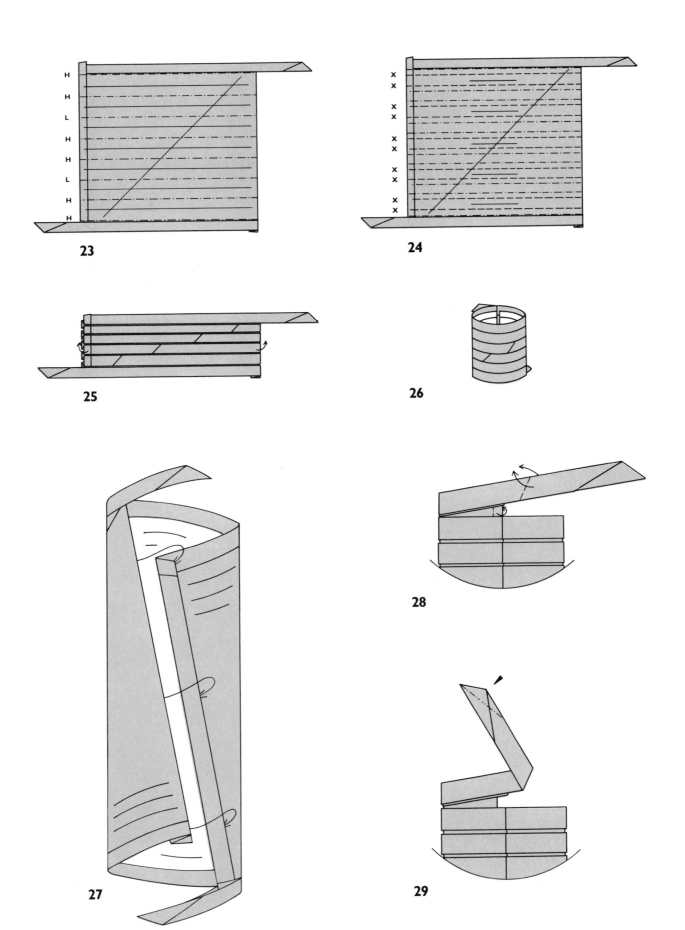

23

24

25

26

27

28

29

30 Spread the sides of the paper.

31 Here through step 33 are front views of the head. Crimp to form the tongue.

32 Pull out the loose paper from behind the head to change the color of the tongue.

33 Close the head.

34 Crimp the head downward.

35 Round the back of the head. Narrow the jaw. Curl the tongue.

36 The head is finished.

37 Here through step 38 are details of the tail. Pleat as symmetrically as possible to form the rattles. Tuck the loose paper into the base of the tail.

38 Narrow the rattles, and curl the tip of the tail upward. Pinch the coils all around to curve the body of the snake.

The completed RATTLESNAKE.

(1984)

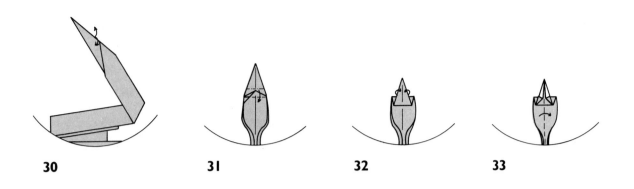

30　　　**31**　　　**32**　　　**33**

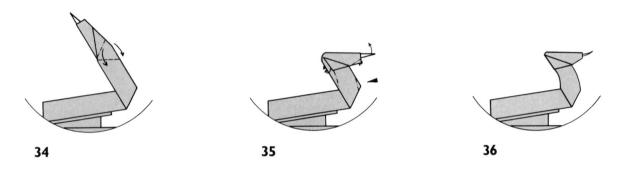

34　　　**35**　　　**36**

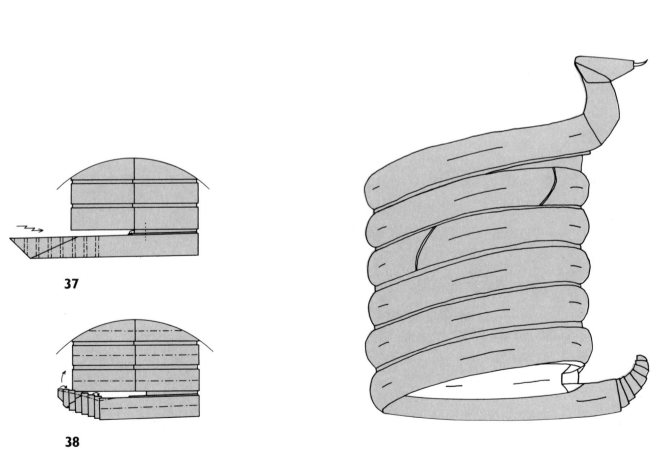

37

38

ALLIGATOR

Use a sheet of paper colored on one side. A 10-inch square will produce a model 6½ inches long.

1 Crease the sides to the centerline and unfold.
2 Valley-fold where the creases meet the edge. This is the familiar kite base.
3 Valley-fold the upper flap so that the crease meets the tip of the shaded flap. Unfold the shaded flap.

4 Inside reverse–fold the sides.
5 The result is a form of off-center preliminary fold. Turn the model over.
6 Valley-fold edge to edge. The hidden paper will stretch.

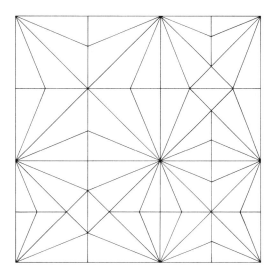

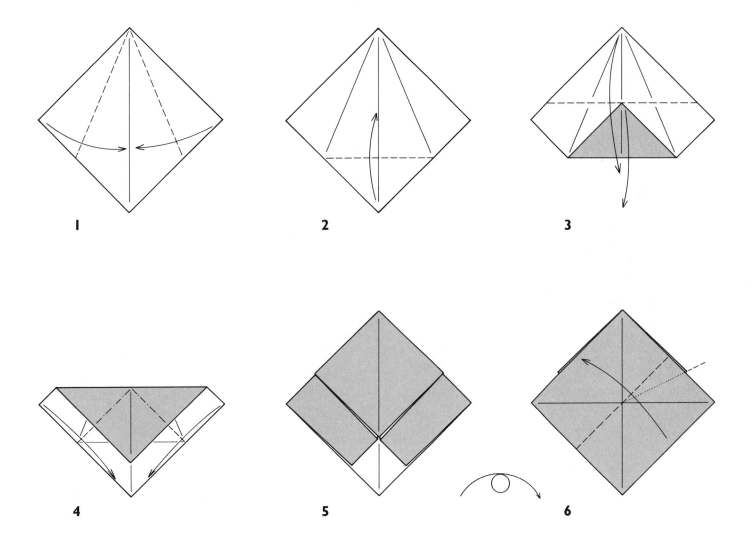

1

2

3

4

5

6

7 Inside reverse–fold to the centerline.
8 Unfold to step 6.
9 Repeat steps 6 through 8 on the opposite page.

10 Inside reverse–fold the sides to the centerline.
11 Lift and flatten. This is a form of petal fold.
12 Inside reverse–fold to the centerline.

13 Valley-fold two flaps over to the left.
14 Following the existing creases, swing the lower corner upward. Only the valley folds are new.
15 Valley-fold two flaps back to step 13.

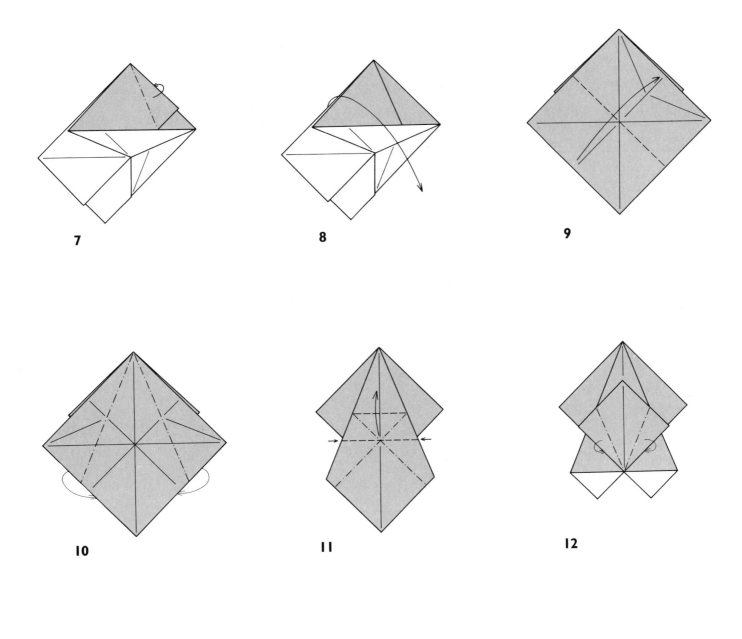

7

8

9

10

11

12

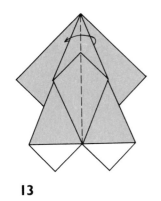

13

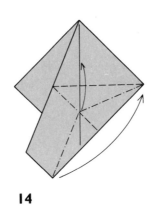

14

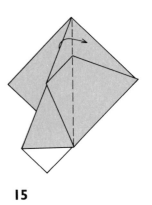

15

ALLIGATOR ■ 223

16 Repeat steps 13 through 15 on the opposite side.
17 Turn the model over.
18 Valley-fold edge to edge.

19 Inside reverse—fold the upper shaded flap to the centerline. In a single motion, pull out the loose paper and swing down the lower shaded flap to the centerline.
20 Valley-fold the shaded flap to the right-hand corner.
21 Valley-fold the shaded flap to the left.

22 Narrow the white portion of the flap with valley folds, and swing the tip to the right.
23 Swivel the entire assembly counterclockwise about point x.
24 Valley-fold horizontally at the midline (this is where the crease falls naturally), and tuck the tip underneath.

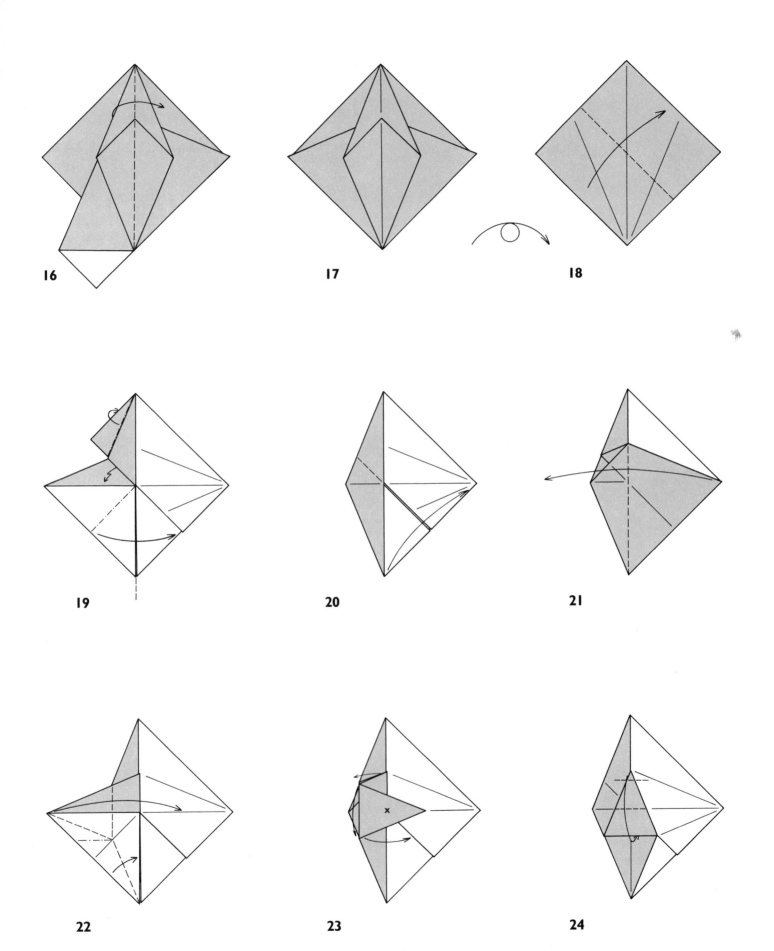

16

17

18

19

20

21

22

23

24

25 Valley-fold to the left. This completes the left hip. The shaded lower flap will be the left hind leg.
26 Return the upper-right-hand flap to position 18.
27 Repeat steps 18 through 26 on the opposite side.

28 Inside reverse—fold the sides to the centerline.
29 Lift and flatten, as in step 11. This is also a form of petal fold.
30 Lift the tip and stretch. This completes the petal fold.

31 Inside reverse—fold the two central flaps. These will be the front legs.
32 Turn the model over.
33 Crease the triangle in half lightly. Valley-fold the tip down to meet the light crease and press firmly. Unfold.
34 Stretch the lower tip as far as it will go but do not flatten. This flap will be the tail.

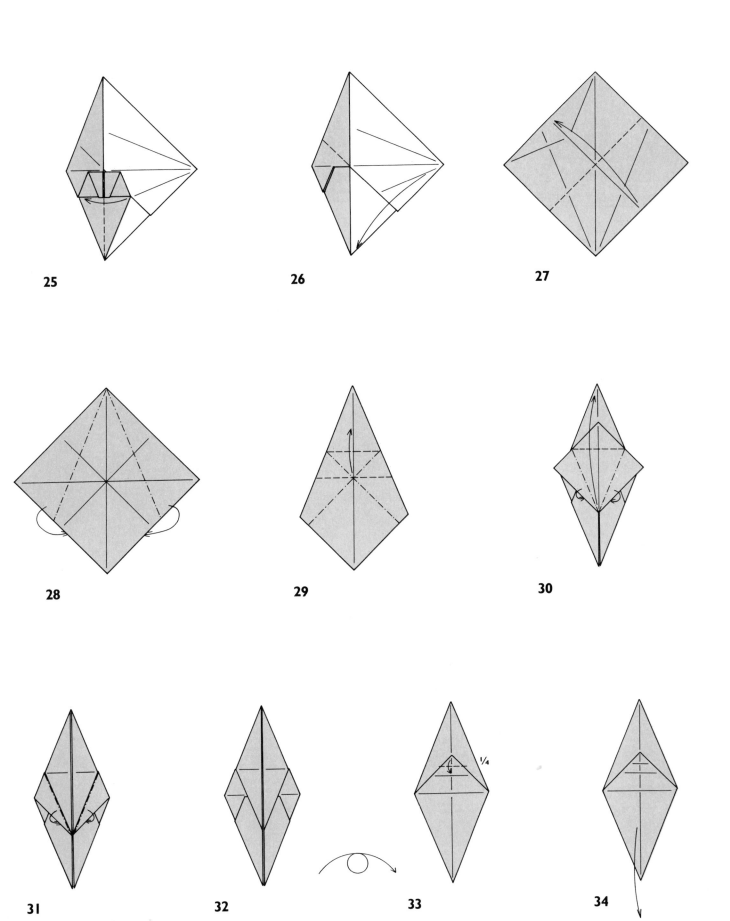

25

26

27

28

29

30

31

32

33

1/4

34

35 Fold the tail back up, forming an open sink along the existing creases.

36 Valley-fold the tail at the base of the sink. Stretch the tip of the tail, but not as far as before. The central, sunk portion will squash. Flatten carefully.

37 Valley-fold the sides toward the centerline, but not to the very tip of the tail.

38 Valley-fold the model in half.

39 Inside reverse—fold the four legs symmetrically.

40 Tuck the four legs into the pockets behind.

41 The two flaps on the right-hand side will be the upper and lower jaws. Crimp the lower jaw and the tail symmetrically. The details show the direction of the creases as seen from below.

42 Outside reverse—fold the upper jaw.

43 The newly exposed flap on the right-hand side will be the tongue. Crimp the legs, tail, and tongue symmetrically.

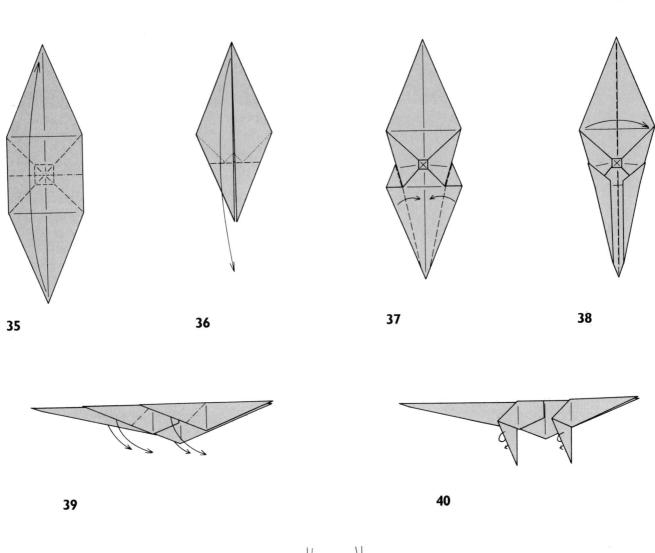

35

36

37

38

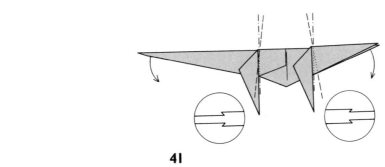

39

40

41

42

43

44 Here through step 49 are details of the head. Valley-fold both sides of the lower jaw. Tweezers may help.

45 Narrow the tongue with mountain folds. Tuck the loose paper inside. Tweezers may help again.

46 Spread the lower jaw to make a spoon shape. Flatten the tongue. Swing the upper jaw back to its original position.

47 Swivel the upper jaw forward, pulling out loose paper from the body.

48 Crimp the upper jaw. Inside reverse—fold the tips of the upper and lower jaws to form teeth.

49 An opening runs all the way along the back of the model. To fatten the 'gator, insert your finger into the opening, and push down the loose paper contained in the belly and the lower jaw. Round the head.

The completed ALLIGATOR.

(1987)

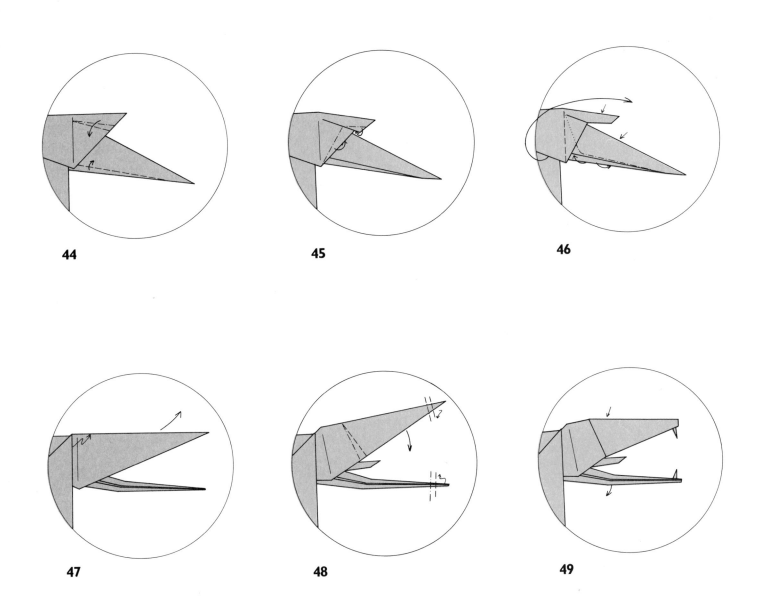

44

45

46

47

48

49

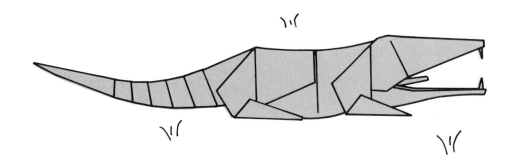

TIGER

Use a sheet of paper colored on one side. A 10-inch square will produce a model 5 inches long.

1 Mountain-fold the lower corners to the center.
2 Valley-fold the top layer only. Crease only as far as the lines indicate.
3 Valley-fold the small white square.

4 Unfold to step 1.
5 Valley-fold the lower edge of the square at the intersection of the existing creases.
6 Valley-fold the upper edge of the square so it meets the lower edge.
7 Mountain-fold the model in half.

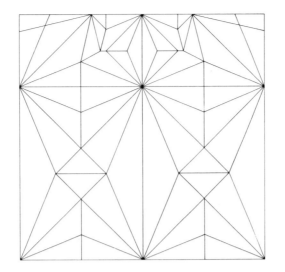

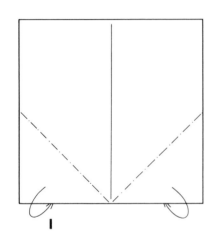

1

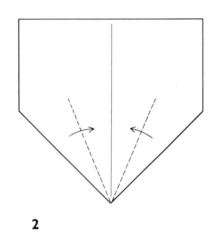

2

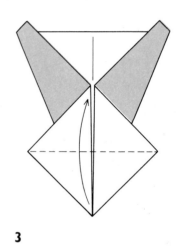

3

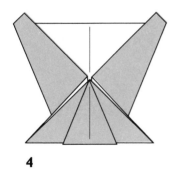

4

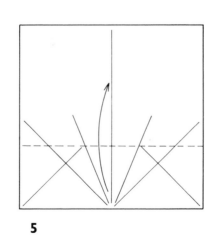

5

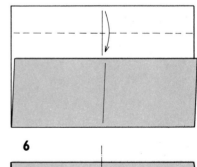

6

7

8 The paper is open at the bottom. Crimp the two sides symmetrically.

9 Valley-fold the two sides. Repeat behind.

10 Unfold to step 1.

11 Following the existing creases, rabbit's-ear the left-hand side.

12 Valley-fold where the crease falls naturally.

13 Following the existing creases, stretch the shaded corner as far as it will go.

14 Again following the existing creases, valley-fold the right-hand flap over to the left. The upper edge of the paper will swing down automatically.

15 Valley-fold the cut edge of the shaded flap to the folded edge.

16 Valley-fold the cut edge of the white triangle to the folded edge.

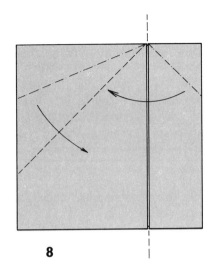

8

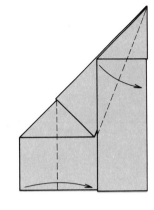

9

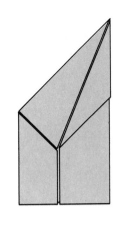

10

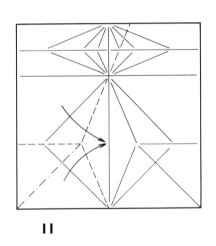

11

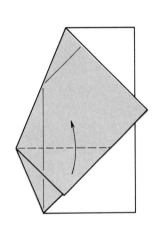

12

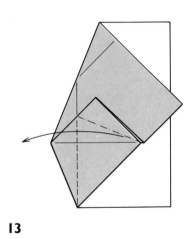

13

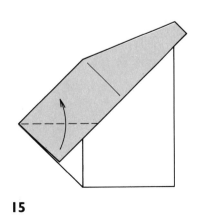

14

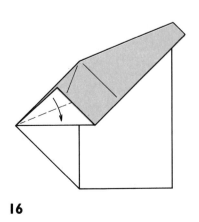

15

16

17 Valley-fold at the intersection of the folded edge and the existing crease.
18 Unfold to step 16.
19 Repeat the valley fold from step 17 on the entire white triangle.

20 Repeat the valley fold from step 16.
21 Tuck the entire assembly underneath.
22 Following the existing creases, rabbit's-ear the right-hand side. This step is the mirror image of step 11.

23 Valley-fold where the crease falls naturally. This step is the mirror image of step 12.
24 Following the existing creases, stretch the shaded corner as far as it will go. This step is the mirror image of step 13.
25 Again following the existing creases, valley-fold the left-hand flap over to the right. The upper edge of the paper will swing down automatically. This step is the mirror image of step 14.

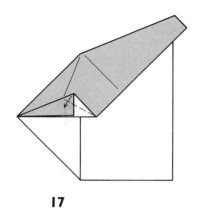

17

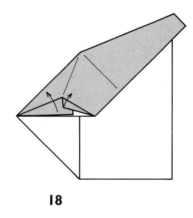

18

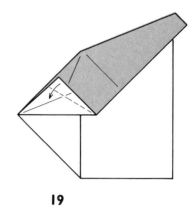

19

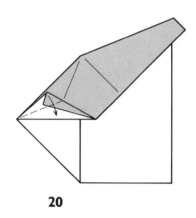

20

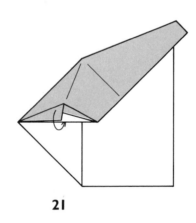

21

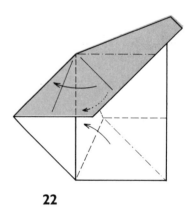

22

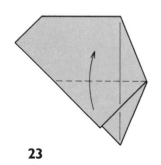

23

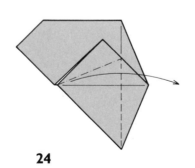

24

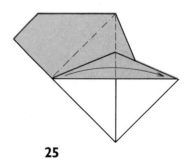

25

26 Repeat steps 15 through 21 in mirror image.

27 Inside reverse–fold the shaded flaps to the center-line.

28 Following the existing creases, collapse this flap in a single motion.

29 Valley-fold the central flaps upward, making the creases where they fall naturally. The loose paper behind the flaps will close automatically.

30 Valley-fold the central flaps back down, keeping the loose paper closed. In a single motion, pull out the loose paper and swing down the lower shaded flap to the centerline, as in step 19 of the ALLIGATOR.

31 Inside reverse–fold the two lower flaps. These will be the hind legs. The folds at the top are formed in a single motion. Find, on each side of the centerline, a discontinuous shaded flap with two layers. The junction of the two layers forms a tiny pocket containing the loose paper needed to make the shaded flap continuous. Inserting a thumb in the pocket on each side, stretch each shaded flap so that it becomes continuous. Following the existing creases, valley-fold each shaded flap to the centerline. The additional mountain and valley folds on the white portion will form automatically. Flatten.

32 The two central flaps will be the front legs. Valley-fold the upper portion down to cover the legs.

33, 34 These two steps are performed almost simultaneously. Rabbit's-ear the entire model carefully to avoid tearing the paper. As the model becomes three-dimensional, swing the front legs to either side, and the loose paper will tighten. Only the single ply underneath the model will have received a rabbit's ear. Flatten. The result appears in step 44.

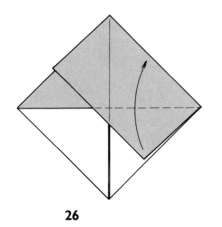

26

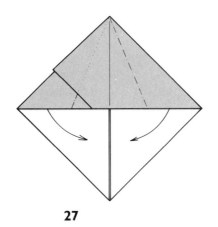

27

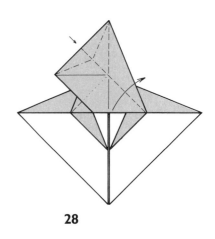

28

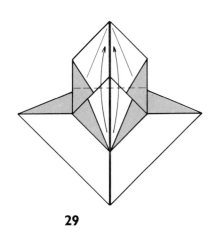

29

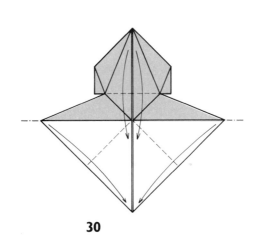

30

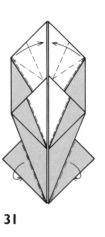

31

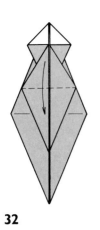

32

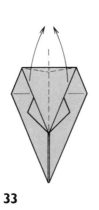

33

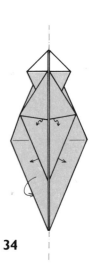

34

35 Here through step 43 are details of the head. Valley-fold where the crease falls naturally. Repeat behind.

36 The long valley fold divides the white flap into four equal angles. Collapse the paper upward. Repeat behind.

37 Inside reverse–fold edge to edge. Repeat behind.

38 Valley-fold the white flap edge to edge, and swing the small shaded triangle to the rear. This will be the right ear. Repeat behind.

39 Crimp the full thickness symmetrically.

40 Pull out the loose paper from either side to form the top of the head.

41 Crimp the lower jaw symmetrically.

42 Outside reverse–fold the lower jaw. Spread the ears. Outside reverse–fold the upper jaw to form the nose and tooth.

43 The head is completed.

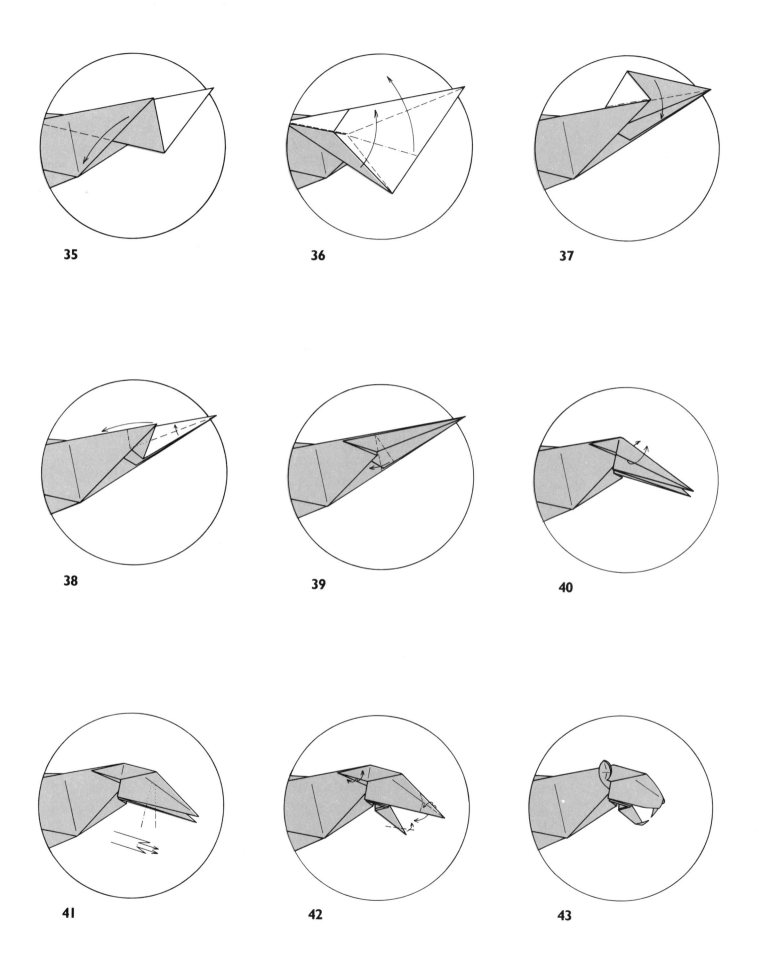

35

36

37

38

39

40

41

42

43

44 Here through step 50 show the body without the head details. Inside reverse–fold the front legs. Crimp the hind legs.

45 Inside reverse–fold the tail. The crease should divide into thirds the angle formed by the upper edge of the tail and the back edges of the hind legs. Crimp the hind legs. Valley-fold the front legs edge to edge.

46 Valley-fold the upper edges of the hind legs. Valley-fold the tail edge to edge, and tuck the loose paper inside. Pull out one ply of loose paper from each of the front legs.

47 Unfold the hind legs to step 45. Rabbit's-ear the tail on either side, and turn it inside out. Swivel the single ply of loose paper from each of the front legs as far forward as it will go.

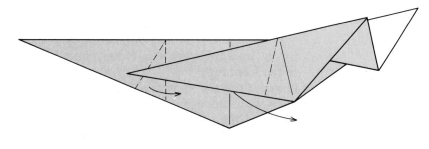

44

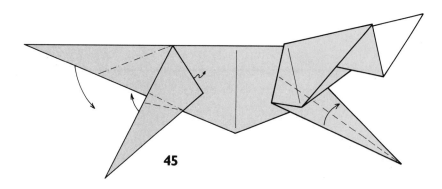

45

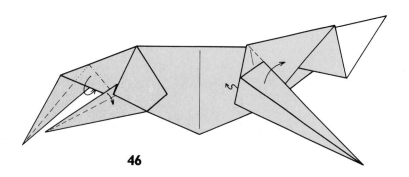

46

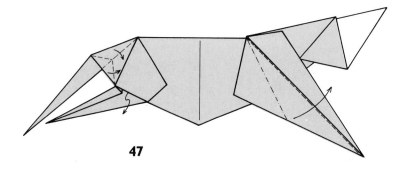

47

48 Following the existing creases, inside reverse–fold and crimp the hind legs symmetrically. Valley-fold the backs of the front legs. Mountain-fold the fronts of the front legs.

49 Narrow the tail with mountain folds. Narrow the belly with mountain folds on each side. Tuck the fronts of the front legs into the adjacent pockets, then valley-fold the front legs to the rear.

50 Narrow the belly again with mountain folds. Crimp the front legs symmetrically. Shape the tip of the tail.

The completed TIGER.

(1987)

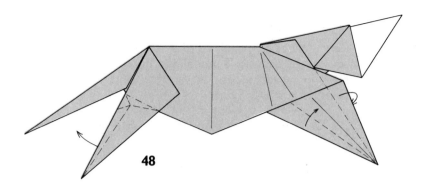

48

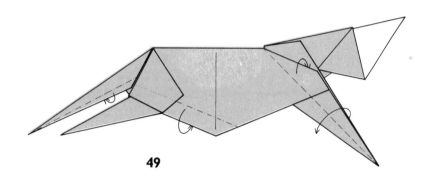

49

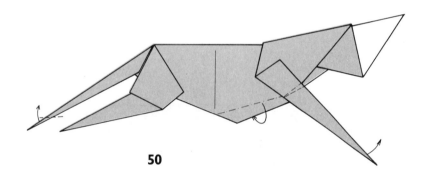

50

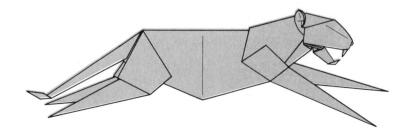

REINDEER

Use a sheet of paper colored on one side. A 10-inch square will produce a model 3 inches long. For your first attempt, use a square measuring at least 18 inches to a side.

1 Divide the square horizontally into quarters. Pleat like an accordion.
2 Crease lightly edge to edge. Repeat behind.
3 Valley-fold the corner so it meets the crease. Repeat behind.
4 Swing the front face down.
5 Valley-fold the left-hand edges to the centerline.

6 Following the edges of the existing flaps, rabbit's-ear behind. Turn the model over.
7 Following the edge of the existing flap, mountain-fold behind.
8 Following the edges of the hidden flaps, inside reverse—fold and close the model.

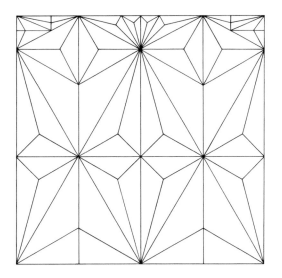

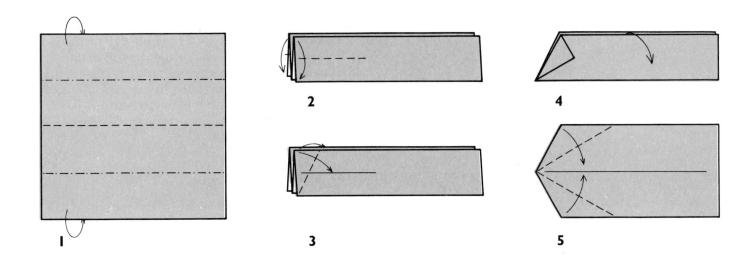

1

2

3

4

5

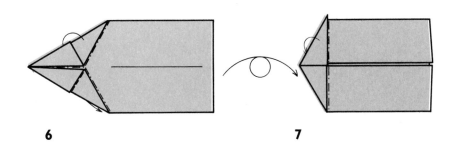

6

7

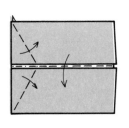

8

9 Following the edge of the hidden flap, valley-fold the lower-left-hand corner to the upper right. Repeat behind.

10 Valley-fold the right-hand edge to the left. The crease should lie on top of the former lower-left-hand corner. Crease firmly and unfold to step 9.

11 Following the existing creases, crimp the entire model symmetrically.

12 Unfold the entire square.

13 Following the existing creases, refold the square. In the middle of the paper are two vertices where many lines meet. These vertices will plunge downward as the left and right sides of the paper swing upward and toward each other.

14 Inside reverse–fold the two flaps projecting from the top. Valley-fold the two side flaps down and to the right.

15 Squash one flap.

16 Lift the loose paper upward, and close the flap.

17 Valley-fold two flaps up and to the left, returning them to their position in step 14.

18 Following the edge of the hidden flap, crease and unfold. Then swivel two flaps up and to the left. When you are done, the model will not lie flat.

19 The model is now three-dimensional. The exposed white portion shows paper that is seen almost directly on edge. Squash the shaded flap.

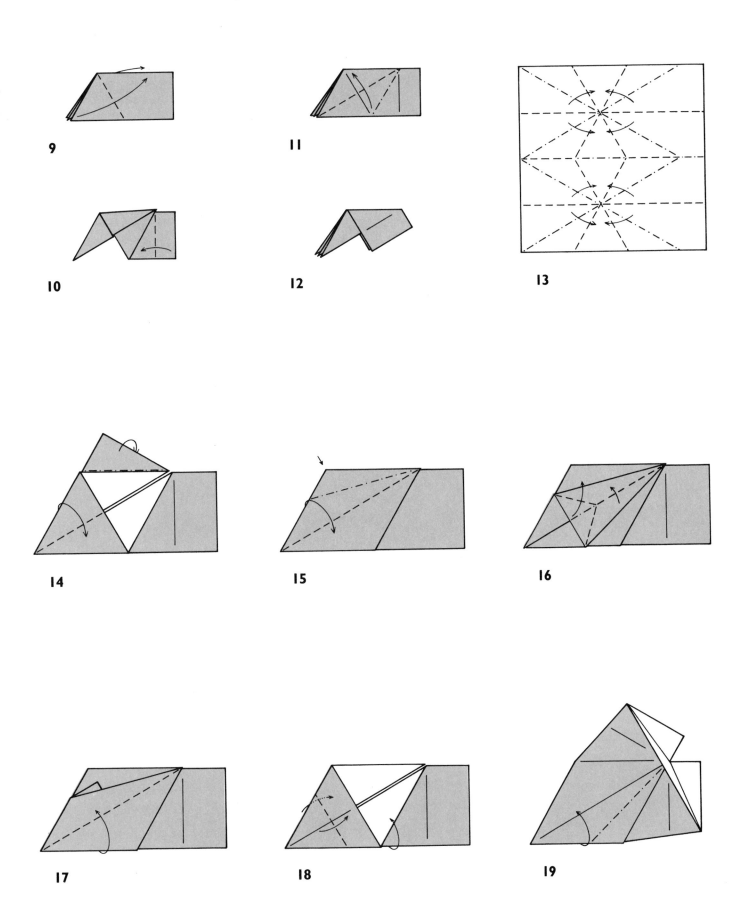

9

11

10

12

13

14

15

16

17

18

19

20 Lift the loose paper upward, as in step 16, and swing two flaps down and to the right.

21 Valley-fold the lower-left-hand corner up and to the right as far as it will go.

22 Push with your finger from behind to form a little pyramid of the shaded square. The square will pop forward and flatten.

23 Valley-fold the tip halfway, and unfold to step 22.

24 Following the existing creases, open double–sink and close the flap in the same motion.

25 This is a form of petal fold. Repeat behind.

26 Open up and spread the loose paper.

27 Following the existing creases, tuck the small triangle into the pocket behind and close the model in the same motion. Use tweezers. Repeat behind.

28 Swivel the flap at the left of the slot counterclockwise. The model will crimp symmetrically.

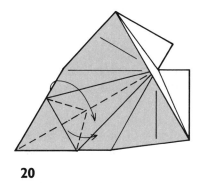

20

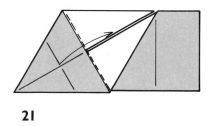

21

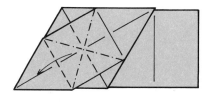

22

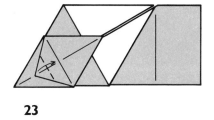

23

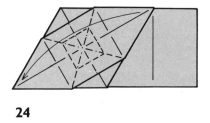

24

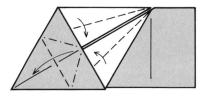

25

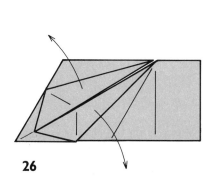

26

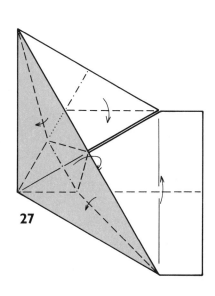

27

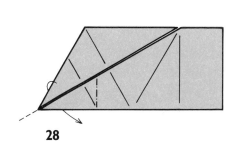

28

29 Open the model slightly and inside reverse–fold the entire assembly at the right. (This procedure could be called a "closed" inside reverse fold, because it pops directly from one position to another.) The central flap turns inside out in the process.

30 Valley-fold the white flap down and to the left. Repeat behind.

31, 32 Make individual creases as shown. Then, in a single motion, push in at the front of the model and collapse it into a three-dimensional rabbit's ear. Massage the creases into place. The result is symmetrical.

33 Valley-fold the shaded flap up and to the right. Repeat behind.

34 Inside reverse–fold through the shaded portion. Repeat behind.

35 Swing the white triangle down and to the right. The shaded portion of the flap will automatically swing down and to the left. Repeat behind.

36 Valley-fold the shaded flap up and to the right. Repeat behind.

37 Bring the three corners of the white triangle together, and collapse the loose paper like a fan. Repeat behind.

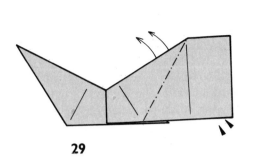

29

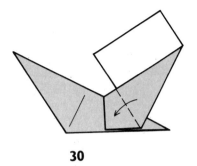

30

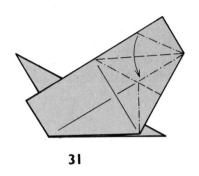

31

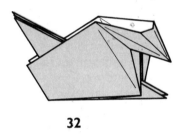

32

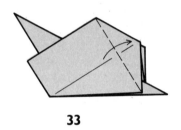

33

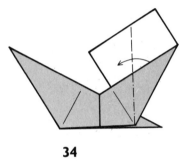

34

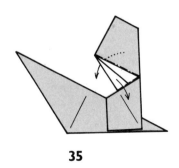

35

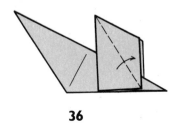

36

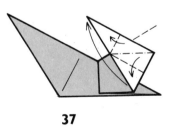

37

38 The flaps pointing up and to the left are the rear legs. Mountain-fold them, leaving the central tail flap in place. Valley-fold the white flap down and to the right. Inside reverse–fold the shaded tip. Repeat behind.

39 Crimp the legs. Swing the tail all the way underneath and forward. Narrow the white flap with valley folds, and swing it up and to the right. The shaded flaps pointing down and to the right are the front legs. Creasing lightly, lift up the flap obscuring the front leg. Repeat behind.

40 The position of the drawing has been rotated slightly. Inside reverse–fold the tail and swing it toward the rear. (This crease is hidden from view). Then, in a single motion, crimp the front legs and rotate the head and neck assembly clockwise. Narrow the hip with a mountain fold. Repeat behind.

41 Narrow the belly with mountain folds, and tuck the loose paper into the adjacent pockets formed by the tail. Narrow the front leg, valley-folding the double thickness. Swing one white flap and one shaded flap over to the left, and tuck the excess paper into the body. Repeat all folds behind.

42 Inside reverse–fold the hind leg. Without making any new creases, slide the top layer off the front leg, and tuck it into the pocket beneath. Cut-away view: Squash. Repeat all folds behind.

43 Narrow the hind leg symmetrically with valley folds, and tuck the loose paper inside with mountain folds. (The mountain folds will pinch the back of the hips slightly.) Slide another layer off the front leg. Turn the valley fold into a mountain fold, and tuck the layer into the pocket beneath. Cut-away view: Closed-sink the big flap. Squash the little flap at the top. Repeat all folds behind.

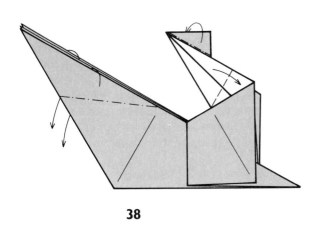

38

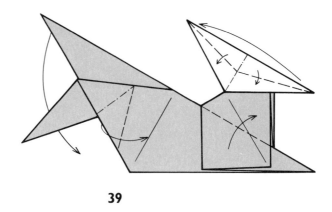

39

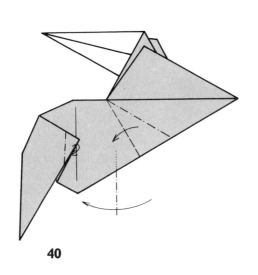

40

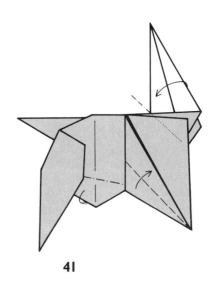

41

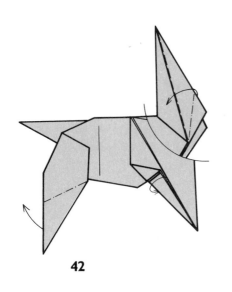

42

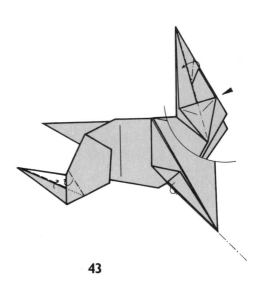

43

44 Inside reverse–fold the hind leg. Close the front leg with a valley fold. Crimp the tail symmetrically. Cutaway view: Closed-sink the little flap. Swing the big flap to the right. Repeat all folds behind.

45 Closed-sink two head flaps. Mountain-fold the top layer of the front leg. (Part of this crease is hidden from view.) Repeat both folds behind.

46 Squash the next head flap, and swing it to the rear. Repeat behind.

47 Lift the tiny triangle inside the squash fold, and collapse it upward. The white flap at the center of the model contains the head and the ears. Swing it into view.

48 Mountain- and valley-fold the head assembly, and collapse it upward. Flatten it. Then pull the front flap down slightly to expose the inside.

49 Open the head assembly slightly, and narrow all the flaps with valley folds. Flatten again.

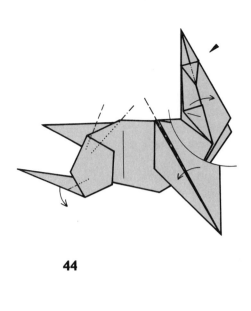

44

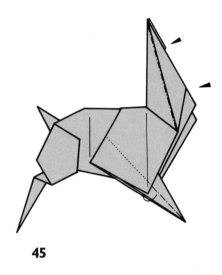

45

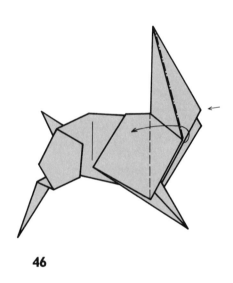

46

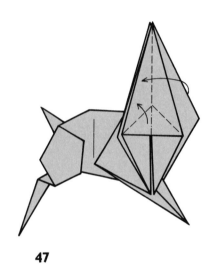

47

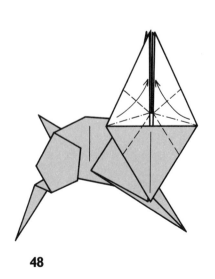

48

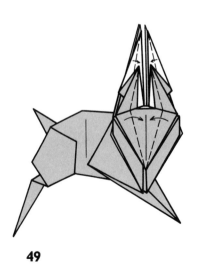

49

50 Open the head assembly slightly, and pull out the loose paper. Following the existing creases, flatten it into a petal fold.

51 Mountain-fold the tip of the single-ply triangle. This will be the eyes. Following the existing crease, swing the entire head assembly upward.

52 Valley-fold the head assembly to the right.

53 The model is now entirely symmetrical. Narrow the front leg with a valley fold. Repeat behind.

54 Narrow the belly with a mountain fold. Swing down the near antler. Repeat both folds behind.

55 Inside reverse–fold the adjacent antler. Repeat behind.

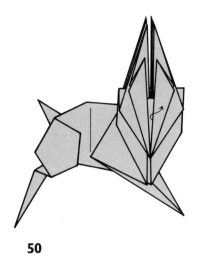

50

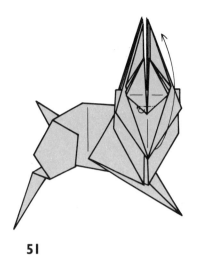

51

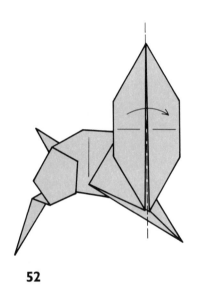

52

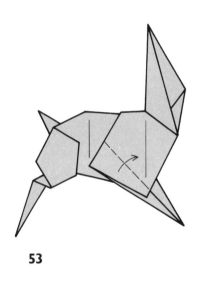

53

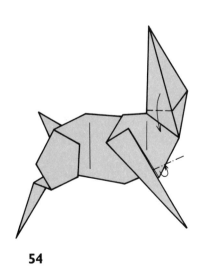

54

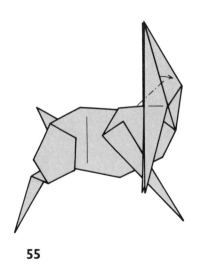

55

56 Here through step 63 are details of the head. Narrow the projecting antler with valley folds. Repeat behind.

57 Swing the projecting antler to the rear. Repeat behind.

58 Inside reverse–fold the rear antler. Swing up the front antler. Repeat behind.

59 Outside reverse–fold the rear antler to form the tine. Inside reverse–fold the front antler. Repeat behind.

60 Narrow the front antler with valley folds, and swing it to the rear. Repeat behind.

61 Inside reverse–fold the upper rear antler. Repeat behind. Inside reverse–fold the head through the base of the ears.

62 Separate the tines of the upper rear antler. Repeat behind. Turn the head flap inside out with valley folds on either side. The ears will pop up.

63 Outside reverse–fold the upper front tines. Spread the ears. Pull out the loose paper from either side of the neck to enlarge the jaw. Roll the tip of the head to form the nose.

The completed REINDEER.

(1976–78)

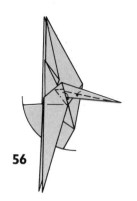

56

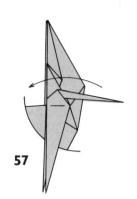

57

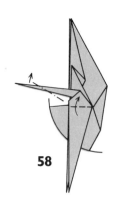

58

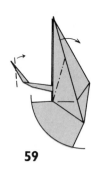

59

60

61

62

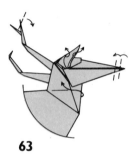

63

ELEPHANT

Use a sheet of paper colored on one side. A 10-inch square of paper will produce a model 2¾ inches long. For your first attempt, use a square measuring at least 18 inches to a side.

1 Valley-fold in half.
2 With the paper completely flat, valley-fold from the center to the corner.
3 Squash.

4 Valley-fold to the centerline and unfold.
5 Petal-fold. Ignore the creases made in the previous step.
6 Following the existing crease, valley-fold the small triangle.

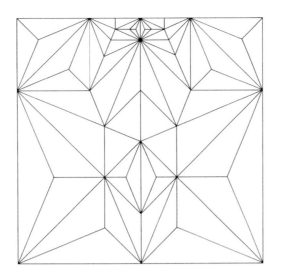

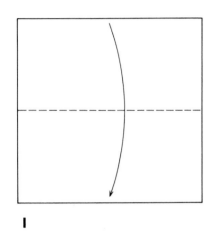

1

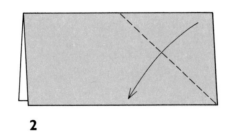

2

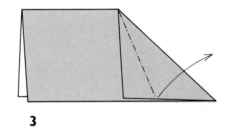

3

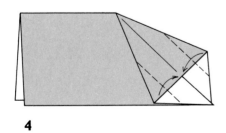

4

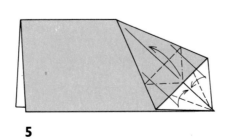

5

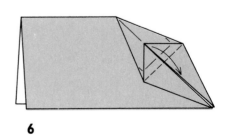

6

7 Open-sink the triangular portion on either side through the creases formed in step 4.

8 Following the existing creases, spread the sinks and valley-fold the loose paper to the centerline.

9 This is the tail. It will reappear later. Unfold to step 7.

10 Open the model slightly, and tuck the small triangle inside.

11 Mountain-fold the shaded flap behind.

12 The model is now symmetrical. Lift one ply, and swing it to the right. Flatten. New mountain folds will form automatically.

13 Valley-fold the left-hand triangle, using the hidden edge as a guide.

14 Valley-fold the right-hand triangle through the two corners.

15 Unfold both triangles. Repeat steps 13 through 15 on the opposite side.

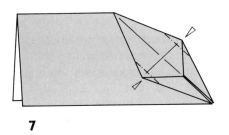

7

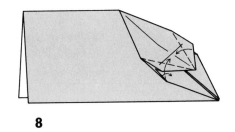

8

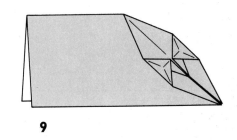

9

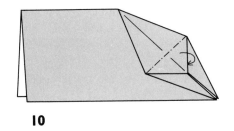

10

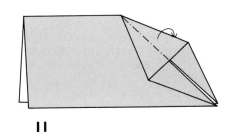

11

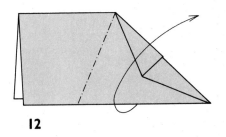

12

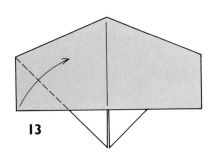

13

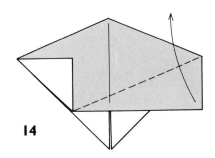

14

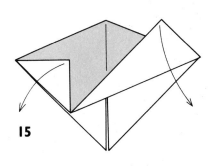

15

16 Turn the model over.
17 Valley-fold the bottom flaps to either side, and swing the entire assembly upward.
18 Swing the left-hand flap to the lower right. The tiny triangular flap at the apex of the model will double over.

19 Swing the left-hand flap back to its previous position. The tiny triangular flap will remain in place.
20 Open the model slightly, and closed-sink the upper layer of the triangular flap. Use tweezers to ease the paper into place. This step is very difficult.
21 Repeat steps 18 through 20 on the opposite side.

22 Swing the two white flaps upward.
23 Narrow the flaps with valley folds, and close them.
24 In the same motion, valley-fold the model in half and pull the tail toward you.

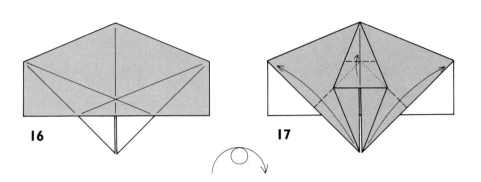

16

17

18

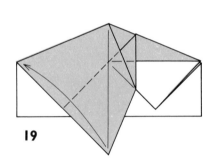

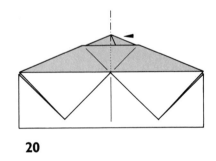

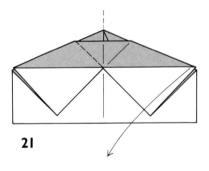

19

20

21

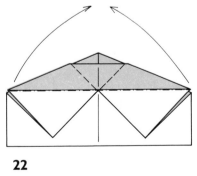

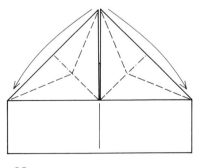

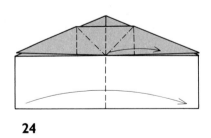

22

23

24

25 Hidden view: Refold steps 7 through 9, narrowing the tail. Repeat behind.

26 Following the hidden edge, inside reverse–fold the lower-right-hand corner.

27 With your right hand, grasp the model at the exposed spot marked *x*. With your left hand, grasp the model at the hidden spot marked *x*. Swivel the upper right of the paper clockwise until new mountain folds form as shown. The result is an open sink that should be performed symmetrically.

28 This is a form of rabbit's ear. Repeat behind so the model remains symmetrical.

29 These are two separate rabbit's ears, one on either side.

30 Spread the paper on both sides, and pull down.

31 Collapse the white portion like a fan. Repeat behind.

32 Swing the right-hand flap as far left as it will go, and it will narrow automatically. Repeat behind. Pull out the loose flap from under the belly.

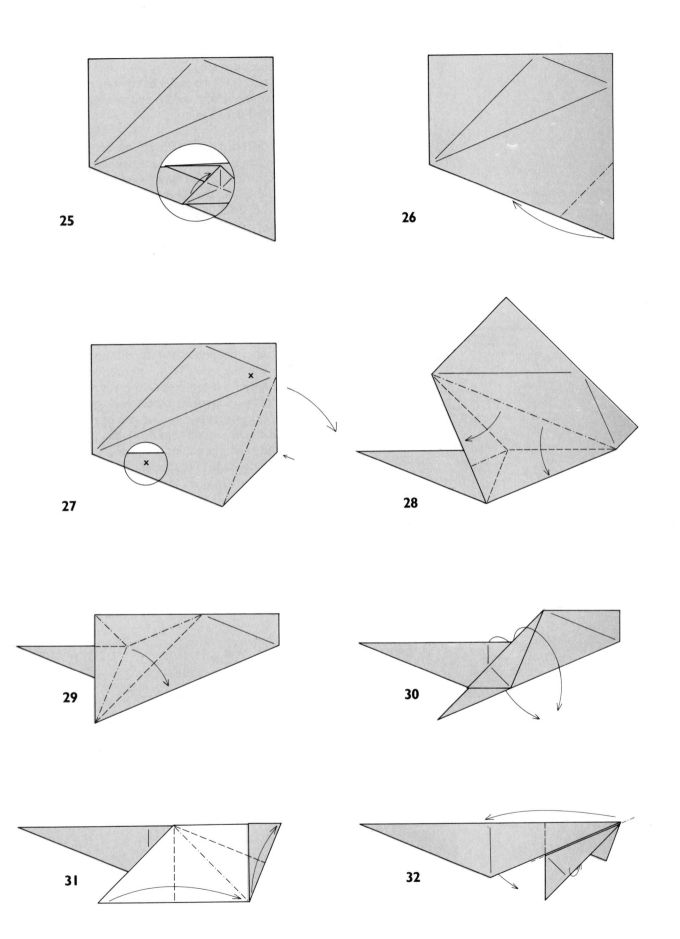

25

26

27

28

29

30

31

32

33 Inside reverse—fold the belly flap and the head flaps on either side.

34 Tuck the two sides of the belly flap into the outer-most pockets on either side. Inside reverse—fold the head flaps again.

35 The horizontal flap at the center is the front leg. Inside reverse—fold the front leg so that one layer falls on top and three below. The horizontal flap at the left is the hind leg. Valley-fold the hind leg; see step 36 for the exact location of the valley fold. Repeat both folds behind.

36 Note that the vertex of the triangular flap on the hind leg touches the vertical centerline. Valley-fold the hind leg back on itself so that the top of the valley fold touches the centerline and is perpendicular to the lower edge of the leg. Repeat behind.

37 Crimp the hind leg symmetrically. The mountain fold is perpendicular to the upper edge of the leg, while the valley fold is perpendicular to the bottom edge of the leg. Repeat behind.

38 This step involves three locking folds. Mountain-fold the loose paper to the left of the rear hip into the body. Mountain-fold the loose paper to the right of the rear hip behind the hip. Narrow the belly with a mountain fold that slightly pinches the belly flap last seen in step 34. Repeat all folds behind.

39 Here through step 54 are details of the head. Valley-fold where the crease falls naturally. This will be a tusk. Repeat behind.

40 Pull out the loose paper.

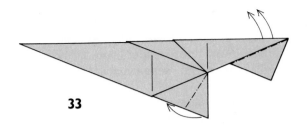

33

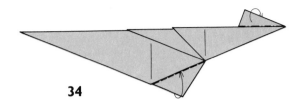

34

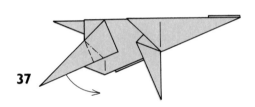

35

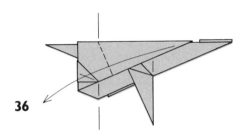

36

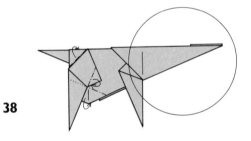

37

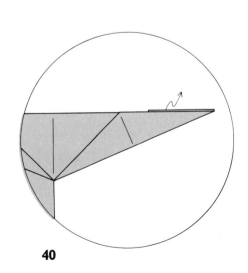

38

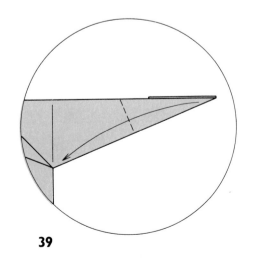

39

40

41 Crimp and swivel. The mountain fold is perpendicular to the upper edge, while the valley fold is perpendicular to the lower edge. Repeat behind.

42 Pull out the loose paper, and valley-fold it as far right as it will go. Repeat behind.

43 Turn the loose paper inside out, and tuck it underneath. Repeat behind.

44 Spread the front of the model slightly.

45 This is a top view. Making the creases where they fall naturally, collapse the loose paper toward the front of the model.

46 Inside reverse—fold the projecting flap, then unfold to step 44.

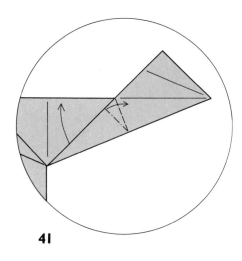

41

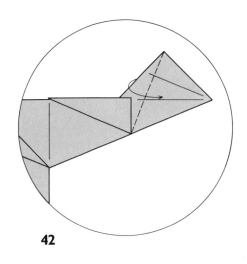

42

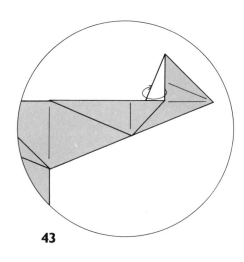

43

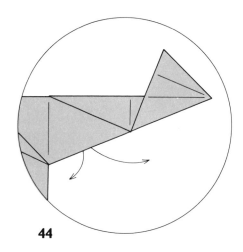

44

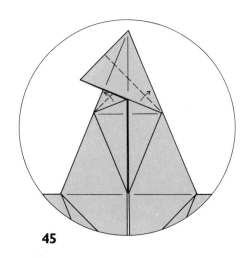

45

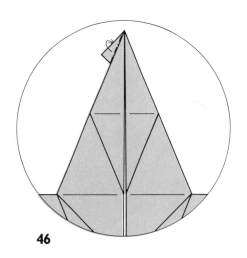

46

47 Following the existing creases, collapse the entire assembly symmetrically.

48 Crimp the neck symmetrically. On each side, the front ply goes outside the leg, the back ply inside. Swing the tusk forward. Repeat behind.

49 Inside reverse–fold the tusk and unfold. The creases are perpendicular to the lower edge of the trunk. Pull out a single ply of loose paper from behind the head, and release it. Repeat both folds behind.

50 Valley-fold the loose single ply to the right. Inside reverse–fold the tusk symmetrically. The creases divide into thirds the angle formed by the upper edge of the trunk and the crease made in the previous step. Repeat both folds behind.

51 Turn the tusk inside out so that white appears on the outside. Spread the flaps evenly on either side. Lift the loose paper at the base of the ear. The tiny mountain fold will form automatically. Repeat both folds behind.

52 Following the existing creases, crimp the tusk. Fold down the base of the ear. Repeat both folds behind.

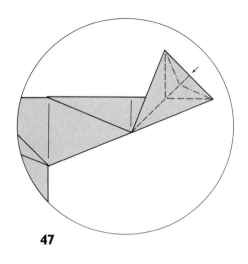

47

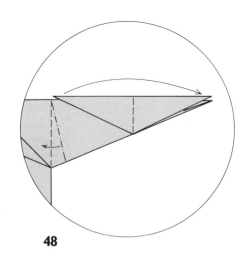

48

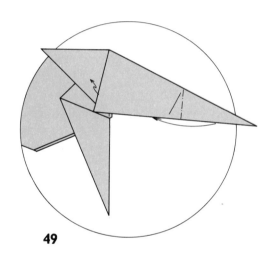

49

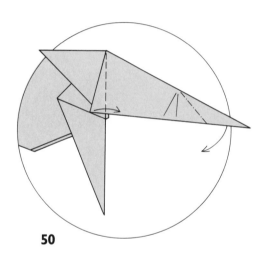

50

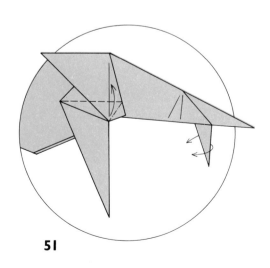

51

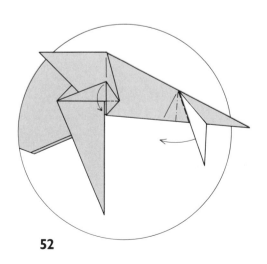

52

53 Open up the ear slightly, and closed-sink the little irregular pyramid. Repeat behind. Crimp the trunk symmetrically.

54 Narrow the tusk with valley folds on either side. Swing to the left the loose paper to the right of the ear. Open the body slightly, and pull out a single ply of paper from behind the leg. Repeat all folds behind. Swivel the trunk to the rear with a tiny, hidden crimp.

55 Inside reverse–fold the tip of the ear. Swing the tusk forward with a hidden inside reverse–fold. Tuck the front leg into the pocket beneath. Repeat all folds behind. Inside reverse–fold the tail.

56 Crimp the legs, and inside reverse–fold the tips to form the feet. Narrow the tail with valley folds, and tuck the loose paper inside. Round the body. Curl the trunk, and separate the "fingers" at the tip of the trunk.

The completed ELEPHANT.

(1985–87)

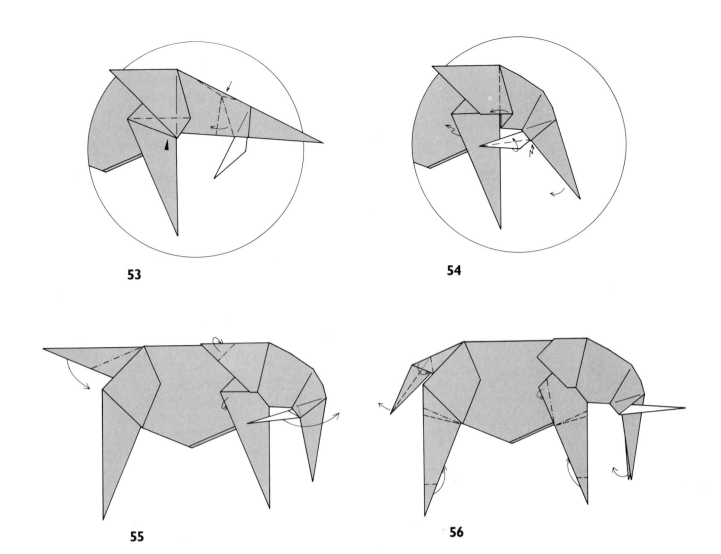

53

54

55

56

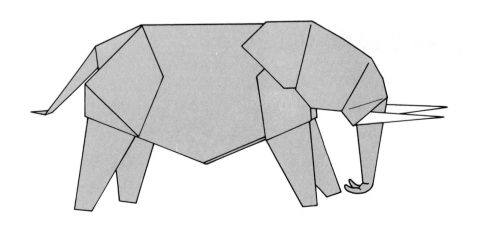

KNIGHT ON HORSEBACK

For this model, I have borrowed a model of a unicorn, designed by Patricia Crawford, and transformed it, minus the horn, into the base for a mounted knight. (Instructions to Crawford's unicorn can be found in Robert Harbin's *Origami: A Step-by-Step Guide;* see Notes and Sources). The knight and the horse are folded from the same sheet of paper and take their colors from the opposite sides. In this version, the knight will appear white and the horse shaded. A 10-inch square will produce a model 2¾ inches tall. For your first attempt, use a square measuring at least 18 inches to a side.

1 Divide the square horizontally into quarters. Pleat like an accordion.
2 Inside reverse–fold the corners.
3 Inside reverse–fold through the center.
4 Open the model completely, and turn the right side inside out.
5 The right side is now white. Inside reverse–fold the left side.

6 Rotate the shaded side to the front and the white side to the rear.
7 Pull down two flaps.
8 Form a preliminary fold from the shaded face only.

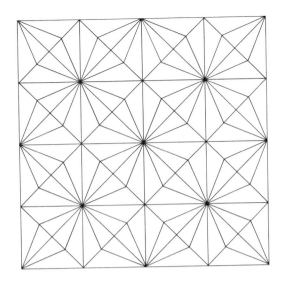

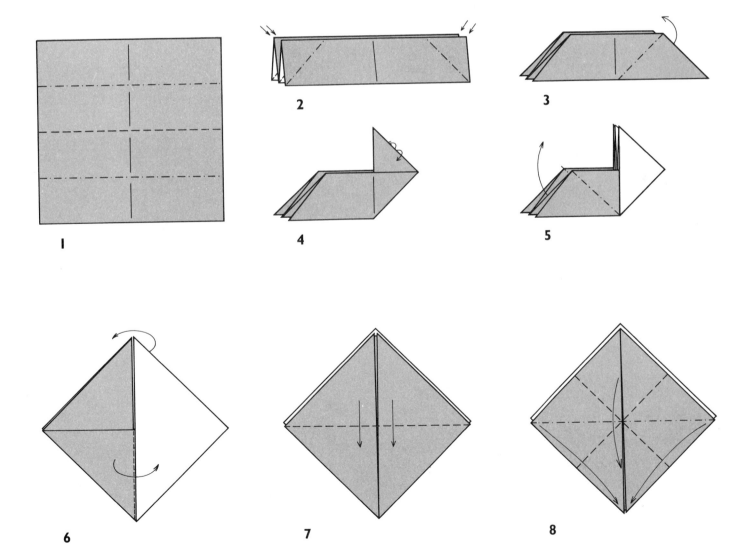

1

2

3

4

5

6

7

8

9 Inside reverse–fold the front shaded layer.

10 Inside reverse–fold the second shaded layer.

11 The result is a form of bird base. Turn the model over.

12 Form a preliminary fold from the white face. Fold all the layers together as one.

13 Inside reverse–fold the sides of the front white layer.

14 Inside reverse–fold the sides of the second white layer. Turn the model over.

15 Lift the front shaded layer, and stretch it as far as it will go.

16 The model is now three-dimensional. Rabbit's-ear the two projecting flaps, and flatten.

17 The model is now flat, and the result is a form of stretched bird base. Repeat steps 15 and 16 on the white side.

18 Valley-fold the entire model in half, but do not press it flat.

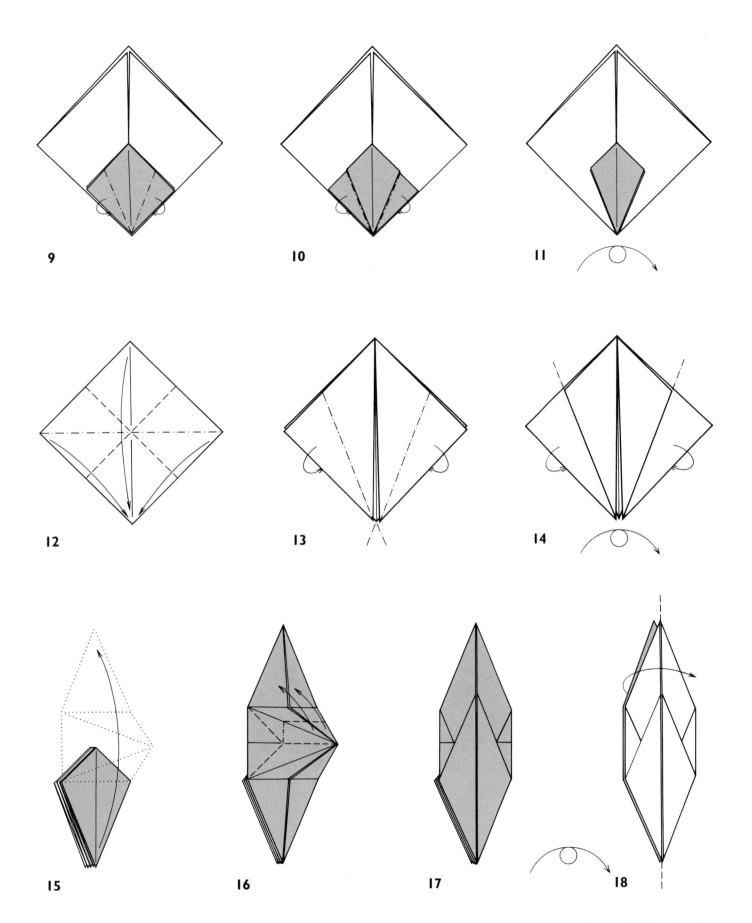

9

10

11

12

13

14

15

16

17

18

19 Slide the white half away from the shaded half.

20 Unfold the inside of the white half.

21 Following the existing creases, turn the white half inside out. Flatten the entire model.

22 The white half will be the knight and the shaded half the horse. Mountain-fold the length of the knight. The crease should meet the intersection of the existing folds. Crease firmly with tweezers and unfold.

23 Spread the white flaps to either side of the horse, and swivel the knight clockwise.

24 Inside reverse—fold two white flaps as far as they will go. These will be the knight's sword and shield.

25 Here through step 27 are details of the sword and shield. Valley-fold the sword and the shield front and back.

26 Swing the top edges of the sword and the shield as far down as possible.

27 Form tiny crimps, as shown in the detail. If possible, avoid crimping the full thickness of the body. Repeat behind.

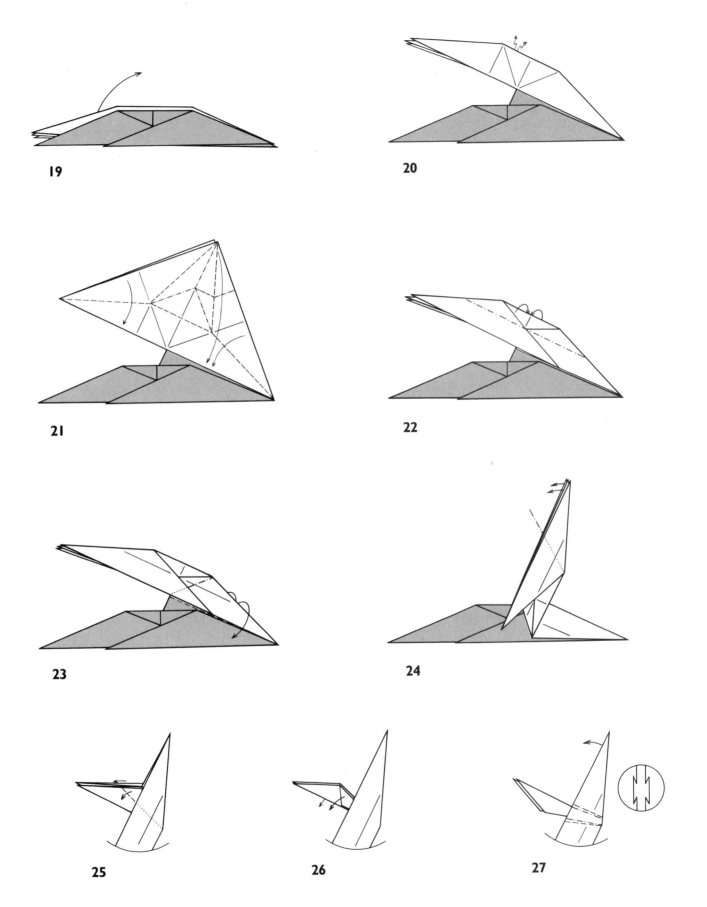

19

20

21

22

23

24

25

26

27

28 Narrow the knight's body by mountain-folding the existing crease. Narrow the knight's head by making a new mountain fold that slopes slightly forward. The valley fold will form automatically. Repeat behind.

29 Crimp the flap hidden inside the knight's body, as shown in the detail. In the same motion, rotate the knight counterclockwise and mountain-fold the white paper at the rear. The model should remain symmetrical.

30 This step is the most difficult in the model. There are two flaps at the rear of the horse that are partly white and partly shaded. Carefully closed-sink these two flaps into the rear of the horse. Reach into the opening at the front of the knight's body with your finger or with tweezers to guide the sink into place.

31 Tuck the exposed white flaps at the rear of the knight into the horse's body. Rabbit's-ear the horse's front legs. Inside reverse–fold the horse's hind legs. Inside reverse–fold the horse's neck. There is a tiny flap at the base of the knight's body left over from the crimp in step 29. Tuck it inside, as shown in the details.

32 Open the horse's neck and front legs completely, and turn the neck inside out. Of the two white flaps protruding from the front of the knight, choose one to be the shield, and squash it downward. (Do not repeat this fold on the other white flap.) Crimp the knight's legs, and form feet. Valley-fold the outermost layer on the horse's hind legs.

33 Closed-sink the horse's neck halfway. Swing the outermost layer on the horse's hind legs toward the front. Repeat both folds behind.

34 Here through step 38 are details of the horse's hind leg. Repeat all folds on the other leg. Mountain-fold to the centerline.

35 Inside reverse–fold through half of the hidden back flap.

36 Inside reverse–fold again, through the same half flap.

37 Narrow the edge of the leg with a tiny mountain fold.

38 This is the back view of the completed hind leg.

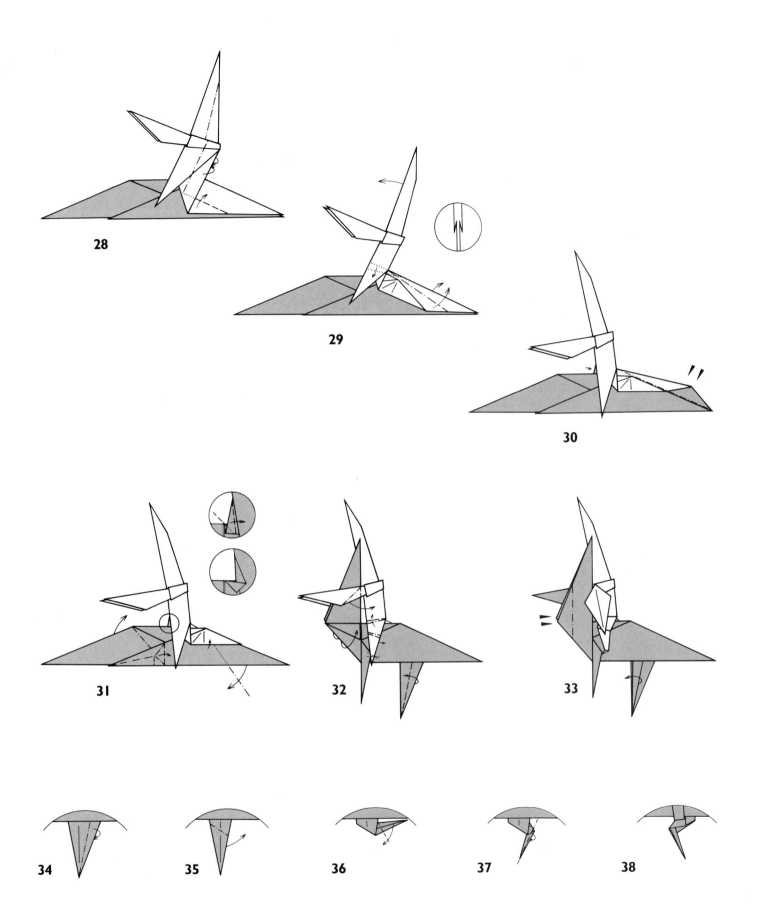

28

29

30

31

32

33

34

35

36

37

38

39 Here through step 45 are details of the horse's tail. Inside reverse–fold the full thickness of the tail. Be careful not to tear the paper. If the paper is bulky, you may have to approximate this step.

40 Inside reverse–fold through the white portion.

41 Crimp the loose paper to form the hip. Repeat behind.

42 Crimp the tail symmetrically, and spread the paper.

43 Note that a small white triangle has appeared. Swing the shaded portion to the right to cover the white portion.

44 Swing one shaded ply back to the left.

45 Crimp the body with tweezers to make the hip more pronounced. Release.

46 Here through step 50 are details of the horse's head. Inside reverse–fold the neck.

47 Outside reverse–fold the end of the neck to form the head. The loose paper will swing back to the right.

48 Pinch the head to form the ears. Inside reverse–fold the head to form the nose and the mouth.

49 Pinch the ears, and tuck the excess paper into the head.

50 The horse's head is completed.

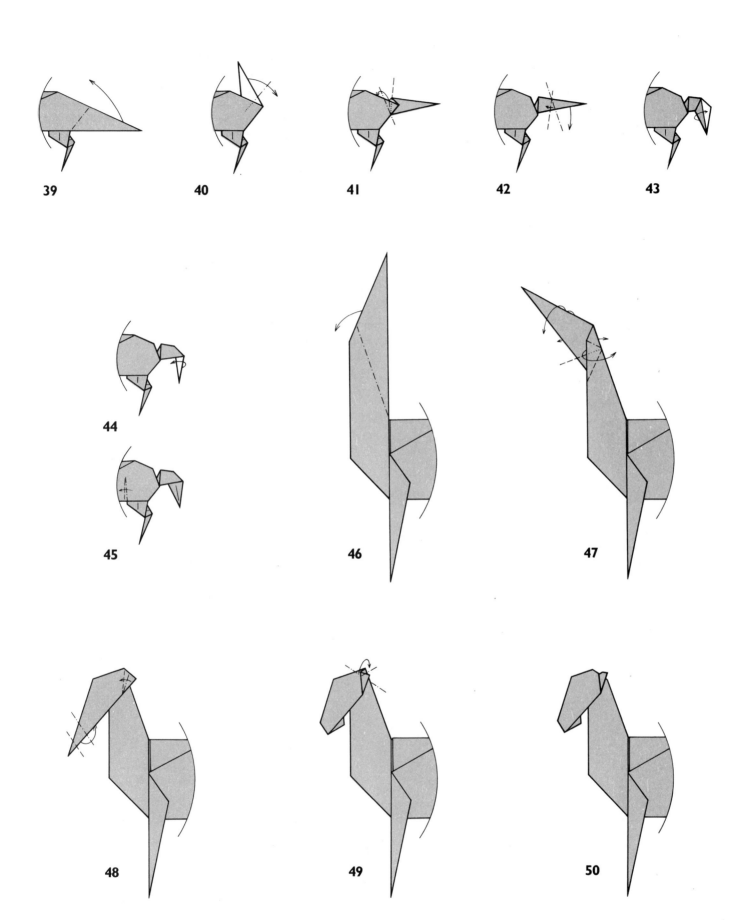

39

40

41

42

43

44

45

46

47

48

49

50

51 Here through step 57 are details of the knight's head and torso. Outside reverse–fold the head to form the helmet. Sink the top of the shield, and lift the entire shield upward. Inside reverse–fold the lower tip of the shield. Mountain-fold the sides of the shield. Curve the body of the shield. Round the knight's arm with tweezers.

52 The shield is completed. Outside reverse–fold the helmet. Pull out the loose paper from under the visor. Repeat behind. Turn the model over.

53 Pull out the loose paper from the top of the visor, and flatten it along the existing crease. Narrow the sword, and pleat it backward toward the body.

54 Pinch the sword to make it three-dimensional. Inside reverse–fold the tip of the visor.

55 Pinch the sword again to narrow it. Crimp the tip of the visor.

56 Round the knight's head, arm, and body. Tilt the sword upward.

57 The knight's head and torso are completed.

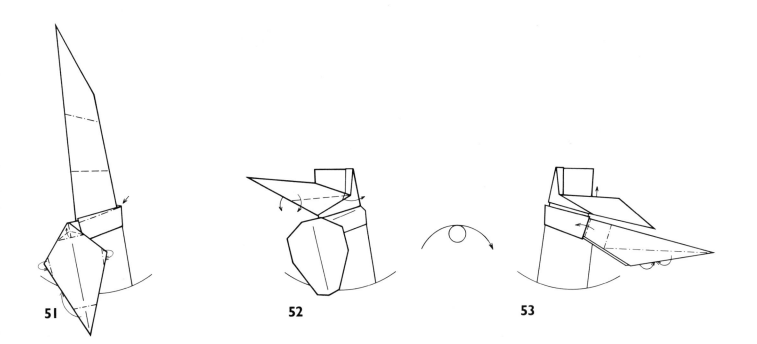

51

52

53

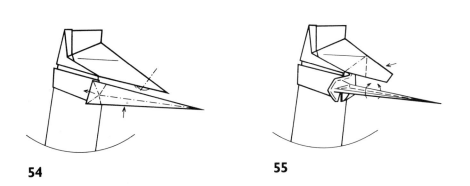

54

55

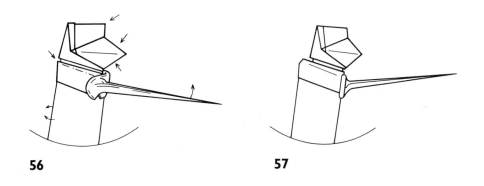

56

57

58 Here through step 66 are details of an alternative helmet. Treat the sword and the shield as in steps 51 through 56. Inside reverse–fold the head.
59 Narrow the paper hidden inside the helmet. Repeat behind.
60 Inside reverse–fold the projecting flap. This will be a plume.
61 Outside reverse–fold the plume.

62 Pinch the end of the plume.
63 Outside reverse–fold the tip.
64 Pull out the loose paper from the tip.
65 Shape the tip. Round the helmet.
66 The alternative helmet is completed.

The completed KNIGHT ON HORSEBACK in battle.

(1975–77, revised 1986)

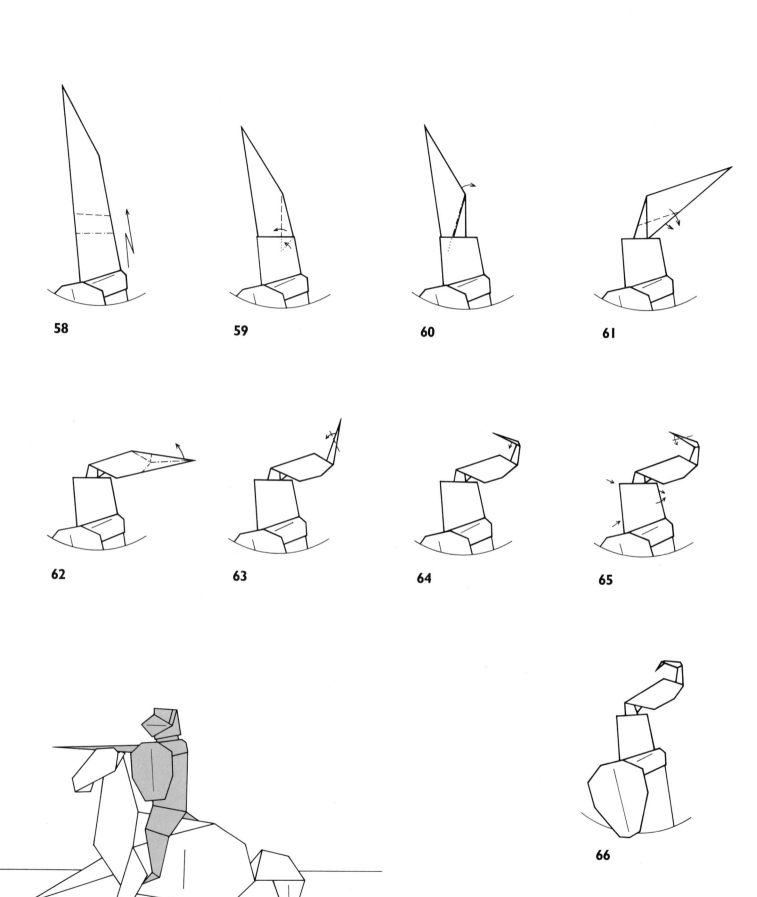

58

59

60

61

62

63

64

65

66

BUTTERFLY

Use a sheet of paper colored brightly on one side. A 10-inch square will produce a model with a 5-inch wing-span. For your first attempt, use a square measuring at least 18 inches to a side.

1 Blintz-fold.
2 Preliminary-fold.
3 Valley-fold the sides to the centerline. Repeat behind.
4 Valley-fold the tip, then unfold the entire square.

5 Valley-fold the corners of the paper to the corners of the small square.
6 Valley-fold the edges to make another square.
7 Collapse the model with mountain and valley folds.
8 Open-sink the shaded square.

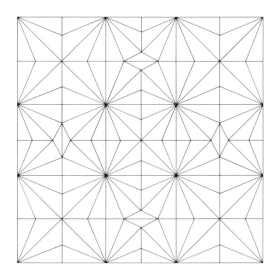

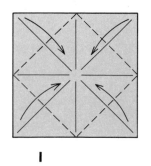

1

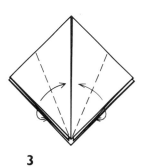

2

3

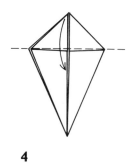

4

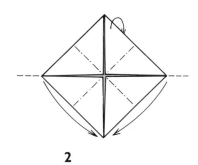

5

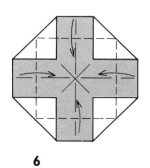

6

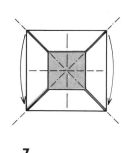

7

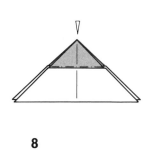

8

9 Two spots marked *x* appear on diagonally opposite sides. Holding each side at *x*, rotate them about the hidden center of the paper. Flatten.

10 The dotted line shows the internal edge. Squash the front and back flaps.

11 Squash the two side flaps, and swing them upward.

12 Inside reverse–fold the two side flaps downward.

13 Note that four-fold symmetry has returned. Inside reverse–fold the eight side flaps.

14 Inside reverse–fold the four top flaps, each of them two ply.

15 Swing two flaps to the right. A hidden triangular flap will stretch automatically.

16 Repeat step 15 on the three other sides. Then unfold the paper to step 6.

17 Following the existing creases, collapse the model but do not flatten it.

18 Repeat the four inside reverse folds from step 14. Flatten the model completely.

19 Swing the white flap down.

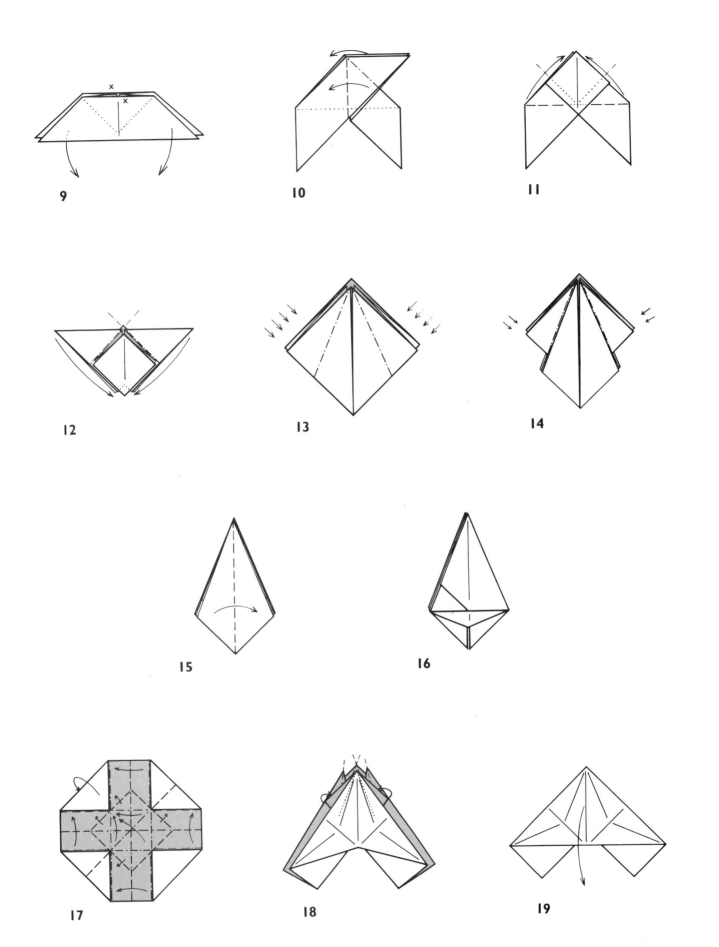

9

10

11

12

13

14

15

16

17

18

19

20 Following the existing creases, swing the front flap to the left.

21 Repeat step 20 on the three other identical flaps.

22 Following the existing creases, collapse the two side flaps symmetrically.

23 In the same motion, swing one ply of the right-hand flap to the left and pinch it flat along the existing creases. The squash should fall into place naturally. Note the hidden crease, indicated by a dotted line.

24 Inside reverse—fold the tip of the front flap. Repeat this and step 23 on the two other visible flaps. Repeat only step 23 on the back. Turn the model over.

25 Squash the lower triangle. Pull out the loose paper from the upper triangle. Note that the upper and lower triangles are identical but face opposite directions.

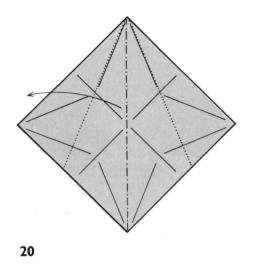

20

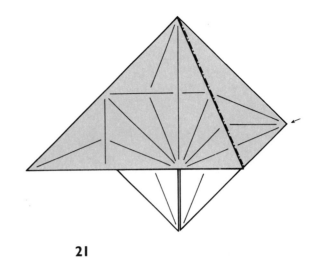

21

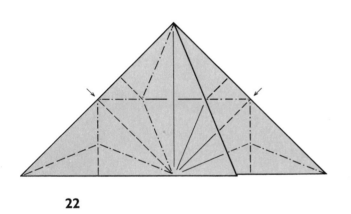

22

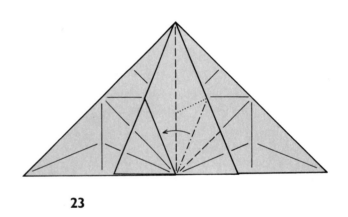

23

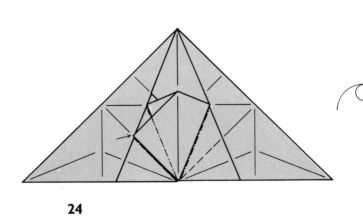

24

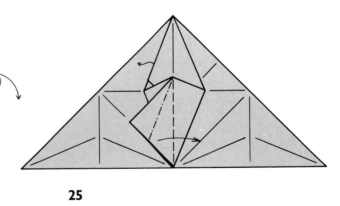

25

26 Here through step 31 are details of the lower triangle. Valley-fold so that the cut edge at the lower left meets the existing crease at the lower right.

27 Valley-fold along the centerline.

28 Valley-fold to the centerline. Repeat steps 26 through 28 on the right-hand side, and unfold to step 26.

29 Following the existing creases, swing the center upward. The sides will narrow automatically.

30 Repeat steps 25 through 29 on this smaller flap.

31 Valley-fold the white portion to the centerline, and tuck the tiny shaded triangle inside. Use tweezers. Repeat steps 25 through 31 on the identical upper triangle.

32 Lift a single ply from the big left-hand triangle and turn it inside out to create a pocket for half of the top assembly. Repeat on the big right-hand triangle.

33 Crimp the two big triangles to form wings. Mountain-fold the existing crease, and swivel the paper until it meets the intersection of two more existing creases, as shown. The model will not lie flat.

34 Narrow the hind wings with small tucks. The valley folds meet the edge of each wing at the existing crease.

35 Unfold the crimps to step 33, and valley-fold the model in half. The model will now lie flat.

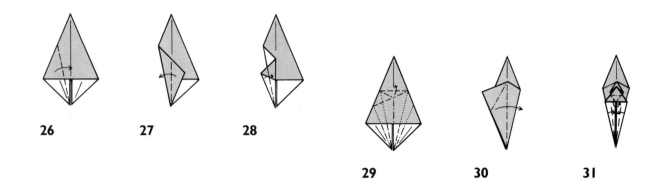

26   27   28

29   30   31

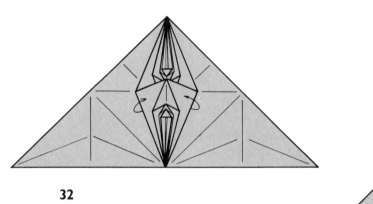

32

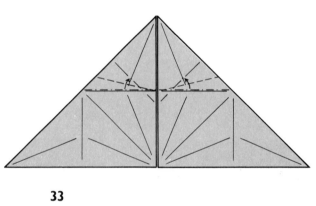

33

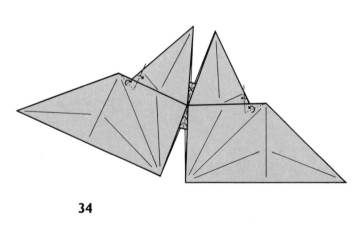

34

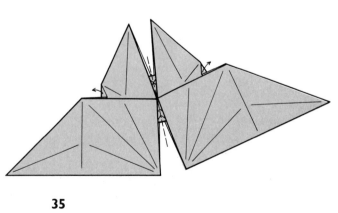

35

36 Fold five flaps upward. Count only the flaps that touch the point *x*. Repeat behind.

37 The top half of the kite-shaped flap is three ply; the bottom half is one ply. Open-sink the long triangular flap. Repeat behind.

38 Valley-fold one flap downward. Repeat behind.

39 Form a rabbit's ear. This will be the middle leg. Repeat behind.

40 Pinch the middle leg at *x*, and pull gently away from the rest of the model. Closed-sink the puffed-out triangular portion. Repeat behind.

41 Pull out the loose paper from between the middle layers at the extreme left side of the model. Mountain-fold the middle leg in half. To the left of the middle leg are tiny protrusions of paper. Mountain-fold the front protrusion and valley-fold the back one. Above the middle leg is a loose horizontal flap. This will be the front leg. Rabbit's-ear the front leg symmetrically, and swing it downward. Repeat all folds behind.

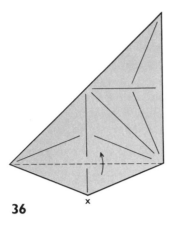

36

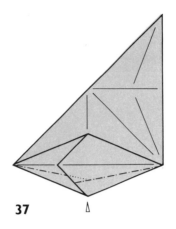

37

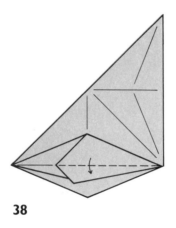

38

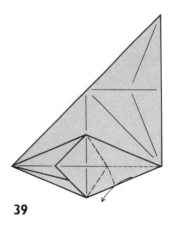

39

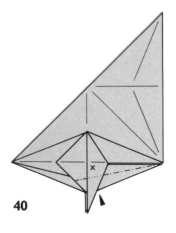

40

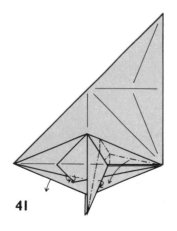

41

42 At the extreme left is the loose paper pulled out in the previous step. Valley-fold the paper to the right as far as possible and unfold. (The model will not lie flat during the fold.) Valley-fold another loose flap to the right to cover the middle and front legs. Repeat both folds behind.

43 Rabbit's-ear the flap at the far left. This will be the hind leg. Repeat behind. Pull out the loose paper from underneath the right side of the model.

44 Narrow the hind leg by swinging the left half over on top of the right half. Repeat behind. Inside reverse–fold the loose paper underneath the model.

45 Here through step 47 are details of the tail and hind leg. Pull the two sides apart gently, and closed-sink the excess paper.

46 Valley-fold in half. Repeat behind.

47 The flap at the extreme left is the abdomen. Inside reverse–fold the tip of the abdomen, and narrow the sides with mountain folds. The thin vertical flaps are excess paper. Tuck them behind with a mountain fold. Pinch the hind leg, and swing it downward. Repeat all folds behind.

48 Two thin layers of paper hang below the body. Crimp them with tweezers, and tuck them up and into the body. Narrow with a mountain fold the loose flap covering the middle and front legs. Repeat all folds behind.

49 Narrow with a second mountain fold the loose flap covering the middle and front legs. Repeat behind. Crimp the front and middle legs. Inside and outside reverse–fold all six legs as symmetrically as possible. Lift a single ply from the big triangle and turn it inside out to create a pocket for half of the body assembly, as in step 32. Repeat behind. Spread the loose paper underneath the model. The following views are from the bottom.

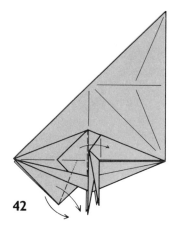

42

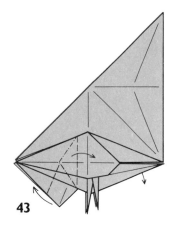

43

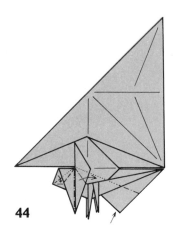

44

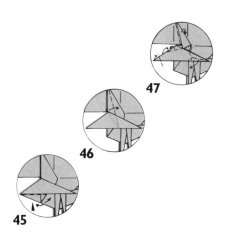

47

46

45

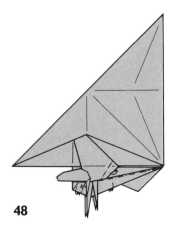

48

49

50 Here through step 68 are details of the head. These steps are difficult, and if the paper is bulky, you may have to settle for an approximation. Petal-fold.
51 Form a rabbit's ear.
52 Pull out the loose paper.

53 Valley-fold the loose paper downward.
54 Swivel the top half of the assembly around the existing crease.

55 Valley-fold to the existing horizontal crease and unfold.
56 This is a very thick crimp. The head will bunch up against the body.
57 Following the existing creases, valley-fold the loose paper toward the center.

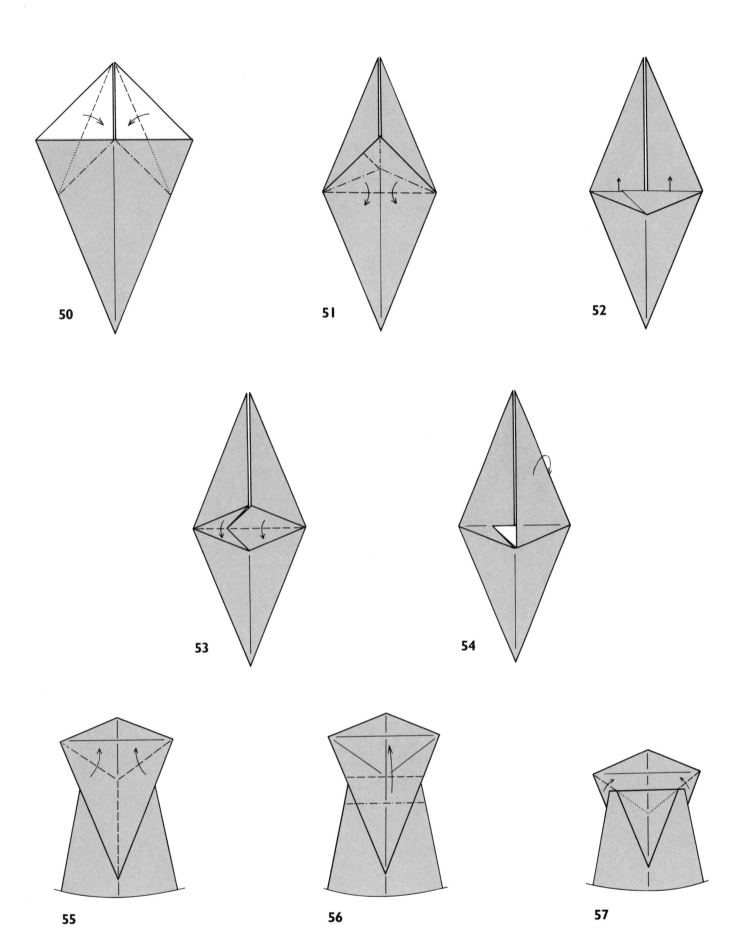

50

51

52

53

54

55

56

57

58 Open the model slightly, and closed-sink the exposed paper into the adjacent pockets.

59 Close the model. The following views are from the side.

60 The horizontal flap will be an antenna. Inside reverse–fold the antenna. Repeat behind.

61 Petal-fold the front face of the antenna, and tuck the excess paper inside. Repeat behind.

62 Valley-fold the front face of the antenna to the right. Repeat behind.

63 Valley-fold the tip as far up as it will go. Mountain-fold halfway from the tip to the valley fold. Narrow the back face of the antenna with a mountain fold. Tuck the loose paper into the head. Repeat behind.

64 Form a five-sided closed sink. Tweezers are a necessity for this step. Repeat behind.

65 Spread the sink. With luck, it will pop up to form a five-sided pyramid. Repeat behind.

66 This is the butterfly's bulging compound eye. Valley-fold the antenna to the rear. Repeat behind.

67 Pinch both antennae, and swing forward. The flap to the right of the antennae will be the rest of the head. Pinch it near the tip, and rotate it clockwise as far as possible.

68 Inside reverse–fold the tip of the head. Narrow the top and back of the head with mountain folds. Repeat behind. Curve the antennae.

69 Here through step 78 are details of the wings. Reform the wing creases from step 35 on the thin outer layers only, not the thick inner layers. It will be necessary to crimp the thick inner layers as shown with dotted lines. Repeat behind.

70 At the junction of the front and rear wings is excess paper left over from the crimp. Tuck it into the pocket behind. Inside reverse–fold the top of the front wing. Mountain-fold the lower-right-hand corners toward each other. The bottom edge meets the intersection of two existing creases. Repeat all folds behind.

71 Inside reverse–fold the top of the front wing asymmetrically to the right. At the apex of the rear wing is a tiny hidden flap. Following the existing crease, swing it into view. Repeat all folds behind.

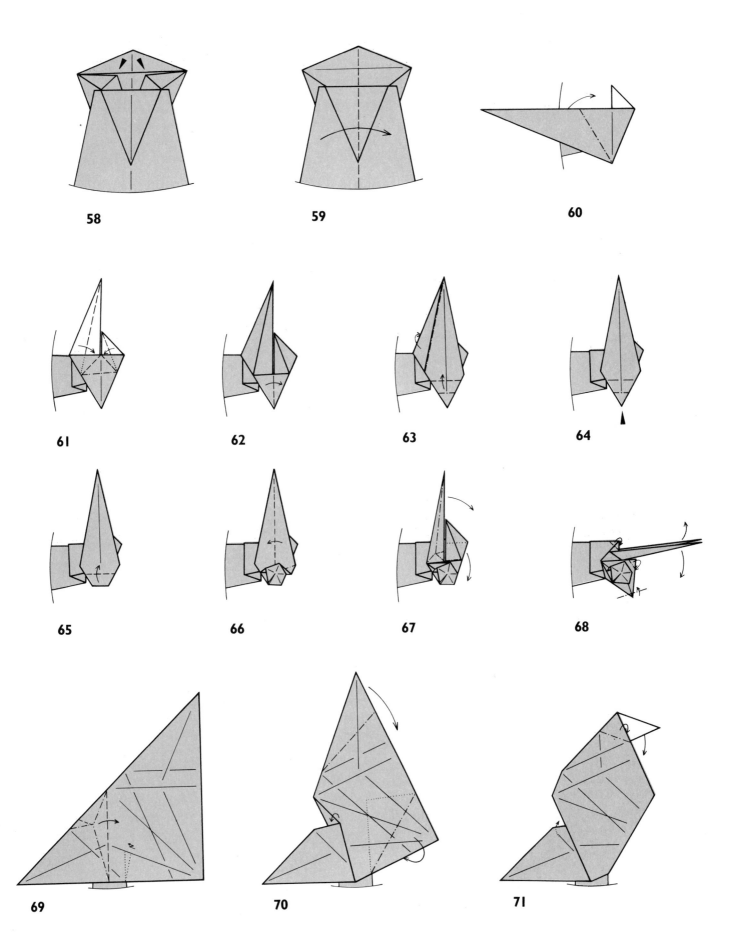

58

59

60

61

62

63

64

65

66

67

68

69

70

71

72 This and step 73 are inside views of a front wing. Valley-fold the tiny white flap up and to the left. Repeat on the other front wing.

73 In the same motion, tuck the tiny white flap into the shaded pocket and close the wing. This procedure locks the top of the wing. Repeat behind.

74 Rabbit's-ear the tip of the rear wing. Following the existing crease, closed-sink the tiny flap at the apex of the rear wing. Narrow the front wing with mountain folds. These folds lie parallel to the cut edge of the paper and meet the intersection of the lower folded edge and an existing crease. Repeat behind.

75 Here through step 77 are inside views of a front wing. Mountain-fold the left and right flaps along the existing creases. Repeat on the other front wing.

76 Valley-fold the right flap in half. Mountain-fold the left flap in half, and tuck the loose paper behind. Repeat on the other front wing.

77 In the same motion, tuck the right flap into the pocket formed by the left flap and close the wing. This procedure locks the front of the wing. Repeat on the other wing.

78 Closed-sink the tip of the front wing. Pinch the tip of the rear wing, and curl it upward. Repeat behind.

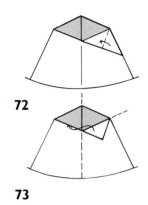

72

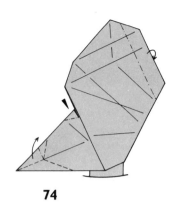

74

73

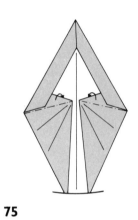

75

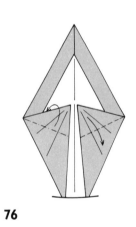

76

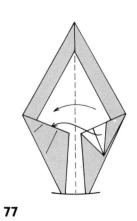

77

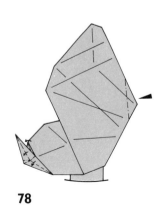

78

The completed BUTTERFLY, ready for flight.

(1982–84)

NOTES AND SOURCES

Innumerable volumes have been written on some of the subjects raised in this book. Other subjects have not, to my knowledge, been discussed at all. This is a selected listing of the sources I have found most important.

The specific works cited in the text are listed in order of their mention. Publications on the same subject are gathered under relevant topic headings. Many of the works on origami are available through the Origami Center of America or through other international origami societies.

CROSSING THE DIVIDE

Escher's quotation "What a pity..." is assembled from two sources. The first half, up to the ellipses, is from

Bruno Ernst, *The Magic Mirror of M. C. Escher* (New York: Ballantine Books, 1976), p. 37.

The second half is from

M. C. Escher, *Regelmatige vlakverdeling* (*The Regular Division of the Plane*, 1958), reprinted in J. L. Locher, ed., *M. C. Escher: His Life and Complete Graphic Work* (New York: Harry N. Abrams, 1982), p. 162.

Escher's quotation "the richest source..." is from his

The Graphic Work of M. C. Escher (New York: Ballantine Books, 1972), p. 9.

Escher's quotation "I consider the indeterminate..." is from Locher, *M. C. Escher*, p. 157.

FOLDING: A COMPACT HISTORY

Information on Japanese and Moorish paperfolding was culled from the following books and pamphlets:

Julia McLean Brossman and Martin W. Brossman, eds., *A Japanese Paperfolding Classic: Excerpt from the "Lost" Kan no mado* (Washington, DC: Pinecone Press, 1961), see introduction, pp. ix–xviii.
Terrence Deignan Farrelly, "Bibliography of Origami" (unpublished), pp. i–ii.
Robert Harbin, *New Adventures in Origami* (New York: Funk and Wagnalls, 1972), see introduction by Samuel Randlett, pp. 1–3.
———, *Origami: The Art of Paperfolding* (New York: Funk and Wagnalls, 1969), see "A Short History of Origami," pp. 1–3.
———, *Origami 3: The Art of Paper-Folding* (London: Hodder Paperbacks, 1974), see introduction by Sidney French, pp. 1–3.
———, *Origami 4: The Art of Paper-Folding* (London: Hodder and Stoughton, 1977), see introduction by Eric Kenneway, pp. 1–3.
———, *Paper Magic: The Art of Paperfolding* (London: John Maxfield, 1971), see "Paper-Folding...Past and Present," pp. 11–15.
Isao Honda, *All About Origami* (Tokyo: Toto Bunka, 1960), see preface.
———, *The World of Origami* (New York: Japan Publications Trading Co, 1967), see "The Origins of Origami," pp. 21–30.
Eric Kenneway, *Complete Origami: An A–Z of Facts and Folds* (New York: St. Martin's Press, 1987). Includes historical information throughout.
———, *Folding Faces* (London: Paddington Press, 1978), see introduction.
Vicente Palacios, *Papirogami* (Barcelona: Editorial Miguel A. Salvatella, 1978), see introduction, pp. 5–26. In Spanish.
James Minoru Sakoda, *Modern Origami* (New York: Simon and Schuster, 1969), see introduction, pp. 9–21.
Michael Schuyt and Joost Elfers, *Origami* (Cologne: DuMont Buchverlag, 1979), see "Ost ist Ost und West ist West," pp. 9–14. In German.
Roger Sheppard, Richard Threadgill, and John Holmes, *Paper Houses* (New York: Schocken Books, 1974), see "Paper and the Paper House," pp. 1–4.
Sadami Yamada and Kiyotoda Ito, *New Dimensions in Papercraft* (Tokyo: Japan Publications Trading Co, 1967), see introduction, pp. 21–22.

Information on Western paperfolding was drawn from the following books:

Edwin A. Dawes, *The Great Illusionists* (Secaucus, NJ: Chartwell Books, 1979), pp. 193–202 (on Harry Houdini).
John Fisher, ed., *The Magic of Lewis Carroll* (New York: Clarkson N. Potter, 1973), see "Origami," pp. 197–205, and extensive bibliography, pp. 276–279.
Martin Gardner, *The 2nd Scientific American Book of Mathematical Puzzles and Diversions* (New York: Simon and Schuster, 1961), see "Origami," pp. 174–185, and bibliography, pp. 249–250 (on Lewis Carroll and Miguel de Unamuno).
Jerry Mander, George Dippel, and Howard Gossage, *The*

Great International Paper Airplane Book (New York: Simon and Schuster, 1967), pp. 11–47 (on Leonardo da Vinci).

Vicente Palacios, *La Creación en Papiroflexia* (Barcelona: Editorial Miguel A. Salvatella, 1979), pp. 5–20, 121–140 (in Spanish; on Unamuno).

Samuel Randlett, *The Art of Origami* (New York: E. P. Dutton, 1966), see introduction by Edward Kallop, pp. 13–19 (on Unamuno and Leonardo). This essay is reprinted from the catalog to "Plane Geometry and Fancy Figures," an exhibition of paperfolding held in 1959 at the Cooper Union Museum for the Arts of Decoration.

I MEET THE MASTER

The printmaker Harunobu:

Sadao Kikuchi, *Ukiyoe* (Osaka: Hoikusha Publishing Co., 1982), p. 28.

Yoshizawa's personal history:

Akira Yoshizawa, "On Creative Origami," *The Origamian*, 3, no. 3 (n.d.): 1–2.

In addition, other excellent books on origami are

Robert Harbin, *Origami: A Step-by-Step Guide* (London: Hamlyn Publishing Group, 1974). Pages 66–68 contain instructions for Patricia Crawford's model of a unicorn, which I borrowed for my knight on horseback.

———, *Secrets of Origami* (Sydney: Angus and Robertson, 1971). Biographies of contributors appear throughout.

Kunihiko Kasahara, *Origami Omnibus* (Tokyo: Japan Publications, 1988).

Kunihiko Kasahara and Toshie Takahama, *Origami for the Connoisseur* (Tokyo: Japan Publications, 1987).

Robert Lang, *The Complete Book of Origami* (New York: Dover Publications, 1989).

Jun Maekawa and Kunihiko Kasahara, *Viva Origami!* (Tokyo: Sanrio Publications, 1983). In addition to containing many outstanding models by Maekawa, superbly illustrated by Kasahara, this book includes a discussion of the geometry of paperfolding. Their treatment parallels, and has influenced, my own thinking on the subject.

John Montroll, *Animal Origami for the Enthusiast* (New York: Dover Publications, 1985).

———, *Origami for the Enthusiast* (New York: Dover Publications, 1979).

———, *Origami Sculptures* (Bethesda, MD: Antroll Publishing, 1988).

Samuel Randlett, *The Best of Origami* (New York: E. P. Dutton, 1963), see preface by Martin Gardner, pp. 1–2, and biographies of contributors, pp. 179–182.

T. Sundara Row, *Geometric Exercises in Paper Folding* (New York: Dover Publications, 1966).

Stephen Weiss, *Wings and Things: Origami That Flies* (New York: St. Martin's Press, 1984).

LEARNING FROM NATURE

The quotation from Arthur Loeb appears in

R. Buckminster Fuller, *Synergetics* (New York: Macmillan Publishing, 1982), p. 823.

Other valuable sources on form and patterns in nature include

George Howe Colt, "The Polyhedral Arthur Loeb," *Harvard Magazine*, March–April 1982, 27–37.

Keith Critchlow, *Order in Space* (New York: Viking Press, 1969).

György Doczi, *The Power of Limits: Proportional Harmonies in Nature, Art and Architecture* (Boston: Shambhala Publications, 1981).

Matila Ghyka, *The Geometry of Art and Life* (New York: Dover Publications, 1977).

Stephen Jay Gould, *Ever Since Darwin: Reflections in Natural History* (New York: W. W. Norton, 1979).

———, *The Flamingo's Smile: Reflections in Natural History* (New York: W. W. Norton, 1985).

———, *Hen's Teeth and Horse's Toes: Further Reflections in Natural History* (New York: W. W. Norton, 1983).

———, *The Panda's Thumb: More Reflections in Natural History* (New York: W. W. Norton, 1982).

Stefan Hildebrandt and Anthony Tromba, *Mathematics and Optimal Form* (New York: Scientific American Library, 1985).

Alan Holden, *Shapes, Space and Symmetry* (New York: Columbia University Press, 1971).

H. E. Huntley, *The Divine Proportion: A Study in Mathematical Beauty* (New York: Dover Publications, 1970).

Arthur L. Loeb, *Color and Symmetry* (New York: John Wiley, 1971).

———, *Space Structures: Their Harmony and Counterpoint* (Reading, MA: Addison-Wesley, 1977).

Caroline H. MacGillavry, *Fantasy and Symmetry* (New York: Harry N. Abrams, 1976).

Thomas McMahon and John Tyler Bonner, *On Size and Life* (New York: Scientific American Library, 1983).

David R. Nelson, "Quasicrystals," *Scientific American* 225, no. 2 (August 1986): 42–51.

Peter Pearce, *Structure in Nature Is a Strategy for Design* (Cambridge, MA: MIT Press, 1978).

Cyril Stanley Smith, *A Search for Structure* (Cambridge, MA: MIT Press, 1982).

Paul Joseph Steinhardt, "Quasicrystals: A fundamentally new phase of solid matter exhibits symmetries that are impossible for ordinary crystals," *American Scientist*, November–December 1986: 586–597.

Hugo Steinhaus, *Mathematical Snapshots* (New York: Oxford University Press, 1969).

Peter S. Stevens, *Patterns in Nature* (Boston: Little, Brown, 1974).

D'Arcy Thompson, *On Growth and Form*, abridged edition, ed. J. T. Bonner (Cambridge: Cambridge University Press, 1977).

Helmut Tributsch, *How Life Learned to Live: Adaptation in Nature* (Cambridge, MA: MIT Press, 1982).

Hermann Weyl, *Symmetry* (Princeton, NJ: Princeton University Press, 1952).

Robert Williams, *Natural Structure* (Moorpark, CA: Eudamon Press, 1972).

X AND X'

The bible of fractal geometry is

Benoit B. Mandelbrot, *The Fractal Geometry of Nature* (San Francisco: W. H. Freeman, 1982). See the excellent bibliography for more sources.

Other accessible sources on fractal geometry and the related fields of chaos theory and catastrophe theory include

Ralph H. Abraham, *On Morphodynamics* (Santa Cruz, CA: Aerial Press, 1985).

Ralph H. Abraham and Christopher D. Shaw, "Dynamics: A Visual Introduction" in F. Eugene Yates, ed., *Self-Organizing Systems* (New York: Plenum Publishing, 1987), 543–597.

———, *Dynamics: The Geometry of Behavior* (Santa Cruz, CA: Aerial Press, 1985). Four volumes.

David Campbell, James P. Crutchfield, J. Doyne Farmer, and Erica Jen, "Experimental Mathematics: The Role of Computation in Nonlinear Science," *Communications of the Association for Computing Machinery* 28 (1985): 374–384.

James P. Crutchfield, J. Doyne Farmer, Norman H. Packard, and Robert S. Shaw, "Chaos," *Scientific American* 255, no. 6 (December 1986): 46–57.

A. K. Dewdney, "Beauty and profundity: the Mandelbrot set and a flock of its cousins called Julia," *Scientific American* 257, no. 5 (November 1987): 140–145, the "Computer Recreations" column.

———, "A computer microscope zooms in for a look at the most complex object in mathematics," *Scientific American* 253, no. 2 (August 1985): 16–24, the "Computer Recreations" column.

———, "Probing the strange attractions of chaos," *Scientific American* 257, no. 1 (July 1987): 108–111, the "Computer Recreations" column.

Irving R. Epstein, Kenneth Kustin, Patrick De Kepper, and Miklós Orbán, "Oscillating Chemical Reactions," *Scientific American* 248, no. 3 (March 1983): 112–123.

Martin Gardner, "Four Books on Catastrophe Theory," in *Science: Good, Bad and Bogus* (Buffalo, NY: Prometheus Books, 1981), pp. 365–374.

———, "In which 'monster curves' force redefinition of the word 'curve,'" *Scientific American*, 235, no. 6 (December 1976): 124–133, the "Mathematical Games" column.

James Gleick, *Chaos: Making a New Science* (New York: Viking Press, 1987).

———, "New images of chaos that are stirring a science revolution," *Smithsonian* 18, no. 9 (December 1987): 122–135.

Douglas R. Hofstadter, "Strange attractors: mathematical patterns delicately poised between order and chaos," *Sci-*

entific American 245, no. 5 (November 1981): 22–43, the "Metamagical Themas" column.

Gina Kolati, "Catastrophe Theory: The Emperor Has No Clothes," *Science* 196 (April 15, 1977): 287, 350–351.

Heinz-Otto Peitgen and Peter H. Richter, *The Beauty of Fractals* (Berlin: Springer-Verlag, 1986).

Tim Poston and Ian Stewart, *Catastrophe Theory and Its Applications* (London: Fearon-Pitman, 1978).

Ilya Prigogine and Isabelle Stengers, *Order Out of Chaos* (New York: Bantam Books, 1984).

Leonard M. Sander, "Fractal Growth," *Scientific American* 256, no. 1 (January 1987): 94–100.

Robert Shaw, *The Dripping Faucet as a Model Chaotic System* (Santa Cruz, CA: Aerial Press, 1984).

Ian Stewart, "The Seven Elementary Catastrophes," *New Scientist,* November 20, 1975, 447–454.

———, "What Shape Is a Catastrophe?" *Analog,* June 1978, 30–48.

"Symmetries and Asymmetries: A Mosaic Special," *Mosaic* 16, no. 1 (January–February 1985). Includes articles on fractal geometry and chaos theory.

René Thom, *Structural Stability and Morphogenesis* (Reading, MA: W. A. Benjamin, Addison-Wesley, 1975).

Arthur T. Winfree, "Rotating Chemical Reactions," *Scientific American* 230, no. 6 (June 1974): 82–95.

Alexander Woodcock and Monte Davis, *Catastrophe Theory* (New York: E. P. Dutton, 1978).

Ralph S. Zahler and Hector J. Sussman, "Claims and Accomplishments of Applied Catastrophe Theory," *Nature* (October 26, 1977): 759–763.

E. C. Zeeman, "Catastrophe Theory," *Scientific American* 234, no. 4 (April 1976): 65–83.

Further thoughts of my own on these topics can be found in

"Against the Currents of Chaos," *The Sciences,* September–October 1984, 50–55. An essay on chaos theory.

"Snowflakes, Coastlines, and Clouds," *The Sciences,* September–October 1983, 63–68. An essay on fractal geometry.

"The Topology of Everyday Life," *The Harvard Crimson,* May 14, 1979, p. 2. An essay on catastrophe theory.

A MUSIC LESSON

Fats Waller's quotation appears in

David Steinberg, "*Bartlett's* Ain't Got It," *Verbatim,* Winter, 1979–80, p. 9. The quotation is often mistakenly attributed to Louis Armstrong.

The reductionist criticism of Beethoven's Symphony no. 7 is by

Leonard Marcus, liner notes to the recording by L'Orchestre de la Suisse Romande, Ernest Ansermet conducting, London STS-15067.

The holistic criticism of Beethoven's Symphony no. 7 is by

Richard Freed, liner notes to the recording by the Philadelphia Orchestra, Riccardo Muti conducting, Angel S-37538.

The theme of reductionism and holism plays a key role in three related books that have greatly influenced my text:

Douglas R. Hofstadter, *Gödel, Escher, Bach: An Eternal Golden Braid* (New York: Basic Books, 1979).
———, *Metamagical Themas: Questing for the Essence of Mind and Pattern* (New York: Basic Books, 1985).
Douglas R. Hofstadter and Daniel C. Dennett, *The Mind's I: Fantasies and Reflections on Self and Soul* (New York: Basic Books, 1981).

A method of notating origami diagrams is outlined in

Alice Gray, "O.I.L.: John Smith's Origami Instruction Language," and Eric Kenneway, "Profile—John Smith," *The Origamian* 13, no. 2, (n.d.), p. 1.

Programming the IBM System 360 Model 91 to produce origami models is described in Kenneway, *Complete Origami*, p. 44.

James Jeans's quotation is taken from his

Science and Music (New York: Dover Publications, 1968), p. 13.

Wilhelm Fucks's correlograms of intervals in music are discussed in

Manfred Eigen and Ruthild Winkler, *Laws of the Game: How the Principles of Nature Govern Chance* (New York: Harper and Row, 1983), pp. 310–313.

Denys Parsons's *Directory* is described in

Robin Maconie and Chris Cunningham, "Computers Unveil the Shape of a Melody," *New Scientist*, April 22, 1982, 206–209.

The fractal structure of music is outlined in

Martin Gardner, "White and brown music, fractal curves and one-over-*f* fluctuations," *Scientific American* 238, no. 4 (April 1978): 16–32, the "Mathematical Games" column.

Hermann von Helmholtz's quotation is taken from his

On the Sensations of Tone as a Physiological Basis for the Theory of Music (New York: Dover Publications, 1959), pp. 306–307.

Additional sources on computers and music:

Pierre Boulez and Andrew Gerzso, "Computers in Music," *Scientific American* 258, no. 4 (April 1988): 44–50.
Heinz von Foerster and James W. Beauchamp, eds., *Music by Computers* (New York: John Wiley, 1969).
Martin Gardner, *Time Travel and Other Mathematical Bewilderments* (New York: W. H. Freeman, 1988), see "Melody-Making Machines," 85–96.
Lejaren A. Hiller, Jr., "Computer Music," *Scientific American* 201, no. 6 (December 1959): 109–120.
———, *Music Composed with Computer: An Historical Survey* (Urbana, IL: University of Illinois School of Music, 1968).
Carleen Maley Hutchins, ed., *The Physics of Music* (San Francisco: W. H. Freeman, 1978). A collection of readings from *Scientific American*.

Additional sources on computers and invention:

Rudolf Arnheim, *Entropy and Art: An Essay on Disorder and Order* (Berkeley: University of California Press, 1971).
Margaret Boden, *Artificial Intelligence and Natural Man* (New York: Basic Books, 1977), see especially ch. 11, "Creativity."
Gregory J. Chaitin, "Randomness and Mathematical Proof," *Scientific American* 232, no. 5 (May 1975): 47–52.
Peter Eisenman, "Biology Center for the J. W. Goethe University of Frankfurt, Frankfurt am Main, 1987," *Assemblage* no. 5 (February 1988): 28–50. The tale of a building designed using computers and fractal geometry.
Herbert W. Franke, *Computer Graphics, Computer Art* (London: Phaidon Press, 1971).
Stanislaw Lem, *His Master's Voice* (New York: Harcourt Brace Jovanovich, 1983). A brilliant novel about human and machine intelligence by the Polish philosopher and science-fiction writer. See also my interview with Lem in the *New York Times Book Review*, March 20, 1983, 7, 34–35. A longer version appears in *Missouri Review* 7, no. 2 (1984): 218–237.
Frank J. Malina, ed., *Visual Art, Mathematics and Computers: Selections from the Journal LEONARDO* (Oxford: Pergamon Press, 1979).
Jacques Monod, *Chance and Necessity* (New York: Vintage Books, 1972).
John von Neumann, *The Computer and the Brain* (New Haven: Yale University Press, 1979).
L. S. Penrose, "Self-Reproducing Machines," *Scientific American* 200, no. 6 (June 1959): 105–114.
John R. Pierce, *Introduction to Information Theory* (New York: Dover Publications, 1980), see especially ch. 13, "Information Theory and Art."
Erwin Schrödinger, *What is Life? and Mind and Matter* (Cambridge: Cambridge University Press, 1979).
Norbert Wiener, *Cybernetics: Or Control and Communication in the Animal and the Machine* (Cambridge, MA: MIT Press, 1980).
———, *God and Golem, Inc.* (Cambridge, MA: MIT Press, 1973).

THE PSYCHOLOGY OF INVENTION

The source for most of this material is

Jacques Hadamard, *The Psychology of Invention in the Mathematical Field* (New York: Dover Publications, 1954).

William James's quotation is in ibid., p. 25.

Francis Galton's quotation is in ibid., p. 24.

John Edgar Teeple's anecdote is in ibid., p. 35.

Henri Poincaré's quotation "Most striking at first" is in ibid., p. 14.

The comparison of illumination to a flash of lightning comes from

Charles Correa, "Planning for Bombay," in *Charles Correa* (Singapore: Mimar Books, 1984), p. 56. Correa attributes the metaphor to Paul Hindemith.

Leonard Eugene Dickson's story is in Hadamard, *Psychology of Invention,* p. 7.

Poincaré's quotation "To create . . ." is in

E. T. Bell, *Men of Mathematics* (New York: Simon and Schuster, 1965), p. 549.

Paul Valéry's quotation is in Hadamard, *Psychology of Invention,* p. 30.

Beethoven's method of invention is described in

Leonard Bernstein, *The Joy of Music* (New York: Simon and Schuster, 1980), pp. 73–93.

Claude Lévi-Strauss's method of invention is described in Hadamard, *Psychology of Invention,* p. 90.

Francis Galton's method of invention is noted in ibid., p. 69.

Theodule Armand Ribot's method of invention is noted in ibid., p. 93.

Albert Einstein's letter is quoted in ibid., p. 142.

Human chess players possess a "vocabulary of patterns," as discussed by

Fred Hapgood, "Computer Chess Bad—Human Chess Worse," *New Scientist,* December 23–30, 1982, 827–830.

Computer chess players examine 175,000 positions a second, as described by

Paul Hoffman, *Archimedes' Revenge* (New York: W. W. Norton, 1988), 196. See also David Waltz, "Artificial Intelligence," *Scientific American* 247, no. 4 (October 1982): 118–133.

Hermann Weyl's quotation appears in Peitgen and Richter, *The Beauty of Fractals,* p. 4.

G. H. Hardy's quotation is from his

A Mathematician's Apology (Cambridge: Cambridge University Press, 1967), pp. 84–85.

The working habits of paperfolders are described in my

"Creativity in Origami: A Panel Discussion," *The Origamian* 16, no. 1 (n.d.), 9–14.

Leonardo da Vinci's quotation appears in Locher, *M. C. Escher,* p. 160.

A discussion of the distinction between creation and discovery appears in

Gunther S. Stent, "Prematurity and Uniqueness in Scientific Discovery," *Scientific American* 227, no. 6 (December 1972): 84–93. It is reprinted in Owen Gingerich, ed., *Scientific Genius and Creativity: Readings from Scientific American* (New York: W. H. Freeman, 1987), pp. 95–104.

The examples of multiple discovery in science are drawn from

Robert K. Merton, *The Sociology of Science: Theoretical and Empirical Investigations* (Chicago: University of Chicago Press, 1973), see especially the essays "Priorities in Scientific Discovery," pp. 286–324, and "Singletons and Multiples in Science," pp. 343–370.

The examples in mathematics are drawn from

Tobias Dantzig, *Number: The Language of Science* (New York: Free Press, 1954), pp. 195–196.
Morris Kline, *Mathematics: The Loss of Certainty* (New York: Oxford University Press, 1982), pp. 81–88.
Howard DeLong, *A Profile of Mathematical Logic* (Reading, MA: Addison-Wesley, 1971), see "Non-Euclidean Geometry," pp. 38–59.

Simultaneous inventions by folders are described in my "Creativity in Origami."

THE CASE OF THE PURLOINED PIG

The exchange between Cerceda and Yoshizawa appears in

Adolfo Cerceda, "A letter from Adolfo Cerceda," *The Origamian* 9, no. 3 (n.d.), p. 1.
"Profile: Akira Yoshizawa," *The Origamian* 3, no. 3 (n.d.), 1–2.
Vicente Palacios, *Fascinante Papiroflexia: Legado del Mago Adolfo Cerceda* (Barcelona: Editorial Miguel A. Salvatella, 1984), 5–15 (in Spanish). See the same author's *La Creación en Papiroflexia,* 14–18, for an interview with Cerceda.

Gert Eilenberger's quotation is in his "Freedom, Science, and Aesthetics," in Peitgen and Richter, *The Beauty of Fractals,* p. 179.

Additional sources on creativity include

David Bohm and F. David Peat, *Science, Order, and Creativity* (New York: Bantam Books, 1987).
Martin Gardner, *aha! Insight* (San Francisco: W. H. Freeman, 1978).
Susan P. Gill, "The Paradox of Prediction," *Daedalus* 115, no. 3 (Summer 1986): 17–48.
E. H. Gombrich, *Art and Illusion* (Princeton, NJ: Princeton University Press, 1972).
Douglas R. Hofstadter, "Can inspiration be mechanized?" *Scientific American* 247, no. 3 (September 1982): 18–34, the "Metamagical Themas" column.

————, "Variations on a Theme as the Essence of Imagination," *Scientific American* 247, no. 4 (October 1982): 20–29, the "Metamagical Themas" column.

Vera John-Steiner, *Notebooks of the Mind: Explorations of Thinking* (New York: Harper and Row, 1987).

Horace Freeland Judson, *The Search for Solutions* (New York: Holt, Rinehart and Winston, 1980), see especially ch. 2, "Pattern." Louis Pasteur's assertion that "chance favors the prepared mind" appears on p. 69.

Scott Kim, *Inversions: A Catalogue of Calligraphic Cartwheels* (Peterborough, NH: Byte Books, 1981), see his discussion of character recognition, throughout.

Thomas S. Kuhn, *The Structure of Scientific Revolutions* (Chicago: University of Chicago Press, 1970), pp. 1–34, 92–135, 146–147.

Imre Lakatos, *Proofs and Refutations: The Logic of Mathematical Discovery* (London: Cambridge University Press, 1977).

Peter Brian Medawar, *Induction and Intuition in Scientific Thought* (Philadelphia: American Philosophical Society, 1969).

Masahiro Mori, *The Buddha in the Robot: A Robot Engineer's Thoughts on Science and Religion* (Tokyo: Kosei Publishing Co., 1981).

Henri Poincaré, *Science and Hypothesis* (New York: Dover Publications, 1952).

Karl R. Popper, *The Logic of Scientific Discovery* (New York: Harper and Row, 1968), pp. 13–56.

Robert S. Root-Bernstein, "Setting the Stage for Discovery," *The Sciences,* May–June 1988, 26–35.

Judith Wechsler, ed., *On Aesthetics in Science* (Boston: Birkhäuser, 1988). See especially Cyril S. Smith's "Structural Hierarchy in Science, Art, and History," pp. 9–53, Philip Morrison's "On Broken Symmetries," pp. 55–70, and Seymour A. Papert's "The Mathematical Unconscious," pp. 105–119.

TOWARD A VOCABULARY OF FORM

Diverse books have influenced my thinking on form. Among these are

Christopher Alexander, Sara Ishikawa, and Murray Silverstein, *A Pattern Language: Towns, Buildings, Construction* (New York: Oxford University Press, 1977). An encyclopedic guide to the patterns of human habitation as well as a how-to book for architects and planners.

Georg Gerster, *Below From Above* (New York: Abbeville Press, 1986). Extraordinary aerial photographs that reveal the patterns of nature and of human habitation.

Philip and Phylis Morrison and the Office of Charles and Ray Eames, *Powers of Ten* (New York: Scientific American Library, 1982). A journey through orders of magnitude from subatomic particles to quasars.

Edward Tufte, *The Visual Display of Quantitative Information* (Cheshire, CT: Graphics Press, 1983). A passionate and lucid guide to the aesthetics of charts and graphs.

Further thoughts of my own on these topics can be found in

"Examining Life at the MBL," *Harvard Magazine,* September–October 1983, 32–42. An essay on the hierarchy of patterns in life.

"Companion Guides to the Universe," *The Sciences,* July–August 1984, 50–54. An essay on the hierarchy of patterns in space and time.

The definition and etymology of *blintz* are taken from

Stuart B. Flexner, ed., *The Random House College Dictionary* (New York: Random House, 1984).

My speculations on the relationship between origami and morphogenesis were stimulated by

Peter J. Bryant, Susan V. Bryant, and Vernon French, "Biological Regeneration and Pattern Formation," *Scientific American* 237, no. 1 (July 1977): 67–81.

Alfred Gierer, "Hydra as a Model for the Development of Biological Form," *Scientific American* 231, no. 6 (December 1974): 44–54.

Tryggve Gustafson and Mark I. Toneby, "How Genes Control Morphogenesis," *American Scientist,* July–August 1971, 452–462.

Shinya Inoué and Kayo Okazaki, "Biocrystals," *Scientific American* 236, no. 4 (April 1977): 82–92.

Marcus Jacobson and R. Kevin Hunt, "The Origins of Nerve-Cell Specificity," *Scientific American* 228, no. 2 (February 1973): 26–35.

James D. Murray, "How the Leopard Gets Its Spots," *Scientific American* 258, no. 3 (March 1988): 80–87.

Rudolf Raff, "The Molecular Determination of Morphogenesis," *BioScience* 27, no. 6 (June 1977): 394–401.

Ronald L. Schnaar, "The Membrane Is the Message," *The Sciences,* May–June 1985, 34–40.

Lewis Wolpert, "Pattern Formation in Biological Development," *Scientific American* 239, no. 4 (October 1978): 154–164.

ORIGAMI SOCIETIES

ORIGAMI IS IN CREASING proclaim the T-shirts worn by the Friends of the Origami Center of America. There are now at least a dozen origami societies in the United States alone, and many more worldwide. Contact one of the organizations listed below to see if there is a group in your area. Addresses are current at the time of publication and may change.

Belgium-Netherlands Origami Society
Mr. L. D'haeseleer
Postbus 100
B-2400 Mol
BELGIUM

International Origami Centre Belgium
I O C B V2W
FR V.D. Berghelaan 171
2630 Aartselaar
BELGIUM

Mouvement Français des Plieurs de Papier
56 Rue Coriolis
75012 Paris
FRANCE

British Origami Society
Mr. Dave Brill
12 Thorn Road
Bramhall, Stockport
Cheshire SK7 I HQ
GREAT BRITAIN

Centro Diffusione Origami
Casella Postale 225
40100 Bologna
ITALY

Centro Italiano Origami
P.O. Box 357
10100 Torino
ITALY

International Origami Centre
P.O. Box 3
Ogikubo, Tokyo 167
JAPAN

Nippon Origami Association
1-096 Domir Gobancho
12-gobancho
Chiyoda-ku, Tokyo 102
JAPAN

The Origami Collection
Lindestraat 22
3581 Ls Utrecht
NETHERLANDS

Origami Society Netherlands
P.O. Box 35
9989 Zg Warffum
NETHERLANDS

New Zealand Origami Society
79 Dunbar Road
Christchurch 3
NEW ZEALAND

Centro Latino de Origami
Caracas 2655
Dpto. 13-Jesus Maria
Lima 11
PERU

Asociación Española de Papiroflexia
C/Pedro Teixeira No. 9
ESC. IZQ - 9 DCHA
2820 Madrid
SPAIN

The Friends of the Origami Center of America
15 West 77th Street
New York, NY 10024
U.S.A.

West Coast Origami Guild
P.O. Box 90601
Pasadena, CA 91109
U.S.A.

PICTURE CREDITS

Page 65: Copyright © 1988 M. C. Escher c/o Cordon Art-Baarn-Holland.

Page 66 top, middle: Figure 87 from *The Penguin Dictionary of Architecture* by John Fleming, Hugh Honour, and Nikolaus Pevsner (Penguin Books, 1966, 1972, 1980), copyright © John Fleming, Hugh Honour, the Estate of Nikolaus Pevsner, 1966, 1972, 1980. Reproduced by permission of Penguin Books, Ltd.

Page 66 bottom: Photograph by Wim Swaan.

Page 67 top: Courtesy of Conway Library, Courtauld Institute of Art.

Page 67 bottom: Photographs by Bruno Balestrini by courtesy of Electa Editrice, Milano.

Page 76: Copyright © 1989 by Scott Kim.

Pages 86, 90, 94, 98, 104, 112, 118, 124, 128, 132, 138, 142, 150, 158, 172, 182, 194, 210, 220, 232, 246, 262, 278, and 292 (c): Photographs by Quesada/Burke, New York.

INDEX TO TERMS

ABOUT THE AUTHOR

PETER ENGEL was born in 1959 and grew up in New York City. Throughout a varied career that has included architecture, writing, graphic design, and origami, he has consistently tried to integrate artistic and scientific points of view, with results that are evident in this book. He studied the history and philosophy of science at Harvard University, where he received the Leonard J. Siff Prize in 1981 for his thesis. In 1987 he graduated from Columbia University with a master's degree in architecture and received a William Kinne Fellows Award to study low-income housing in India, research that has also been supported by an Indo-American Fellowship from the Fulbright Program. His writing has appeared in *The New York Times*, *The New Republic*, *The Sciences*, *Scientific American*, *Harvard Magazine*, *Connoisseur*, *Discover*, and other publications. He has traveled extensively in Asia and is currently working as an architect in India.